The Sixty-Ninth Annu of the General Service Conterence of Alcoholics Anonymous

"Our Big Book — 80 Years, 71 Languages"

2019 Final Report

Crowne Plaza Times Square, New York, NY – May 19–25, 2019

www.aa.org

50M – 8/19 (RP)

■ Contents

Confidential — full names used

Since this report is a confidential A.A. document, for members only, it contains members' full names and addresses.

This usage — to facilitate communication within the Fellowship — was approved by the 1975 Conference. Such confidential use respects our Tradition of anonymity in public communications and with media (press, radio, TV, etc.).

About the Cover: *Front* — a sampling of Big Books published by A.A.W.S., Inc. The Big Book is currently published in 71 languages. *Back* — a collection of buttons and other memorabilia shared and exchanged informally among Conference members.

Our Big Book — 80 Years, 71 Languages

Notre Gros Livre — 80 ans, 71 langues

Nuestro Libro Grande — 80 años, 71 idiomas

■ The 69th General Service Conference Convenes

"Our Big Book — 80 Years, 71 Languages" was the theme of the recently concluded 69th General Service Conference, held in New York City May 19–25. As the Fellowship's original "oldtimer in print" — also available digitally and as an audiobook — *Alcoholics Anonymous*, our basic text, has sold over 40 million copies, is available in 71 languages, and has helped carry the A.A. message in more than 180 countries around the world.

Working closely with Dr. Bob and the Fellowship's earliest members, Bill W. recognized that in order to keep the program from getting "garbled" or misinterpreted, it would be necessary to put the process down on paper — to make clear what the first 100 members did to achieve and maintain their sobriety. The process was not without difficulty, of course, with many disagreements over what should be in the book. Nevertheless, together, those early A.A.s constructed a pathway to sobriety that was broad, enduring and inclusive.

With our basic text as the backdrop, the 69th General Service Conference was made up of 93 delegates, 27 trustees and corporate directors from A.A.W.S. and Grapevine, along with 15 General Service Office, Grapevine and La Viña staff members.

Following a warm welcome Sunday morning from Michele Grinberg, Class A (nonalcoholic) chairperson of the General Service Board, and the official roll call by G.S.O.'s general manager Greg Tobin, Anthony Flores of South Dakota, delegate chair of the Conference, referenced the Conference theme: "Seventy-one languages — I have to admit, I wonder how translators do it. 'Whoopee party'? Really, Bill? I'd sure like to know how that got translated into Navajo. Or how it just got translated to our French-speaking friends." Additionally, Anthony contemplated one of the many issues slated to come before the Conference, noting, "In 1939, when the book was first published, I'm guessing none of them imagined we would be here deciding on a possible fifth edition."

Delayed temporarily by bad weather that disrupted her travel plans, the Conference keynote address was delivered on Monday by Yoli Flores, Southwest regional trustee. In her talk, Yoli shared an anecdote about the Big Book from her early sobriety: "My first awakening of the value of the Big Book and translations came from a story by Fran P. in the July 1990 Grapevine titled 'Grupa Una,' about a woman in Romania named Juliet who was in search of recovery from alcoholism during the oppressive years of 1984–85. Fran writes, 'Their faith in A.A. regularly moved me to tears. The first weekend Juliet had the literature, for example, she stayed at home. On Monday, I noticed she seemed quite tired. When asked why, she said she had been sitting up copying the Big Book by hand. Shocked, I told her that I was giving her my copy to keep forever, that she didn't need to copy a single word.'"

Beginning on Sunday afternoon and running through

to Saturday, Conference week is long and often arduous, punctuated by board and committee reports, presentations and discussions, area service highlights, workshops, sharing sessions and a visit to G.S.O. Additionally, the trustee elections, which took place on Wednesday, allowed Tom Ardolf and Lucien Jean, the trustees' and Conference committee chairs respectively, to sharpen their comic deliveries as they filled some of the silence between votes with a selection of jokes from the new Grapevine book *Take Me to Your Sponsor*. Also providing a little comic relief to the week-long proceedings was a performance by the 475 Riverside Players, a ragtag thespian ensemble (comprised of G.S.O. and La Viña staff), who staged a homegrown production of "Dorothy Goes to the International Convention," based on the all-time classic "The Wizard of Oz."

The main focus of each Conference, however, is on the deliberations of each of the 13 Conference committees, and it is during committee meetings that the major work of the Conference is done. With comprehensive background provided for each agenda item (made available for advance distribution to the Fellowship in English, French and Spanish), Conference committees discuss numerous issues of interest to the Fellowship as a whole and come up with recommendations, some of which result in Conference Advisory Actions.

Addressing some difficult issues — issues of growth and unity as a Fellowship in the digital age — the 69th Conference worked its way through agenda items, slowly and carefully formulating a path forward for the Fellowship. Not all Conference discussions resulted in Advisory Actions, though; many of the important matters addressed at the Conference were articulated in the "additional considerations" of each committee — more informal suggestions and guidance on how best to carry the message.

By Friday evening, with discussion and voting on committee agendas and floor actions finally complete, as has become the custom at each Conference, rotating Panel 68 delegates lined up around the room for emotional two-minute farewells, often recounting their gratitude and expressing confidence in the remaining delegates to carry on the meaningful work of the Conference and the Fellowship.

On that poignant note, the 2019 General Service Conference officially concluded with the Serenity Prayer in three languages, led by Marge Miller (English), Eric Parent (French) and Jesus Olivas (Spanish). Reconvening briefly on Saturday morning for a final brunch featuring emotional talks by rotating trustees, Conference members bid one another a fond farewell and began to turn their attention toward next year's Conference with its theme, "2020: A Clear Vision for You."

Greetings

Good morning. My name is Anthony Flores, alcoholic and the Panel 68, Area 63 delegate from South Dakota. I want to welcome all of you to the 69th General Service Conference. I have the privilege of serving as your Conference Delegate Chair because my name was picked out of a hat. Something I still believe was a set-up by the delegates in my region. A conspiracy, plain and simple. But I digress…

Our theme this year is "Our Big Book — 80 Years, 71 Languages." At our regional service conference in Moorhead, Minnesota, we had a breakout session on translating the book. I was fascinated by how this process typically gets done. I won't bore you with the details; I happen to find things interesting that others perhaps don't. (Just ask my 7th and 8th grade students what it is like when Mr. Flores goes off on a tangent… and I've never found a tangent I didn't take.)

Anyway, 71 languages — I have to admit, I wonder how translators do it. "Whoopee party"? Really, Bill? I'd sure like to know how that gets translated into Navajo. Or how it just got translated to our French-speaking friends. In the chapter "A Vision for You," one can hear the optimism jump off the page when it tells the reader, "To duplicate, with such backing, what we have accomplished is only a matter of willingness, patience and labor."

In 1939, when the book was first published, I'm guessing none of them imagined we would be here deciding on a possible fifth edition. One of the founders of the United

States, Benjamin Franklin, said, "We must, indeed, all hang together or, most assuredly, we shall all hang separately."

Their very lives depended on unity — as do ours. However, I would be remiss to not mention something that has concerned me in Alcoholics Anonymous. In the chapter "We Agnostics," Bill writes, "But his face falls when we speak of spiritual matters, especially when we mention God, for we have re-opened a subject which our man thought he had neatly evaded or entirely ignored."

It seems to me that we have slowly been evading God. We no longer close with prayer, but instead with a declaration. So, it seems to me this issue is about the Lord's Prayer. I have to admit, I was agitated. I was doubtful. I had to realize I am not running the show. I was forced to my knees asking for the right thought or action. And it hit me. The answer is in our Big Book. Why not pray the prayers found in it? The Third Step Prayer asks God to relieve me of the bondage of self. I don't know about you, but I could use that type of relief. Or how about the Seventh Step Prayer? "I pray that you now remove from me every single defect of character that stands in the way of my usefulness to you and my fellows."

I'll tell you what, that's powerful stuff — much more powerful than a bunch of "I" statements. But, just like the book, what I say here is meant to be suggestive only. I realize I know only a little. My point is: Let us be careful not to change that which saved our lives.

May God bless each of us this week and bless the 69th General Service Conference.

Thank you.

Anthony Flores, South Dakota, Delegate Chair

Keynote Address

Greetings, everyone. I would like to thank Patrick for his loving invitation to share my thoughts and experience on the topic "Our Big Book — 80 Years, 71 Languages." It is a privilege to be among such a distinguished group that normally would not mix. My name is Yoli, and I am an alcoholic.

When I came to A.A., I was not sure where my decision was going to take me or what to expect out of the kind of "treatment" I was about to receive. I was waiting for a doctor to lead us in some kind of group therapy. Instead, I was given a message of desperation and hope by two men in a house that was cluttered with books and small magazines on every table as well as the mantelpiece. I was asked to come back for a 5:30 meeting that evening. They also told me that I would meet other women with whom I could talk about my drinking.

So, I went back, and the first woman I saw was standing near the meeting room door, eating baby food. (I learned later that alcohol had damaged her throat and she could not eat normal food easily.) She talked to me for a while and then walked away while others introduced themselves to me. She appeared again just before meeting time with a book in her hand. She explained that it was a textbook called *Alcoholics Anonymous* and that it was necessary for

a successful recovery from alcoholism. She then informed me that it would cost me $5.50 (the year was 1980). My thought was that three months of group therapy was all I needed and for this I did not need a book. So I answered that I had no money for the book. She left and placed it in a closet as we all walked into the meeting. Later, this woman repeated her actions and received the same answer from me. About the third or fourth time with my same answer of no money, she said, "You take the book and when you get some money you can pay for the book." My ego told me that I was not about to have a debt with these people. So I searched my purse and, voilà, I found the $5.50. Later I learned that the book was the basic text of our lifesaving program.

Bill started writing the A.A. Big Book in 1938, when there were only two groups in existence — one in Akron and another in New York City. He would handwrite his notes while Ruth Hock typed them for the manuscript. She then mimeographed 400 copies and mailed them out for evaluation and comments. One comment was to have a physician write the introduction to the book. Another was to add personal stories to the completed book. Still another important contribution came from an argument made mostly by Hank and Fitz about the "God" word. The argument was settled by a compromise, with the addition of the phrase "as you understand Him." And 30 stories were added to provide personal experience.

As the manuscript moved forward, a title needed to be given to the book. Many titles were suggested, but "Alcoholics Anonymous" and "The Way Out" were the standout names voted by the two existing groups. "The Way Out" received a slight majority, but a review of the records of the Library of Congress revealed that 12 books had already been published with that title.

Harper & Brothers offered to publish the book, but Hank P. convinced Bill that they should publish the book themselves and finance it by selling shares under Works Publishing Company. Unfortunately, sales were slow and disappointing. It was Jack Alexander's March 1941 *Saturday Evening Post* article that gave the book prominence, and it ultimately began to sell. The first printing of the A.A. Big Book was released with 4,730 copies on April 10, 1939. Since its publication, we have seen the book help millions of men and women recover from alcoholism when its suggestions are followed.

The book itself explains the purpose of its existence. The foreword to the First Edition states, "To show other alcoholics precisely how we have recovered is the purpose of this book." The chapter "There Is a Solution" reinforces the purpose by recognizing that an alcoholic may ask, "What do I have to do?" It goes on to say, "It is the purpose of this book to answer such questions specifically. We shall tell you what we have done."

Being bilingual, I would often make meetings at various Spanish-speaking groups. I noticed that there was a need to participate and share references from the Big Book and other literature to emphasize the importance of our recovery tools. After five years in my home group, I decided that I could be more useful in Spanish-speaking groups. In the years serving the Spanish-speaking membership, I discovered that there were several problems in the translations of the A.A. Big Book and the "Twelve and Twelve." What happened was that I found myself in the middle of a translation uproar from the Spanish-speaking members. To top it off, the problem was compounded by the use of three different translations of the Big Book that were being used. One of these books was from the G.S.O. in Mexico. A team of readers in South Texas volunteered to write down some very evident differences of each book, including the English-language book, side by side. These notes were given to the area delegates for submittal to the Publishing Department at G.S.O. The end result was that the Third Edition of the Spanish Big Book experienced a rigorous multinational review process, including by Mexico, when it was published and distributed.

The French Canadians found similar translation difficulties with the A.A. Big Book. The first translation of the French-language Big Book came about in 1952 from a member who asked and received permission to translate the first 11 chapters of the book. The translation was made in a language that could bring the A.A. message to the French-speaking province of Québec. Later in 1959, a literature committee was created that focused on the obstacles in the translation, and in 1961 it was named Les Editions Françaises A.A. ("A.A. French Editions"). After many years and many evolutions, French-language translations are now handled entirely through G.S.O.

My first awakening to the value of the Big Book and its translations came from a story by Fran P. in the July 1990 Grapevine entitled "Grupa Una," about a woman in Romania named Juliet who was in search of recovery from alcoholism during the oppressive years of 1984–85. Fran writes, "Their faith in A.A. regularly moved me to tears. The first weekend Juliet had the literature, for example, she stayed at home. On Monday, I noticed she seemed quite tired. When asked why, she said she had been sitting up copying the Big Book by hand. Shocked, I told her that I was giving her my copy to keep forever, that she didn't need to copy a single word." I, too, was stunned. My mind raced with gratitude that I was able to go to any group, and more than likely they would have one that I could use or buy. At home I have about five copies in English and two in Spanish.

The Big Book has been the single most important piece of literature for keeping our message consistent throughout the world. As our languages change, so does the literary intent of words. As we move from generation to generation, the difficulty of translating the message of a book that was published in 1939 could bring some challenges. But with improved processes, G.S.O.'s Publishing Department has coordinated translations and publication of the Big Book in 71 languages, and through checks and balances manages to keep the integrity of the original message. Most recently, in 2018 the Navajo Big Book was introduced. And still in progress are about 20 additional languages in a growing list of translations and retranslations of our A.A. Big Book.

There will be many alcoholics who will come through the program. Some will find recovery in our program as described in our book; others will look for other programs and succeed; and still others will be part of a religion and also succeed. However, others will reject all as they search for an easier, softer way. Nonconformity may cause the alcoholic's death and affect the lives of others who cross his or her path. Should we continue to keep the program as outlined in the first 164 pages of the Big Book? I say yes. We should remain one of the choices provided to the suffering alcoholic.

I will conclude my presentation with a reading from the A.A. Big Book, "A Vision for You," where it states, "Our hope is that when this chip of a book is launched on the world tide of alcoholism, defeated drinkers will seize upon it, to follow its suggestions. Many, we are sure, will rise to their feet and march on. They will approach still other sick ones and fellowships of Alcoholics Anonymous may spring up in each city and hamlet, havens for those who must find a way out."

Thank you very much.

Yolanda Flores, Southwest Regional Trustee

■ Presentations

International

Before introducing the two presenters, Eva Sanchez, moderator and staff member on the International assignment at G.S.O., opened the session with the words of former Class A trustee board chair, Dr. Milton Maxwell, who addressed the 6th World Service Meeting in 1980:

"A.A. unity is based not upon authority but upon accepting differences, allowing freedom, and keeping our focus on the primary purpose of helping one another achieve and maintain sobriety.

"Basically, the spiritual part of the program means an unself-centered approach to everything, not insisting on having our own way but accepting what is best for A.A. as a whole. The A.A. way is to give each individual his dignity and freedom, each group its dignity and freedom, and each country or region its dignity and freedom.

"Our U.S./Canadian experience is not binding on any of you, but we join in these World Service Meetings to share our experience and your experience, and through that sharing to help A.A. grow stronger in all parts of the world."

Following this introduction, the two trustees-at-large from the U.S. and Canada offered their presentations.

'The 1969 Project' —
History of the World Service Meeting

For his last major project, Bill W. felt that an international exchange of experiences was necessary to meet the growth of general service problems:

The problems of public relations, of anonymity, of self-support, of relations with medicine and religion — these are all keenly felt in many A.A. countries. The problem of printing and distributing literature is another one that can best be solved by exchange of experience and policies.

With the authorization of our General Service Board, Bill sent a letter dated November 15, 1967, to representatives of 13 other countries and regions with the largest A.A. populations — including the United Kingdom, Australia, New Zealand, France, Belgium, Germany, Finland, Central America, South America, Mexico, Norway, South Africa and the Netherlands — to gauge the interest in convening a World Service Meeting (WSM) in New York to run for three days in the autumn of 1969. Each country or zone would be allowed two delegates: one being the principal A.A. service head, with the other perhaps the chair of the general service board, whether alcoholic or nonalcoholic. The first WSM would be financed by voluntary contributions of the participating countries according to each country's ability to pay into a "world treasury," in addition to paying the first $200 of expenses for each of its delegates.

Following an enthusiastic response from the countries polled, Bill presented a position paper to the General Service Board at its January 1968 meeting and to the 1968 General Service Conference to secure approval for "The 1969 Project." Bill stated in part:

I would like to offer what I believe to be our present views of the problem of more general services in overseas countries, to suggest steps that might be taken to strengthen general service work existing abroad, to increase the number of such overseas centers, and to provide for them an orderly plan of evolution according to the several needs of the many countries that now

ought to become in various degrees involved in these activities.

First, let me distinguish between local services and general or world services. While A.A. is a loosely knit society, we do know, nevertheless, that properly authorized and organized A.A. services are necessary to enable groups, local areas, and A.A. as a whole to function. In no other way can we carry our message to the alcoholics who still suffer. Hence, our groups customarily name rotating committees, and in larger metropolitan centers, we choose local or central committees which provide offices or answering services where calls for help may be received, sponsorship and hospitalization provided, etc. All this activity is designed to meet strictly local needs and area problems. Most A.A.s are familiar with such local arrangements and clearly see the need for them; indeed, many members still think that group and intergroup services are all that A.A. needs for its total functioning. However, this is not really so.

As early as 1938, it was recognized that A.A. as a whole must have top international leadership, and that this leadership would have to create those vital services that could not be provided locally on a haphazard basis. Had we failed to do this, A.A. would have fallen into schism, if not anarchy. Thus, sorely crippled, our message could never have been effectively carried anywhere. The bulk of our present-day membership would still be drinking or dead.

After reviewing the history of general services in the U.S. and Canada and the linking of those services to the Fellowship through the mechanism of our General Service Conference, Bill looked to one more needed development in our world service structure:

We must now proceed to establish other world service centers; these in addition to the few that have been taking form in recent years. Long ago, it became apparent that New York could not forever provide complete general services to all the A.A. countries that occupy such vast regions of the world. The reasons for this are not hard to understand; our present centralized structure would develop serious defects:

- If continued, growing centralization would tend to make New York and its service leadership the "world capital" of A.A. Psychologically, such an ever-growing concentration would be most unwise.

- It would foreclose the creation of effective world leadership overseas.

- It would deprive other countries of the healthy responsibility of manning their own overall services.

- Administratively, an increasing centralization at New York would also prove faulty. For example, just how could New York actually manage and conduct public relations in remote Europe or distant Australia? We can continue to give advice on request, but never could we personally render service as we do in the North American region.

- The financial problem of supporting an activity lodged mostly in New York would finally become difficult, if not impossible.

Once approved by the 1968 General Service Conference, the first WSM was held in New York in 1969, and attendees included Bill W., Class A trustee Dr. Jack Norris, general manager Bob H. and two U.S. delegates. The delegates unanimously agreed that the meetings were worthwhile, and the idea of holding future meetings with rotating delegates was approved. The next meeting was held in 1972, when it was recommended that future WSMs be held every two years. At the third WSM in London in 1974, the following statement of purpose was adopted:

The primary purpose of the World Service Meeting is the same as that of all A.A. activity — to carry the message to the alcoholic who still suffers, wherever in the world he may be, whatever the language he speaks. The World Service Meeting seeks ways and means of accomplishing this goal by serving as a forum for sharing the experience, strength and hope of the delegates who come together every two years from all corners of the world.

It can also represent an expression of the group conscience on a worldwide basis. Experience teaches us that organizing ourselves into a sound structure enables us to develop and deliver our services more effectively. The World Service Meeting encourages the planning of a sound service structure suited to the needs and capabilities of the various countries, and the exploration of expanding A.A. services to reach the alcoholic through internal communication, literature distribution, sponsorship, public information, community relations and institutions work.

Newton Pritchett, Trustee-at-large/U.S.

25th World Service Meeting

The 25th World Service Meeting (WSM) took place in Durban, South Africa, from October 7 to October 11, 2018, with the theme "Our Twelve Traditions: A.A.'s Future in the Modern World."

Our U.S./Canada service structure was represented by Newton P., trustee-at-large/U.S., as first-term delegate and myself as second-term delegate. We were also very well represented by our general manager, Greg T., who co-chaired the meeting, and Mary C., Clement C., Eva S. and Sandra W., who served as committee secretaries.

Bolivia and Turkey had delegates present for the first time. Iran and Cuba were present for the second time, each with two delegates. The delegates from Iran were delayed with some visa issues. However, when they did arrive, they were met with a standing ovation.

This was just one of a number of examples of A.A.'s supportive spirit that was evidenced at the WSM. This meeting was not only about presentations and workshops, but also about how A.A.s everywhere support each other's recovery and growth, whether as individuals or as structures. It is the same kind of experience we have here at our Conference and in each of our assemblies.

At the WSM we saw some of this support in financial terms. A number of countries and regions, including Great Britain, Sweden, German-speaking Europe, Denmark, Mexico, Norway, Belgium and French-speaking Europe, provided financial sponsorship for other countries to attend. This WSM established a World Service Meeting Fund to which countries can contribute funds in order to provide financial assistance to countries that may request financial assistance to attend the WSM. Like the International Literature Fund, this new fund will be administered by A.A.W.S.

Similar to what we do here at the Conference, at the WSM, countries give highlights. Some of the high points of those highlights for me included:

1. Cuba announced that it is close to official legal recognition and now has an official website and email account. They are in the process of restructuring to conform with the laws of Cuba.

2. Finland spoke of an active YPAA that had recently hosted a EURYPAA and of their structure's efforts to reach out to retired alcoholics.

3. The Netherlands is developing an image plan to help improve the reputation and image of A.A. in order to reach more alcoholics.

4. Turkey spoke of how A.A. began in 1988 and how they operated without a legal identity until February 7, 2018. They are now known as Alcoholics Anonymous Solidarity and Support Association and are able to work in hospitals and prisons and with other government associations.

There were presentations on a number of topics, including the relevance of our Traditions in this modern world; how service is investing in A.A.'s future; the future of our national magazines; and the safety of the vulnerable member. This led to a discussion relating to inclusion that touched on the effect of sexually predatory behavior — behavior that causes some to be excluded from an opportunity for recovery. My own view was that we ought to stop legitimizing this kind of behavior by referring to it as "13th stepping," which simply sounds cute rather than criminal. It also touched on the need and responsibility of those members who are in the room to look for who is *not* in the room.

There were also presentations around the topics of attracting members into service and of special purpose groups. Workshops were held on the topics of how to use the Internet wisely; Country-to-Country Sponsorship; and leadership in A.A.

The WSM closed with the Serenity Prayer being said in 24 languages.

What I witnessed was an enthusiasm for Alcoholics Anonymous and the lifesaving work we do. It does not seem to matter where an alcoholic lives, what language he or she got drunk in, or how old or young he or she is: The message of Alcoholics Anonymous reaches across the barriers of culture, language and time.

I heard many stories of the incredible lengths that members go to help the still-suffering alcoholic and the actions being taken to help the still-suffering find hope. We witness this on every international trip that our trustees-at-large and office staff make.

We also see friends of A.A. going to great lengths with a passion to help the suffering alcoholic. An example of this in this past year was one doctor friend in Cuba who traveled 12 hours on a bus to celebrate A.A.'s 25th Anniversary in Cuba. She was also instrumental in securing the first-

Our Twelve Traditions: A.A.'s Future in the Modern World

ALCOHOLICS ANONYMOUS 25TH WORLD SERVICE MEETING
Durban, South Africa | October 7-11, 2018

ever invitation for Alcoholics Anonymous to officially participate in a Health Conference in Cuba. This conference also witnessed the credibility that our Class A trustees bring to Alcoholics Anonymous with other professionals. Our own Dr. Peter Luongo spoke the language of the professionals assembled at that conference in relating how A.A. helped him better serve his clients.

What is clear to me from both the experience of the WSM and the experiences of our other international travel for A.A. events is how important it is for us to continue our role — important for the world of A.A. and for the health of A.A. in our own structure.

As the most senior A.A. structure, we are a little like the longtimer in the rooms of A.A. Others want and need our experience, strength and hope, but we also have much to learn and need the experience and enthusiasm of others — whether it is the vibrancy of the Fellowship in Lithuania spurred by a very active YPAA; or seeing Russia reach out to support the emergence of A.A. in some of the countries that were former Soviet Republics; or seeing the leadership, both financial and spiritual, of structures like Mexico and the U.K.; or the WSM delegate for Iran saying that his structure is looking forward to the day when they can help others the way they have been helped. It may be the chance experience of meeting with a member from Serbia to discuss translation procedures, or a discussion with board members from Portugal about how our app may be able to help them, or seeing how other structures are harnessing the use of social media within our Traditions: We have much to give. And by giving, we are given the opportunity to continue to grow in love and understanding. May it always be so.

Scott Huyghebaert, Trustee-at-large/Canada

Yesterday's World — Our Legacies Begin

Hello, everyone, my name is Sara Plansky-Pecor and I am an alcoholic. I am honored to be serving Area 74 Northern Wisconsin and the Upper Peninsula of Michigan as Panel 68 delegate to the General Service Conference.

Thank you to Patrick C. for the loving invitation to present on the topic of "Yesterday's World — Our Legacies Begin." The Three Legacies of our beloved program of Alcoholics Anonymous are Recovery, Unity and Service. These Legacies have been passed down to us from our co-founders, Bill W. and Dr. Bob, and the oldtimers of A.A.

Recovery is our Twelve Steps. The Twelve Steps were first presented in 1939 with the publishing of our Big Book of *Alcoholics Anonymous*. The foreword to the First Edition of the Big Book of *Alcoholics Anonymous* states, "To show other alcoholics precisely how we have recovered is the main purpose of this book."

Unity is our Twelve Traditions. A.A.'s Twelve Traditions present the principles that support the unity of the A.A. Fellowship at the group level. The Traditions were first presented in a series of articles by our co-founder, Bill W., in the late 1940s, which appeared in AA Grapevine.

The foreword in *Twelve Steps and Twelve Traditions* states, "A.A.'s Twelve Traditions apply to the life of the Fellowship itself. They outline the means by which A.A. maintains its unity and relates itself to the world about it, the way it lives and grows."

Service is our Third Legacy. "A.A.'s Twelfth Step, carrying the message, is the basic service that our fellowship gives; it is our principal aim and the main reason for our existence. A.A. is more than a set of principles; it is a society of recovered alcoholics in action. We *must* carry A.A.'s message; otherwise we ourselves may fall into decay and those who have not yet been given the truth may die. This is why we so often say that *action* is the magic word. Action to carry A.A.'s message is therefore the heart of our Third Legacy of Service." (*A.A. Comes of Age*, pp. 139–40)

Altogether, the Twelve Steps, Twelve Traditions and Twelve Concepts represent what we know as the Three Legacies of Alcoholics Anonymous: Recovery, Unity and Service. The Three Legacies of A.A. began in yesterday's world and I am forever grateful that they continue in my world today. I practice the Twelve Steps; I follow the Twelve Traditions; and I continue to take action in my life in carrying the message of our Twelfth Step. I will tell you that my life is not balanced. Alcoholics Anonymous takes up a lot of my time! However, I have no doubt in my mind that without A.A. in my life and left to my own devices I wouldn't be breathing. I am the person I am today because of our beloved program. Everything I have learned has come from someone who has walked before me in this program and has taken the time to pass it on to me. I have learned through my recovery as well as my journey in general service that I am not unique; I am not intelligent. As a matter of fact, it was told to me very simply at the beginning of my recovery that I am just another bozo on the bus.

I believe it is my responsibility as a member of Alcoholics Anonymous to pass on what I have learned from others who walked this path before me. Today more than ever I believe in the importance of a home group and passing on the message to the women I sponsor as well as of communicating our group conscience down the triangle of the structure of the Conference. The theme of the 69th General Service Conference is "Our Big Book — 80 Years, 71 Languages." Our Three Legacies of Recovery, Unity and Service began in yesterday's world; however, today, after 80 years, our Big Book is being read in 71 languages. This tells me the instructions were given to us in our Twelve Steps, Twelve Traditions and Twelve Concepts for World Service, and they need to be followed if we want this program to continue forever. I agree that A.A. will be destroyed from within — and not from anything outside of us — if we don't follow our principles. We need to be responsible not only for our personal recovery programs but also for the program of Alcoholics Anonymous as a whole.

I would like to direct your attention to a paragraph in *A.A. Comes of Age* that I find remarkable and which is a quote from the late Bernard B. Smith, nonalcoholic, past chair of our board of trustees and one of the architects of the Conference structure. "And I thought of the finger of God determining our course — as individuals, as a fellowship, and in our relation to the world about us. Clearly, I thought, the Twelve Steps of A.A. must have been spiritually conceived to meet a serious and growing challenge to all of us, nonalcoholic as well as alcoholic. What is that challenge? It is the challenge to a generation that would deny the spiritual basis for human existence and accept in its place a currently socially accepted basis that is mechanistic and materialistic. It is a challenge to which A.A. will never yield, for the tenet of its faith and, indeed, its existence is founded on the certainty of a spiritual basis for life on earth." (*A.A. Comes of Age*, pp. 274–75)

As we move forward this week with this humbling opportunity to participate in the 69th General Service Conference, I challenge you to think about the question posed by Bernard Smith and how it fits in today as to whether Alcoholics Anonymous is moving toward a "mechanistic and materialistic" society. Our Legacies began in yesterday's world, and we need them to continue to ensure the recovery of the alcoholic who still stumbles in the darkness one short block from this room. After serving my first year as Area 74 Panel 68 delegate to the General Service Conference, I have felt very disillusioned by this experience. It appears to me that A.A. is moving toward a society that is mechanistic and materialistic in thought and action and taking on the ways of the world. Are we today still following our spiritual principles, which have been firmly embedded in our Legacies and which began in yesterday's world?

I would like to close with a quote from Concept XII Warranty Six, "Freedom under God to grow in His likeness and image will ever be the quest of Alcoholics Anonymous.

May our General Service Conference be always seen as a chief symbol of this cherished liberty." (*The A.A. Service Manual 2018–2020*, pp. 72–73)

Sara Plansky-Pecor, Northern Wisconsin and the Upper Peninsula of Michigan

Today's World — Demonstrating Integrity, Anonymity and Service

Greetings to all attendees of the 69th General Service Conference. My name is Jon Phillips and I'm an alcoholic. I am gratefully serving as the Panel 68 delegate for Area 64, Tennessee. Thank you, Patrick and Nay, for the loving invitation to present on the topic "Today's World — Demonstrating Integrity, Anonymity and Service." With advances in technology and the ever-evolving methods of communication from our members, last year's Conference theme "A.A. – A Solution for All Generations" and the presentation topic I've been given this year couldn't be more vital to our present and our future. I would like to use my five minutes to touch on two areas that I have had to work on to keep an open mind so that I do not stay stuck in what some might consider a rigid approach to our way of life. Those areas are social media and sponsoring A.A. members from our younger generation.

Let's start with social media. I had the opportunity to give a presentation at the Southeast Regional Forum on "A.A. and Social Media" last November. In my presentation I focused primarily on Facebook secret groups for A.A. members. I experienced a sigh from the audience when I announced my topic in Sterling. I think there are two reasons this topic is laced with controversy. The first is fear coupled with a lack of understanding when it comes to technology. The second is the lack of integrity shown by some A.A. members when participating in secret Facebook groups. It seems as though some people may not be as concerned about practicing our principles while sitting behind a keyboard! I've probably been guilty myself.

By a show of hands, how many people in the room have Facebook accounts? How many of those with their hands up belong to secret Facebook groups for A.A. members? How many people in the room fully understand all of Facebook's settings? Even further, how many of you have Instagram, Twitter or Snapchat? I can understand skepticism when it comes to social media being a tool to carry the A.A. message because I've experienced it myself. A few years ago, my friend and now alternate delegate for Area 64 convinced me to join Facebook so I could participate in the secret groups discussing various A.A. topics. Apprehensively I joined and quickly fell in love with secret groups for A.A. members. I became an admin for the secret group SES and I still am today. Learning how to deal with people misbehaving in the group, people wanting their way and people constantly taking shots at the admin has been a lot like my home group business meetings! Explaining to A.A. members that these groups do not break your anonymity at the public level has been an adventure as well. I am about as tight as they come about personal anonymity, so I have had to remain open to learning when it comes to Facebook settings. When I saw someone post, "I am so grateful that A.A. has kept me sober for 10 years" or saw someone post their medallion on their timeline, I used to become very judgmental. Although we can certainly break our anonymity on Facebook, as people quite often do, I didn't realize at the time that a lot of these posts were set so that only A.A. friends of the person could see them. It just took me being willing to step down from my pedestal to learn what was really going on.

Overall, I would say the behavior of some individuals has turned a lot of us against secret groups and made A.A. very slow to move into the social media realm. Let's not throw the baby out with the bathwater, because I've seen A.A. member's maturity level grow by leaps and bounds over the last few years when it comes to social media behavior. Though it will never replace face-to-face work with another alcoholic, if we don't stay up to date we may not be able to reach many alcoholics to initiate that face-to-face work.

Now I'll address sponsoring our younger members. I have been accused of being militant when it comes to my sponsorship methods. That approach has worked well with guys my age and older but not so well with our younger crowd. Kids don't communicate the same way I did at 18. I was in the car with my sponsor and his teenage daughter one day and listening to her argue about how phone calls don't make sense and that everyone should always communicate through text. This made me think about how I didn't allow my sponsees to text me. Instead I required them to call. For some reason I wasn't hearing from my younger guys very much. I started allowing them to text me instead, and guess what? They wouldn't leave me alone!

I've had to try to put myself in the younger generation's shoes while at the same time sticking to our principles. I sponsor a guy who just celebrated seven years sober and who got sober when he was 16. For four years I couldn't even get the kid to join a home group. As my attitude changed about how to handle him, his attitude changed as well. He is now the alternate D.C.M. for his district and is as active in general service as anyone I sponsor. I just had to learn to meet our younger A.A. members where they were.

I'd like to thank you all again for allowing me to present on this topic. It has been a blessing to serve at my second Conference with some of you and to meet all of the new 69s. I hope you all enjoy the rest of your week here in New York!

Jon Phillips, Tennessee

Tomorrow's World — Courage to Be Vigilant

Vigilant: to be attentive, careful; watchful. This word is typically associated with danger or difficulties. Another aspect of the meaning of *vigilant* is to be on the lookout for opportunities. Continuous improvement is a way of life for A.A. Inventories are tools used to see where we're at and how to move forward. The Communications Audit can be a useful tool in helping to improve our effectiveness. Our task is to look for and seize our opportunities when they arise — to be ready and willing to change, adapt and update in real time, or as soon as possible. The solution to recovery from alcoholism has not changed in 80 years. However, the way people access the information to that solution has! We will need courage — and an open mind — to utilize new ways to carry the A.A. message into tomorrow's world. Fear of change can stifle growth. The spiritual opposite of fear is courage. We must not let fear of making mistakes or our shortsightedness interfere with our ability to reach the still sick and suffering alcoholic.

The Fellowship is rapidly embracing technology and with much enthusiasm. The news about A.A.W.S.'s redesigned website and the addition of the Meeting Guide

app has been well received in my area. How can we get better at reaching people where they're at — on their cell phones, tablets and in the digital world? Imagine if you will, Bill on Skype, or Bob with a laptop. Or Bill tweeting his new ideas and concepts to the Fellowship! I have little doubt that they would have used every resource available to them in carrying this lifesaving message!

The September 2010 Grapevine featured an interview with Reverend Ward B. Ewing entitled "A Vision for Us" in which he noted, "The Fellowship must develop and utilize effective and innovative approaches to a new generation of alcoholics whose communication pathways have shifted over the last decade or so. 'We're awfully print-heavy, and there's a new generation coming that doesn't use books. So, how do we evolve and find effective means through information technology to carry the message?'"

How indeed? The Communications Audit echoes this as well. It also points out "the need to use familiar or relevant language to key audiences, especially the still-suffering alcoholic."

What about singleness of purpose in tomorrow's world?

In recent years there has been a plethora of twelve-step programs created to fix an assortment of issues. The Communications Audit notes, "The public sees little differentiation between A.A. and other recovery/sobriety programs, and that A.A.'s value is getting lost in 'crowded competition.' There's a lot of affiliation going on, and with a membership growing weaker in their knowledge of our Twelve Traditions it seems acceptable behavior."

I recently had a conversation with a G.S.R. about linking A.A.'s name to N.A. and other things. We discussed how this directly affects our singleness of purpose and confuses newcomers and the public. While other groups and organizations may seem to be closely aligned to our primary purpose, they are not A.A. We talked about why we don't use literature or speakers from outside A.A., and how we check ourselves, not only for affiliation and endorsement, but for the appearance of it. If we (A.A.) allow ourselves to give our endorsement, our name or our resources, we lose the power of our message. We cannot afford to compromise on this. We must stay true to our primary purpose and not try to be all things to all people. Without adhering to these Traditions, A.A. can quickly become something it is not. It was a fruitful discussion and we both came away with a deeper appreciation for our Traditions.

Another area highlighted in the Communications Audit is the ongoing relationship between Alcoholics Anonymous and religion. A.A. is perceived by many as religious. A.A. is a spiritual program and not a religion, yet some A.A. practices make it hard to tell the difference between the two.

My hope for A.A.'s future is that we have the courage to see — and act — on these areas of opportunity. Effective communication will be key to our successful outreach to those looking for a solution to their alcoholism and to the evolutionary growth of A.A. As members of A.A., *we* are responsible for the delivery and the quality of these services. We don't need a service position to do so. We already have one. It's called *A.A. member*.

Vera Farrell, Oregon

Presentation/Discussions

The following topics were presented for discussion by all Conference members.

Equitable Distribution of Workload

The topic of equitable distribution of workload for Conference committees has been under discussion for several years — all the way back to the 1960s, when the Admissions function was moved from the Agenda Committee to the Policy Committee. The '90s saw the creation of two secondary committees: Regional Forums and Archives. At the 2013 General Service Conference, the Conference Policy/Admissions Committee discussed combining the Agenda and Policy/Admissions Committees. However, the sense of the committee was that it wouldn't be that beneficial and that the time currently allotted for each committee's deliberation seemed appropriate. In addition, joining the two committees might have created too heavy of a workload for the resulting committee. Finally, the committee considered the complications involved in merging the committees, which would include updating *The A.A. Service Manual/ Twelve Concepts for World Service* as well as other literature, adding to the responsibilities of staff, and changing the composition and scope of the committees.

All these concerns, as well as the effect any significant change in the scope of the Conference committees would have on the relationship with the corresponding trustee committees and the joint meetings, have been considered throughout the years.

Thus, the structure of 13 Conference committees has remained relatively unchanged since the 1990s. The number of agenda items per committee has also stayed relatively the same — until the last two years, when the total number of agenda items jumped from an average of 72.5 to 108 in 2017, and to 91 total items in 2018. The Literature Committee experienced the largest jump over that period, going from about eight items to 13 in 2017, and to 21 total items in 2018. The Public Information Committee has had the highest average number of agenda items over the last ten years.

Within this same period, for the most part, committees have handled their workload in the allotted time. There are a few, however, that have had to extend that time, such as Public Information (an average allotted 6.4 hours vs 9.1 hours taken in committee). Literature (an average allotted 6.4 hours vs 9.0 hours taken in committee) and Agenda Committees (an average allotted 6.2 hours vs 7.6 hours taken in committee) have also needed more time on average to deal with their workloads.

At their January 28, 2017, meeting, the trustees' committee on the General Service Conference (TCGSC) made the following recommendation to the General Service Board:

In order to assist the Conference committees in handling their workload, if a Conference committee feels it is helpful to complete the work of their committee, they are welcome to meet via conference call in the 60 days prior to the Annual Meeting of the General Service Conference. They may use the call for such things as deciding how to conduct their business, including the means of voting within the committee, reordering the items on their agenda if needed, and holding preliminary non-voting discussions on what they consider to be priority items. Conference committee secretaries would be available to facilitate these meetings.

The General Service Board approved the recommendation at their January 30 meeting.

Each 2017 Conference committee was asked to "consider a request to add text to the committee's Composition, Scope and Procedure regarding the option to meet by conference call prior to the Annual Meeting of the General Service Conference." The committees that discussed this item provided Additional Committee Considerations to take no action noting that the committees already had this prerogative.

Conference calls among the committee members and their secretaries have occurred over the last couple of years to discuss "housekeeping" items.

At that same 2017 General Service Conference, the Trustees' Committee on the General Service Conference also forwarded a recommendation to develop a Plan for the Equitable Distribution of Workload to the Conference Policy and Admissions Committee, which made a recommendation for such a plan to be developed and asked for a report back in 2018.

The trustees' committee on the General Service Conference tasked the committee staff secretary with creating a workable plan. No plan was forwarded; however, the trustees' committee on the General Service Conference requested more time to create a plan by combining and/or creating committees and sent a report with history and options that was presented to the 2018 Conference Policy/Admissions Committee. The 2018 trustees' committee on the General Service Conference also cautioned that if there would be a significant change in the number, composition and scope of Conference committees, it might be better to include both the Conference and trustee committee structure (with approval from the General Service Board before proposing major changes).

This last year the trustees' committee created a subcommittee to come up with a plan. After reviewing the history and considering the options, the subcommittee concluded that a broader discussion is needed on this issue that would include the following questions:

- Does this topic on equitable workload require a larger working group, potentially a General Service Board ad hoc committee?

- Could this occur during the January General Service Board weekend (when delegate chairs are present), setting aside an hour or an hour and a half?

- Should the committee get input from staff, the trustees' committee on the General Service Conference, management and Conference Agenda Committee chair and all delegate chairs in a brainstorming session?

Ultimately, we decided to allocate time at the 69th Conference to gain clarity on the issue.

What exactly is the problem we are trying to fix? Do we want all the Conference committees to have an equal workload, and is that even possible considering the nature of our agenda item process? Since agenda items come from many sources, the number per committee would be difficult to project under our current structure. Or is there another issue at play that would benefit from a closer review? Let's have this discussion and see if we can set a way forward that will allow each committee and the Conference a chance to develop an informed group conscience.

Cathy Beckham, Southeast Regional Trustee

Note: Additional commentary from the discussion following this presentation will be provided for the trustees' ongoing evaluation.

A.A.W.S. Audio/Video Strategy

My name is David Rosen and I am an alcoholic. I currently serve in the professional position of publishing director of A.A. World Services, Inc., a post I have held since mid-2016.

It is my privilege to present to you today an update on our work toward the formulation of a cohesive strategic approach by A.A.W.S. toward creating, distributing and maintaining our multimedia content — all with an eye toward best achieving our mission in this digital age.

We invite the members of the Conference to assist and guide us in this significant endeavor. I will be brief, in hopes that this valuable opportunity for sharing can be made the most of.

The Multimedia Explosion

As we all know, today's audiences — young and old and everyone in between — are hungry for content across formats and forms, from print to e-book, audio to video, information that's accessible in short takes and longer takes, via every means available, including smart devices and voice-activated ones alike.

Before us are pressing matters of how to best share A.A.'s message in forms that reach the sick and suffering alcoholic, the newcomer to A.A., those in service, and those who may not be… yet.

A New Strategic Direction for Audio and Video

We are describing here an A.A.W.S. Audio/Video Strategy to bring together clear focus and resources (existing and emerging), under the active management of the A.A.W.S. Publishing Department, in collaboration with the staff desk assignments — and utilizing professional industry-standard best-practice freelance assistance, as projects warrant.

Here are some recent trends that we are all seeing in the culture at large and in our Fellowship as well: what we are fondly calling the move toward "snackable" content (delightfully short audios and videos, podcasts and the like); the fondness for digesting content via website,

YouTube and podcast; apps for information sharing; the audiobooks explosion; and, throughout, the emphasis on *storytelling* in all content (*personal storytelling* — as in, "what it was like, what happened and what it is like now" — a narrative arc that's dear to every A.A. member's heart). Add to this list visual memes; sophisticated animation and graphic novels; live video streaming; virtual reality video, smart, voice-assisted command control (at home and in cars); online learning and community-building; and more.

We are mindful that in all our efforts to extend the hand of A.A. via our Conference-approved and service literature and other communications, we strive to ensure the integrity of the A.A. message; anonymity; accessibility; attraction and inclusion.

E-book, audio and video production and distribution projects today

Here's what it was like in the old days:

- 30-second video spot from the old "Your A.A. G.S.O."

Here are short samples of recently completed works and works in progress:

- ASL video clip (1 minute)
- PSA short culled from *A New Freedom* video (1 minute)
- Twelve Concepts audio on aa.org (one short sample in Spanish) (1 minute)
- Changes (30 seconds)
- 3 samples (English, French and Spanish revised *Daily Reflections* audio/video project (2 minutes)

Other projects we are moving forward include: converting books, booklets and pamphlets to audio and e-book digital format (to best reach professionals, schools, libraries and prison populations and treatment settings; veterans and members of the armed services; remote communities); Braille Big Books and other content in Québec French and Spanish; a type of virtual Regional Forum for aa.org;

and contracting industry-standard distribution channels for greater reach in e-book, audiobook, video and more.

We have our work cut out for us.

Questions and directions for A.A.W.S. Audio/ Video Strategy

I will conclude by positing these first few questions, which I hope may springboard us toward robust discussions today — and ongoing:

- Where do we start? *Daily Reflections* audio/video project? How can we best address all the imperatives — matters of contemporization, literacy, accessibility, attraction and inclusion?

- How may we best bring the fruits of content conversion and new content creation through group conscience decision making?

- How can we work together with local committees (Corrections, H&I, PI, CPC and so forth) to offer end products that folks actually want and can use?

- What anonymity-protection concerns are involved in each of these formats, platforms and channels?

- How much funding and how many work hours are we talking about? How many additional resources (internal and external) will be needed?

These are just a few of the many questions... Ideas and opportunities abound.

David Rosen, A.A.W.S., Inc. Publishing Director

2020 International Convention

In just a little more than a year, we will meet to celebrate A.A.'s 85th Birthday at our International Convention in Detroit. July 2–5, 2020, are the dates — so mark your calendar! Plans are well underway to make this a joyous and memorable event.

Detroit is a vibrant city, filled with a rich history and its very own soundtrack. The downtown area, where we will be, has undergone a major transformation. The riverfront has been completely revitalized and the convention center entirely renovated. The Detroit downtown core and the areas around the hotels and facilities that we will be using reflect the incredible recovery the city has made, and it is breaking stereotypes by being one of the safest among Midwestern convention cities. When we get there, we'll pack the Cobo Convention Center with handshakes, hugs, kisses and lots of meetings, panels and workshops. And of course, we'll have those extraordinary Big Meetings in the Ford Field Stadium.

The festivities start on Thursday night with a party in Hart Plaza, right next to the Convention Center. Music will fill the summer night, and you will enjoy a beautiful view of downtown Windsor, Canada, right across the river. You can dance in the park under the stars, in the Convention Center or in one of the nearby hotels.

At midnight on Thursday, marathon meetings will start and will continue through Sunday morning. Friday morning, hundreds of meetings will begin at the Convention Center, and Friday night in the Ford Field Stadium, we will hold the exciting Parade of Flags of countries represented at the Convention, followed by the three-speaker Big A.A. Meeting. The wonderful Oldtimers Stadium Meeting will take place on Saturday night, where oldtimers will be selected from the hat to share with us. What a great way to honor our history and hear firsthand what we used to be like, what happened and what we are like now. Sunday morning, we will have our customary three-speaker Big Meeting to close out the weekend, and we will say farewell until 2025 in Vancouver, British Columbia.

Early International Conventions were focal points for important moments in A.A. history. At the first Convention, in Cleveland in 1950, our Twelve Traditions were confirmed, helping to ensure the future of our Fellowship, and at the 1955 Convention in St. Louis, Bill W. and the oldtimers turned the leadership of the Fellowship over to the General Service Conference.

International Conventions offer the occasion for rich and varied experiences, some dramatic and historic, others quiet and serene. Those who talk about attending an International Convention speak of it as a highlight of their sobriety, and the emotion universally expressed is one of gratitude — gratitude for sobriety in A.A. and for having had the opportunity to celebrate that sobriety with tens of thousands of A.A. members and their loved ones in a spectacular gathering.

Many who travel to Detroit with old friends, sponsors or home group members will have those on-the-road meetings that form such an important part of our Fellowship sharing. Those A.A. "coincidences" will occur — a beloved friend you lost track of will show up sober. Someone on your Eighth Step list will appear and provide you with the opportunity to make amends; perhaps you'll be on their Eighth Step list, as well. New and lifelong friendships will be made — perhaps in the wee hours of the morning, as we fellowship over ice cream and coffee. And Twelfth Step work will take place — we have all heard the stories of alcoholics who got sober during an International Convention.

These events affect not only the A.A. members in attendance, but they also provide a chance for the public to see us firsthand. In 1950, a cab driver in Cleveland stated that we were the nicest convention they had ever had. A female taxi driver in Seattle in 1990 commented, "You people have something special. You make me feel good. I'm usually dragged out by these summer conventions, but this time I'm looking forward to each run. Even when one of you gets cranky, the others talk him out of it. I've never seen anything like it. I wish I could send my kids."

In Toronto, one of the city department managers — who was there to demand that every city ordinance be followed to a tee — ran up to a group on Sunday afternoon and practically shouted, "I have one thing to say to you guys! ... Don't go home." During the weekend, the love and fellowship expressed among the attendees had converted her into an A.A. fan. She said that in all her years of city service, she had never seen such cooperation and harmony among such a varied group. In Atlanta, a police officer "complained" that he had never been hugged and thanked so much in the line of duty.

As you may be aware, when planning International Conventions, we try very hard to emphasize to hotels and convention centers in Convention cities the magnitude of our event, yet the message doesn't always get across: During one Convention, disaster struck when all the major facilities in the city ran out of coffee — we drank them dry. But worse was yet to happen: In the same city, they ran out of toilet paper. These International Conventions are also opportunities to let the newcomer and the world know we are not a glum lot.

And now we are celebrating A.A.'s 85th Anniversary! The theme is "Love and Tolerance Is Our Code." The inspiration for the theme appears in the chapter "Into Action" on page 85 of the Big Book. The original phrase is "Love and tolerance of others is our code," and it is part of Bill's sharing on Step Ten, which suggests "we continue to take personal inventory and continue to set right any new mistakes as we go along." It is worth noting that the phrase right before it states, "Then we resolutely turn our thoughts to someone we can help."

The International Convention truly enables attendees to live the spirit of love and tolerance, and to witness the success and growth of A.A. around the world. Not only does this event affect members in attendance and provide the opportunity for a rededication to A.A.'s primary purpose, it also lets the world know that A.A. is still alive, flourishing and available as a community resource, locally and internationally.

You, the members of the Conference, will have a large part to play in the success and tone of the Convention. Most of the speakers will come from your recommendations. You have already received requests to suggest non-A.A. speakers from professional fields. This fall, we will be asking you to send us suggestions for A.A. members to participate in the over 700 meetings taking place over the weekend.

Another major part in organizing this event is working with the Volunteer Welcome Committee. We would not be able to welcome so many members from around the world without an able and enthusiastic Welcome Committee. The core of the committee is in place. They are eager to start, and will begin gathering names of volunteers with a kick-off event in January. We anticipate that upwards of 4,000 volunteers will be welcoming convention-goers to Detroit.

All of this information will be communicated on G.S.O.'s A.A. website, in *Box 4-5-9*, and in special Convention mailings. In August, we will be mailing out the registration forms for the 2020 International Convention to all Conference members, to the G.S.R.s of all active groups, and to others in the service structure, as well as to intergroups, central offices and general service offices around the world.

Registration and housing will open on September 9, 2019. We will be making rooms available on a first-come, first-served basis. As in the past, members will be able to register by mail or online. Once you have registered, you will be able to book your hotel room.

So, one day at a time, we are preparing for an international celebration of A.A.'s 85th birthday. We know this Convention will be a powerful example of the joy of living. And amid the festive crowds, I hope each of us is reminded that "In spite of the great increase in the size and the span of this Fellowship, at its core it remains simple and personal. Each day, somewhere in the world, recovery begins when one alcoholic talks with another alcoholic, sharing experience, strength, and hope." (*Alcoholics Anonymous*, p. xxii)

Julio Espaillat, International Conventions Coordinator

AA Grapevine and La Viña

My name is Albin and I am an alcoholic. It is my privilege to perform the duties of publisher at your AA Grapevine, Inc.

AA Grapevine, Inc. staff is currently comprised of the publisher, controller, director of operations, senior editor, La Viña editor, production coordinator, outreach coordinator, web coordinator, customer relations coordinator, junior accountant, executive/customer service assistant, Grapevine and La Viña editorial assistants, production and office assistants as well as Grapevine and La Viña art directors. Ten of these positions are full-time; the rest are part-time and freelance. It takes a lot to make this organization run smoothly: This is a hard-working team, and each staff member wears many hats through the course of each day.

AA Grapevine, Inc.'s vision is that "Grapevine and La Viña publish/share the voices of the Fellowship of Alcoholics Anonymous, reflecting the diverse experience of recovery using the principles of our program. In all formats, Grapevine and La Viña are lifelines connecting one alcoholic to another in a solution that works."

As such, our mission statement says, "AA Grapevine, Inc. is a multi-media publisher of the International Journals of Alcoholics Anonymous and related content. Its primary purpose is to carry the message to everyone interested in alcoholism, reflecting the stories of experience, strength and hope of its members and friends on topics related to recovery, unity and service. It strives in all its activities to operate in accordance with the Twelve Steps, the Twelve Traditions, and the Twelve Concepts of AA, without soliciting monetary contributions from AA members or groups to fund operating expenses."

Our current business goals, as reflected in the 2018–20 strategic plan, are to:

a. enhance paths of communication, dialogue and outreach to the Fellowship about Grapevine and La Viña;

b. continue to explore all possible revenue streams to ensure viability;

c. make fully informed decisions using Fellowship Feedback input, members' current media usage and habits, industry best practices and usability of all products;

d. adjust Grapevine and La Viña editorial and other content to generate more interest in participation and subscription;

e. create a stronger digital presence to serve the A.A. community wherever they may be, on whatever computer or mobile device;

f. update existing subscription models and delivery platforms to ensure GV is easy to find, subscribe to and use; and

g. fulfill AAGV Inc.'s mission statement.

In addition, we are concentrating on a high level of customer satisfaction. In the fall of 2018, a 15-minute survey was provided to both readers and potential readers of Grapevine and La Viña with the goal of measuring attitudes toward the existing publication, their current/intended usage and their preferences for the future. Many "firsts" were accomplished with this survey: first survey to report on readers who have never subscribed; first to include La Viña questions; first digital survey; and first survey to experiment with fielding through a mobile app. Responses helped us identify the opportunity to streamline both digital and print subscriptions and materials to meet needs, as well as allowed us to conduct enhanced data explorations to answer new questions from subscribers and nonsubscribers alike.

Among our goals, we are continuing to develop our Outreach Program across all areas: Outside Sales, GVR Network, Communications, Carry the Message, A.A.W.S. Cooperation, Workshops, Events.

What are Grapevine and La Viña reps? They're the essential links between groups and the AAGV office who make sure that your groups are aware of the magazine's content each month, of how the features support recovery, of how to write and/or submit stories and more.

In response to the needs of the Fellowship, Grapevine has expanded its media library to include magazines in print, digital and audio formats, GV app, books, e-books, CDs, Grapevine Daily Quote, Grapevine Story Archive, wall calendar, pocket planner and other items.

Your meeting in print is always on the web. Currently, the website is undergoing a significant upgrade for a more user-friendly experience. The Grapevine website invites you to submit your story, artwork, jokes, cartoons or photography through the website. Fun can be had in calculating your sobriety or by writing a caption for a cartoon contest. Perhaps you are interested in trying an online subscription? There's a seven-day free trial for GV's online subscription — including two new online stories each week. Maybe you are searching for a recent GV or LV book? The La Viña store is now available!

The GV audio project continues and now includes over 900 seven-minute shares by members who have recorded them and sent them to GV. Staff is currently developing a plan to utilize the variety of recordings we currently have. GV's most popular book, *The Language of the Heart,* is available as an audiobook, downloadable MP3 or MP3 CD.

If I may, a few points about La Viña, now in its 23rd year of publication. The La Viña Story Archive will be coming soon. We are in the process of converting all physical issues manually into digital format.

The La Viña SMS project, established in 2015, now reaches over 2,300 members through weekly text messaging.

The La Viña Weekly Quote is published in Spanish. I will translate this one for you from *The Best of La Viña*:

Today I only have immense gratitude for my fellow AAs and for all the alcoholics of the world; but especially for my Higher Power, God as I conceive it, for having put me on the path of AA, so that I could save my life, my family and everything I was about to lose.

In celebration of Grapevine's 75th anniversary, a "Toolkit" was developed to encourage groups to share in honor of Bill W.'s hope that Grapevine would connect members and groups. This Toolkit is a comprehensive package of recovery tools that includes a one-year Grapevine Complete subscription; 12 issues of GV print and online; 12 issues of audio recordings; one-year access to the GV Story Archive; the GV book *One on One*, about sponsorship in action; 75th anniversary stickers and bookmarks; and information on becoming a Grapevine or La Viña representative.

Here is the first of a series of YouTube videos in our digital library that will focus on introducing the Grapevine Toolkit and speak a little on how we hope it will help carry the message to English- and Spanish-speaking members. This is the first example of how we want to incorporate the video medium into our GV and LV offerings.

The Carry the Message program functions as one of our mission's "lifelines" connecting one alcoholic to another. This year we have streamlined the process of giving subscriptions to inmates by asking the Fellowship to contact the Outreach Coordinator directly, who will then provide the contact info for the desired number of gift subscriptions. Please see the postcards available at the display table.

In March 1946, Bill W. wrote a letter to Royal Shepard of the law firm Naylon, Foster, and Shepard in New York, which was drafting the Certificate of Incorporation for the AA Grapevine. In it he listed some of the guiding principles that should shape the future of the Grapevine. Bill's first two suggestions were, "The Grapevine should become the Voice of AA as a whole," and "The Grapevine staff should be primarily responsive to AA Group opinion and tradition."

Forty years later, at the 1986 General Service Conference, an Advisory Action was approved that stated, "Since each issue cannot go through the Conference approval process, the Conference recognizes AA Grapevine as the international journal of Alcoholics Anonymous."

A little over 30 years ago, my sponsor handed me a copy of Grapevine, and, in reading it, the nagging sense of loneliness seemed to lessen. The identification and interest in the stories and articles helped fill the vacant uncertainty of early sobriety. Over the years this little magazine has become a Twelfth Step instrument in my journey and a reliable source of inspiration in the daily challenges of life. I hope you take a well-deserved moment to see how it just might provide "a quiet place in bright sunshine" for you.

Albin Zezula, Publisher

Reports from the General Service Board, A.A.W.S., and Grapevine Corporate Boards

General Service Board Report

Greetings and welcome to the 69th General Service Conference, especially to those who are attending for the first time. Also, welcome to our unsung associates — the G.S.O. employees working quietly behind the scenes to make the Conference run smoothly, the staff who are working with us and are also doing their work as Conference members, and, of course, our talented interpreters making sure we all have access to the information presented here this week, regardless of the languages we may be most familiar with.

This week, as we address the many important issues before us, we will be fulfilling our great responsibility passed down from our co-founders and the Fellowship's early members to ensure that the Conference guides and advises upon all matters presented as affecting A.A. as a whole (Conference Charter, paragraph 4). Further, as the Conference Charter states in paragraph 3, "The Conference will act for A.A. in the perpetuation and guidance of its world services, and it will also be the vehicle by which the A.A. movement can express its view upon all matters of vital A.A. policy and all hazardous deviations from A.A. Tradition." And somehow, we collectively agree to make this work even though the Conference has no legal authority over the General Service Board. How does that happen? We do this through the "spiritual handshake" that our founders and early leaders crafted between the General Service Board and the Conference, as expressed in the Conference Charter, the General Service Board Bylaws and in the development of the Twelve Concepts for World Service, adopted in 1962. Read, for example, the long form of Concepts VI and VII.

Thus, this week we embark together on work grounded in the spiritual principles embodied in the Steps, Traditions and Concepts and celebrated in our Big Book — which, as our Conference theme indicates, is now 80 years old and available in 71 languages!

Since the last Conference, your General Service Board has met four times: for the annual Members' meeting in April 2018, and for its regularly scheduled quarterly board meetings in July and October 2018 and January 2019. In addition, the board had three specially scheduled meetings to evaluate and discuss the Communications Audit provided by our consultants, Impact Collaborative, which I'll talk about more fully in a moment.

Over the past year, the work of the board has covered a broad range of issues and, as I review some of the highlights, I would like to call your attention to the in-depth trustees' committee reports that appear in your Conference Manuals. These reports will provide greater detail into the work the board has undertaken throughout the year with much assistance from our talented staff. Indeed, much of what the board and its committees do is to define the work that the G.S.O., under our general manager Greg Tobin, performs — responding to literally tens of thousands of requests for information and guidance per year; publishing an impressive array of books, pamphlets, PSAs and other important materials; and coordinating events such as this Conference, Regional Forums throughout the U.S. and Canada, and international events such as the International Convention and the World Service Meeting. We ask a tremendous amount of our staff and employees, many of whom are not alcoholic. So, please be sure to thank them this week.

In April 2018, following the 68th General Service Conference, the General Service Board welcomed two new Class B trustees: Jan Lembke, Eastern Canada regional trustee, and Kathi Fowler, Pacific regional trustee. We also welcomed Beau Bush, general service trustee, to the board. And, at the end of this year's Conference five trustees will rotate: Northeast regional trustee Rich Purtell, Southwest regional trustee Yolanda Flores, trustee-at-large/Canada Scott Huyghebaert, and Class A trustees David Morris and Ivan Lemelle. We are grateful for the dedication, self-sacrifice and tireless service these trustees have exhibited and the many miles traveled in fulfilling their duties on behalf of the Fellowship. I will miss working with them. Yet, as our principle of rotation keeps us moving ever forward, later in the week, new trustees will be elected for these openings, and new slates of Class As and corporate officers will be presented for disapproval, if any.

Our two corporate boards, A.A.W.S., Inc. and AA Grapevine, Inc., have been busy throughout the year, addressing a broad range of business concerns and developing plans for the future. You will hear from each of these boards individually regarding their activities over the past year. In the interim, I want to report to you that communication among the three board chairs has been excellent during the year and is instrumental to the ongoing collaboration that has been developing among the three arms of our current corporate structure.

Since the 2018 General Service Conference, Regional Forums have been held in the Western Canada, Eastern Canada, Pacific and Southeast regions; and one Local Forum was held in Area 08 San Diego Imperial, CA. Almost 2,100 members attended Regional Forums, including over 1,300 first-time attendees who were able to participate and learn more about our Fellowship services and how the General Service Board, General Service Office, A.A.W.S. and AA Grapevine operate. I was privileged to attend all these Forums, and I can tell you that the love for the Fellowship was much in evidence. The discussions were lively and principled. The Pacific region had a record number of Spanish-speaking attendees. We hope that many more people will become involved in service as a result of attending forums. I enjoyed every minute of this service to you. Also, I want to mention that your trustees have attended and participated in many other A.A. events this year. At many of these events, we strive to expand the Fellowship's knowledge of opportunities for service. In accordance with our strategic plan of outreach, the board looks for non-service events where we might spread the word about the fun and importance of service. For more information on the scope of these events, look at the last page of the General Service Board minutes from each quarter, where an extensive list of trustee travel is noted.

One item of special interest was the invitation we received from the Cuban Health Ministry to participate in November 2018 at the Third International Meeting Against Drug Addiction, held in the city of Guantánamo,

Guantánamo Province, Cuba. One of our Class A trustees, Dr. Peter Luongo — whose experience in the alcoholism treatment field extends for over 30 years — was asked to present on the topic "Healthcare Professionals and A.A.," in which he outlined ways A.A. and the medical profession can work together to help address the problem of alcoholism. Scott Huyghebaert, trustee-at-large/Canada, and Julio Espaillat, staff member at the General Service Office, also attended. They were accompanied by Hernán Merea, former La Viña editor, who acted as translator. A.A. in Cuba has an estimated 1,700 members and 100 groups, and this was a great step toward more active and effective relationships with Cuban professionals in the healthcare arena. In addition, a number of Cuban A.A. members were there as registered participants, and at one venue, local A.A. members spoke to the professionals about how A.A. works and shared briefly about their personal experiences. A.A. meetings were even held in the empty offices of the Health Ministry — a further example of the growing cooperation between health professionals and A.A.

Another important moment occurred this year, with the completion of the translation of the Big Book into Navajo, a spoken language. The CD set of the Big Book was presented at the Red Roads Convention in Albuquerque, New Mexico, to the president of the Navajo nation. The president spoke passionately about the need for the Big Book among his people. Many A.A. members from the Pacific region helped moved this project forward over the last 25 years, and Seventh Tradition dollars funded the project. I was honored to represent all of us in extending the hand of A.A. where a desperate need exists.

Additionally, the General Service Board hosted the 25th World Service Meeting (WSM), which was held in October 2018 in Durban, South Africa, with 72 delegates representing 45 countries or zones in attendance. Established in 1969 "to carry the message to the still-suffering alcoholic, wherever in the world he or she may be," the World Service Meeting has been held every other year since 1972, alternating between New York and a city outside the U.S./Canada structure, as chosen by the WSM itself.

The Final Report of the 25th WSM has been distributed in print form, and an anonymity-protected digital version was posted in February on aa.org. In October 2020, the 26th WSM will be held in Rye Brook, New York, prior to the General Service Board Weekend, with the theme "The Purpose of Our Service: Sobriety within Everyone's Reach."

Throughout the year, G.S.O. and General Service Board representatives also attended a number of other events around the world, including the 55th General Service Conference, in Buenos Aires, Argentina; the Hungarian National Convention, in Szolnok, Hungary; the Middle East Regional Committee of A.A., in Dubai, U.A.E.; and the 31st General Service Conference, in Moscow, Russia. These events and others marked important milestones for the A.A. Fellowship around the world and offered many opportunities to exchange valuable experience of how A.A. can continue serving suffering alcoholics, wherever they may be.

Since the 68th General Service Conference, the General Service Board has held three General Sharing Sessions, which have covered the topics "Love and Tolerance of Others Is Our Code — Philosophy or Practice?", "Rigidity in Alcoholics Anonymous: Our Greatest Danger" and "Social Media — the Colossus of 21st Century Communication." The presentations each sparked thoughtful discussion, highlighting important issues throughout the Fellowship. Complete copies of these presentations are available and may be requested from the staff coordinator at G.S.O.

The most recent sharing session took place as part of the January 2019 Board Weekend, where the General Service Board welcomed Conference committee chairpersons and the Conference delegate chair, as it has been doing since 1991. During the weekend, delegate committee chairpersons attended an orientation at G.S.O., met with their committee staff secretaries, and participated in sessions of corresponding trustees' committees. The practice of inviting Conference committee chairs to the January board meeting continues to benefit the Conference process in helping delegate chairs fulfill their responsibilities to the Conference and to A.A. as a whole, and has enhanced communication throughout the Conference structure. Additionally, at the suggestion of the 2018 Conference Agenda Committee, a new element was implemented this year with a scheduled conference call between each Conference committee and the chairs of the corresponding trustees' committees to review items submitted as agenda items and to talk about items still being considered by the trustees' committees. By all reports this latest evolution was well received.

And, as has been done since 2008 as an ongoing communication tool, the G.S.O. Conference coordinator created a grid of all proposed agenda items as each moved through the board committee process, with regular updates posted on the Conference Dashboard keeping delegates apprised of the status of each item.

As we move closer and closer to the next International Convention in Detroit, Michigan, in 2020, planning is gaining steam, and the board has been kept abreast of developments by A.A.W.S., which has been tasked with overseeing and managing the day-to-day details of the Convention.

The stated objectives of the International Convention are:

- To provide opportunities for a rededication of attendees to the primary purpose of A.A.

- To enable attendees to witness the success and growth of the A.A. program around the world.

- To let the world know that A.A. is alive, flourishing and available as a community resource, locally and internationally.

And so we look forward to Detroit in 2020 — and to Vancouver, British Columbia, in 2025, and St. Louis, Missouri, in 2030!

The theme of our Conference this year is "Our Big Book — 80 Years, 71 Languages." Many of us here will remember just a few short years ago, in 2015, at the 80th Anniversary International Convention in Atlanta, Georgia, the 35 millionth copy of the Big Book, *Alcoholics Anonymous*, was presented to the Sisters of Charity of St. Augustine, the religious order to which Sister Ignatia belonged.

And going back even further in time, the story of A.A.'s basic text — how it was written, published and promoted — like the story of the Fellowship itself, is a story of how, through many failures, the seeds of success were planted. It is the story of a truly alcoholic venture — a plan so crazy and so improbable, as some would say, "it might just work." And, from the vantage point of today, it certainly has.

Adding to the celebration of our Big Book, we can also add publication of our first original book in three decades, *Our Great Responsibility*, a collection of talks given by Bill W. at General Service Conferences between 1951 and 1970. Perhaps we can all take a moment to pause and reflect on those powerful moments Bill shared with Conferences past, on talks held in rooms just like this, with trusted servants just like us. We are links in a powerful chain of recovery.

Another highlight of the year has been the incredible support provided through Seventh Tradition contributions from the Fellowship. The Seventh Tradition remains a cornerstone in any and all discussions about finance, yet beyond the dollars and cents of contributions is the all-important aspect of participation, for which the board is most grateful. We know that a group's first need is to take care of the rent and other basic service expenses that enable its meetings to be held, and to support other local A.A. entities such as intergroup/central offices, as well as district and area service committees that work tirelessly to make A.A.

resources available wherever they are needed. So, these contributions to the General Service Board from groups and individuals, whether by putting checks in the mail or making online contributions, have great meaning within our structure, as they represent a trust placed in us by the Fellowship to expand on

Published in May 2019, this new volume features sixteen of Bill W.'s previously unpublished Conference talks.

move forward to enhance our ability to reach the still-suffering alcoholic. Along the way, we also hope to improve communication up and down the service structure.

Following this Conference, a new ad hoc committee comprised of the Internal Core Team plus a number of trustees will be formed. That commit-

the important work started and maintained in each A.A. group — the work of helping alcoholics get and stay sober.

Much of the board's focus this year has been on communication, a key component of the board's strategic plan. We have an overarching or "umbrella" goal of reaching out the hand of A.A. to all who suffer from alcoholism. One of the particular sub-goals is to improve the effectiveness of our communications to the different populations we serve. We also have a goal of identifying new places and audiences where the A.A. message of hope can be shared. We see the link between effective communication and reaching new groups of suffering alcoholics with our message of hope. Finally, in the communications area, we are committed to being more effective with all the service constituencies we serve, for example, areas, individuals, boards, committees and office communications. As many of you know, this goal of the strategic plan led us to work with Impact Collaborative (IC), a professional communications firm, on a comprehensive communications audit. They undertook and completed such an audit in 2017, and one primary focus of the board throughout this past year has been on what the audit revealed, and what our part is in being more effective. From here, we plan on evaluating how over the next three years the office and staff, the boards and affiliate corporations can strengthen our communications. The '80s are over; the digital era is here. How do we use the giant colossus of communication to talk to each other and to reach the still-suffering alcoholic?

Immediately following the Conference last year, I appointed an ad hoc committee of the General Service Board comprised of trustees, A.A.W.S. and AA Grapevine board directors, with staff representation from both operating corporations, to begin the process of evaluating the recommendations contained in the communications audit. This committee — in collaboration with the Internal Core Team, comprised of A.A.W.S. and AA Grapevine management and personnel who have been working with IC from the start of the audit — was able to review and categorize in a general way the recommendations, to provide some direction relative to ongoing discussion among the various A.A. entities involved, and to develop some priorities to present to the General Service Board. Since then, and following additional meetings dedicated to discussion of the audit and what we might do, the General Service Board and the General Service Office and Grapevine have begun the development of a three-year strategic communications plan that will be our road map for how we will

tee will be tasked with preparing the plan, which will be reviewed by the board and shared with you for input. For now, these are the two key work items for the coming year: create a three-year communications plan, and develop a plan for a communications hub that will coordinate external communications and be charged with overseeing the implementation of the three-year plan. The plan will include such things as protocols for Class A presentations with professionals; a media plan to reach alcoholics in underrepresented populations; protocols for public relations messaging to the general public and friends of A.A.; and development of digital tools to reach the service structure.

Additionally, in our role as good service leaders (Concept IX), the board has been focused on other aspects of its strategic plan — presented in 2016, updated in 2018 and continuously reviewed by the board — to help us focus our limited time and energy. We have developed an informal grid of work undertaken by committees and boards in support of our plan objectives. I can report that the board, through its committees, is working on seven goals. The first goal is that we will model inclusivity and acceptance in accordance with the Third Tradition. Each trustees' committee with staff secretary is inventorying its relevant pamphlets and other materials to suggest what might need to be updated to be more welcoming. The International Conventions/Regional Forums committee and staff are looking at the presentations, handouts and email blasts with an eye toward being welcoming to all. They are also taking a close look at all the materials that will announce our International Convention to the world. If you haven't seen it, take a look at the video inviting you to the International. It's on the aa.org homepage.

The second major goal for the board is to work on our relationships with professionals — being friendly with our friends. The trustees' C.P.C. committee and staff have been working on identifying new nonprofit groups that might want to hear about A.A. The Grapevine outreach coordinator is working with C.P.C. to see how Grapevine publications and services may complement the information provided at professional conferences that we attend. The Corrections Committee is looking at the training programs for corrections personnel to see if there is any way we might make presentations to them about what A.A. is. We recognize local committees do great work, but at the national level the board and staff may be able to open doors that thus far have remained closed.

The third goal is effective communications. I have already reviewed that in my discussion about the board's work on communications this year.

The fourth goal is identifying new places and audiences to bring the A.A. message of hope. Some of this work overlaps with the second goal. However, under this goal we are also looking at whether we might embrace more direct sponsorship of countries with emerging A.A. services. And, we are exploring asking delegates and others to think about populations that could be better served. For example, I know one area that did an inventory and realized that they were not reaching the elderly living in facilities. Bringing our message of hope and recovery has no age limits!

Our fifth goal relates to improving internal communications among the three boards. This has led to discussions on our stated objective under this goal to explore alternative meeting cycles, revamp Board Weekends, consider more efficient use of resources across the three boards; and assuring good communications among the three entities and the office. We also have an objective to study the current size and composition of the General Service Board and each of the affiliate boards, including the rotation schedule, to find the most effective model to support our mission. The trustees' Nominating Committee has been working on this last issue and is developing an evaluation tool with regard to workload and effectiveness.

Our sixth goal is for the General Service Board to act as a role model in promoting the importance of our Tradition of anonymity as expressed in the Eleventh and Twelfth Traditions. We had good presentations and good discussion at our January board meeting on anonymity and social media, and on unity and social media.

Finally, our seventh goal speaks to the financial health of the three boards and the office. While that is largely up to the Fellowship, it is important for the boards to continue to find ways to communicate the work that G.S.O. does as a result of Seventh Tradition contributions, including updating the Seventh Tradition flyer and adding a QR code so individuals can obtain more in-depth information on an item. We are also thinking about sharing more stories that the office receives about how individuals have been touched by our message of hope.

These, then, are just some of the highlights of a very active year — a year that has brought the future into greater focus and that culminates in the discussions that will take place here this week as we search for an informed group conscience on the many matters before us.

And so, as we begin our work, let us reaffirm our commitment to carrying A.A.'s lifesaving message. The General Service Conference is a gift passed on to us, and each of us has an obligation to keep the doors of A.A. open to those who so desperately need it — now and in the future — no matter who they are or where they are from, what their background may be, or what language they speak or sign.

Along these lines, here is a quote from Bill W. that has meant a lot to me over the past year:

In A.A. we are supposed to be bound together in the kinship of a common suffering. Consequently, the full individual liberty to practice any creed or principle or therapy whatever should be a first consideration for us all. Let us not, therefore, pressure anyone with our individual or even our collective views. Let us instead accord each other the respect and love that is due to every human being as he tries to make his way toward the light. Let us always try to be inclusive rather than exclusive; let us remember that each alcoholic among us is a member of A.A., so long as he or she declares.

Our resolve to communicate effectively with each other both as listeners and speakers, and to bring forward what is best for the future of A.A. and our primary purpose should be our guideposts and the measure of our successes this week.

I look forward to an extremely productive and rewarding week, and I sincerely thank you for my opportunity to serve this wonderful Fellowship.

Michele Grinberg, Chair of the General Service Board

Alcoholics Anonymous World Services, Inc.

Alcoholics Anonymous World Services, Inc. (A.A.W.S.) is a not-for-profit corporation composed of nine directors. Members of A.A.W.S., Inc. are the 21 trustees of the General Service Board, who elect the nine directors responsible for oversight of the General Service Office (G.S.O.), group services, printing and distribution of Conference-approved literature and service material. A.A.W.S. holds copyrights in A.A. literature, and is responsible for translations of A.A. literature, including titles licensed to A.A. boards in other countries.

A.A.W.S. directors include two general service trustees

Meeting room where the Conference Committee on Treatment and Accessibilities deliberated on their agenda.

and two regional trustees; three nontrustee directors; G.S.O.'s general manager; and the G.S.O. staff coordinator. Essential nonvoting support personnel attend each board meeting: G.S.O. services staff, finance director, publishing director, human resources director, G.S.O. archivist, board secretary and others.

Each year, directors serving on Alcoholics Anonymous World Services, Inc. report to the General Service Conference on A.A. publishing, group services provided by G.S.O., and other activities linked directly to A.A.'s primary purpose. I am privileged to present this report on behalf of my fellow directors. The purpose of the publishing activities and group services provided by A.A.W.S. and G.S.O., as requested from the Fellowship, is to support members' and groups' Twelfth Step efforts to reach the still-suffering alcoholic. The structure, composition and responsibilities of Alcoholics Anonymous World Services, Inc. are described in Chapter 10 of The A.A. Service Manual.

The A.A.W.S. Board has met seven times since the 68th Conference to receive reports from G.S.O. management and staff, review updates on services, track progress on implementation of Conference and board recommendations related to A.A.W.S., review financial reports, price new and revised publications, consider publishing operations and G.S.O. administrative matters, discuss requests from A.A. members and non-A.A.s seeking permission to reprint A.A. copyrighted literature, and to address other pertinent matters. (Concurrent with the seven board meetings, the A.A.W.S. Board met twice to conduct strategic planning sessions.)

The A.A.W.S. Board utilizes the committee system to address extensive agendas, to gather background material, and to consider requests of various kinds. The board, in turn, discusses committee reports and votes on any recommendations presented by board committees in these reports. In addition, the board conducts long-range and strategic planning. Committees of the A.A.W.S. Board are: Technology/Communication/Services, which addresses the needs of service assignments, reviews G.S.O. communications with the Fellowship, and oversees G.S.O.'s A.A. website; Publishing, which reviews sales results, format requests, reprints, international translations of literature and other publishing matters; Finance, which oversees budgeting and financial results and considers self-support matters; Internal Audit, which reviews all internal audit processes and documentation and sets parameters for any audit changes; and Nominating, which recommends candidates for A.A.W.S. nontrustee director and general service trustee vacancies.

Two ad hoc board subcommittees have worked on specific issues throughout the year: Self-Support, which reviewed self-support materials and continues to develop new approaches to enhance the board's self-support communications with the Fellowship; and Literature Discounts, Handling Charges and Pricing (known as the Delta Project), which reviewed our current and historical pricing structure and continues evaluating possible pricing/discount mechanisms for all A.A.W.S. literature.

Group Services — There were 1,641 new A.A. groups in the U.S. and Canada listed with G.S.O. Each new group's general service representative (G.S.R.) or contact receives A.A. literature and basic information to encourage the group to link with their local structure and support Twelfth Step activities. The service piece "Services Provided by G.S.O./A.A.W.S." describes in detail the services provided by the A.A. staff assignments and other employees at G.S.O.

G.S.O.'s A.A. Website — Oversight of G.S.O.'s A.A. website is the responsibility of the A.A.W.S. Board of Directors, acting through its Technology/Communication/Services and Publishing Committees and in accordance with the Twelve Traditions of Alcoholics Anonymous. The website received an estimated total of 15,254,461 visits for the year 2018, an increase of 14% from last year's total of 13,396,071. A website design project has been underway throughout the year, led by an in-house working group with input from a number of professional consultants.

Approximately 431 emails were received through the online Website Feedback Form in 2018. G.S.O.'s Website Committee reviewed this feedback, with each email receiving a response.

Some highlights of new features for 2018 include: posting of the new Experience, Strength and Hope pamphlets following Conference approval in April 2018; posting of press release for the 25th World Service Meeting; posting of YouTube Information and FAQ pages; posting of the Meeting Finder onboarding announcement; and posting of the "A.A. Around the World" feature on the International page.

The board approved that a basic A.A. app, to include the Meeting Guide, Big Book, Daily Reflections and alert/messaging capabilities, be launched in conjunction with the new A.A. website.

YouTube Channel — The YouTube channel for A.A. World Services, Inc. and the General Service Office was launched in the summer of 2018. The purpose of the channel is to provide an additional platform from which A.A.W.S.-produced videos can be shared with a broader audience in order to enhance carrying the message to alcoholics, the general public and the professional community. Development of the channel began in early fall of 2017 as a response to an Advisory Action of the 2017 General Service Conference to create a YouTube channel with comments disabled that could be analyzed for effectiveness. The channel was started with three Conference-approved PSAs: "Doors," "My World" and "I Have Hope" (available in English, French and Spanish). Expansion of the YouTube collection is in process, with the ultimate goal of hosting all A.A.W.S. video content.

Forums and Other Events — Throughout the year, G.S.O. staff members are invited to attend and participate in many local and area service events, conferences and conventions. These trips help provide information about G.S.O. to A.A. gatherings and help staff to gather local experience to add to other collected experience available from G.S.O.

• *Regional Forums*: A.A.W.S. directors and G.S.O. staff participated in four Regional Forums in 2018: the Western Canada Forum in Saskatchewan in June; the Eastern Canada Forum in Québec in July; the Pacific Forum in

California in September; and the Southeast Forum in Virginia in November.

- *National A.A. Archives Workshop*: G.S.O. Archivist Michelle Mirza participated at the 22nd National A.A. Archives Workshop, September 28–30, presenting on the topic "Dr. Bob: Early Days and Early Writings" and moderating a hands-on workshop titled "Taking Care of Your Repository: Using the Archives Workbook." A total of 160 registered attendees participated.

- *Intergroup/Central Office, A.A.W.S., AA Grapevine*: The Annual Intergroup/Central Office seminar was held in early October 2018. Members of the A.A.W.S. and AA Grapevine Boards attended, as well as management and staff from both offices, including the G.S.O. staff member serving as liaison to intergroup/central offices.

- *National A.A. Technology Workshop:* Representatives from G.S.O. attended the 2018 National A.A. Technology Workshop and presented a panel discussion on the website, YouTube channel and app development. The purpose of this event is to share the message of Alcoholics Anonymous through technology to help the next alcoholic.

International — The 25th World Service Meeting took place in Durban, South Africa, October 7–11, with 72 delegates from 45 countries, including Bolivia and Turkey, who attended for the first time. Established in 1969 "to carry the message to the still-suffering alcoholic, wherever in the world he or she may be," the World Service Meeting has been held every other year since 1972, alternating between New York and a city outside the U.S./Canada structure, as chosen by the WSM itself.

Trustees, G.S.O. management and the international coordinator received invitations from A.A. in other countries to share information and experience with A.A. groups and trusted servants in local service structures. Highlights include:

- 55th General Service Conference,
  Buenos Aires, Argentina, June 2018

- 30 Years of A.A. in Lithuania/Int'l Round-up,
  Palanga, Lithuania, June 2018

- Hungarian National Convention,
  Szolnok, Hungary, July 2018

- Medical Conference,
  Guantánamo, Cuba, November 2018

- Middle East Regional Committee of A.A.,
  Dubai, U.A.E., November 2018

- Mexico's 12th National Convention,
  Puebla, Mexico, March 2019

- 31st General Service Conference,
  Moscow, Russia, April 2019

- 30th General Service Conference, Peru, April 2019

Financial — Complete audited financial details for 2018 are included in the Conference Manual and Conference *Final Report*. Here is an overview:

- Contributions for 2018 were $8,384,721. This was $184,721 (2.25%) greater than budgeted and $24,731 (0.29%) less than 2017.

- Net sales of $14,020,149 were $240,149 (1.74%) more than budgeted and $326,777 (2.39%) greater than 2017.

- Gross profit from literature was $9,452,615 and represented a 67.4% gross profit percentage, compared with 68.4% for the year 2017.

- Total revenue (gross profit from literature plus contributions) was $17,837,336 or $377,091 (2.16%) greater than budgeted and $65,953 (0.37%) greater than 2017.

- Total expenses for the year of $17,382,733 were $424,181 (2.5%) greater than budgeted and $1,370,186 (8.56%) greater than 2017. The increase in expenses was due to open positions being filled, along with increased costs of professional fees, IT systems, the communications audit, and financial controls improvements, such as legal reviews of our numerous contracts. Professional fees were $15,820 higher than budget and included the $135,000 settlement for the manuscript case.

- Net profit for the year 2018 was $454,603; $47,090 less than budgeted and $1,304,234 less than 2017.

2019 Budget: The A.A.W.S. Board approved the budget of the General Service Office for 2019, which reflects gross sales of $15,000,000 and a bottom-line profit of $501,221. After review by the trustees' Finance and Budgetary Committee, the 2019 budget was approved by the General Service Board.

Publishing

International licensing and translation: The Big Book is available in 71 languages, which includes the original English plus 70 translations. The latest translation, now available as an audiobook, is the Navajo Big Book.

For the period January through December 2018, international translation and licensing continued to demonstrate a marked uptick of activity compared with the same period in 2017. A notable surge in activity includes renewal licenses issued and new licenses granted to reproduce and distribute items of translated copyrighted literature, with 265 total licenses fully executed in 2018, as compared to 73 in 2017.

Australia, Belgium, Chile, Finland, Latvia and Mexico have requested license renewals; the license renewals for Bolivia, Colombia, Ecuador, Great Britain, Lithuania, Thailand and Turkey are in process. Other notable international licensing and translation activity is taking place in Bahrain, Cuba, Denmark, Hungary, Iran, Iceland, India, Russia and Ukraine.

Our Great Responsibility: A Selection of Bill W.'s General Service Conference Talks, 1951–1971: Estimated availability of finished books in English, French and Spanish is on track for mid-April 2019. An announcement flyer is in development and an introductory article for *Box 4-5-9* is scheduled for the Spring 2019 issue.

G.S.O. and Staff Operations

Employees: At the end of 2018, G.S.O. had 91 employees: 38 administrative, A.A. staff, supervisory and exempt professionals and 53 supporting personnel.

G.S.O. Visitors: In 2018, G.S.O. welcomed more than 3,000 visitors (up from 2,312 in 2017), including many English- and Spanish-speaking groups ranging in size from 10 to 40. Visiting members and guests often attend the open A.A. meeting held at G.S.O. at 11:00 a.m. on Fridays and tour the office. This is an opportunity to see and hear "how G.S.O. works" and for the G.S.O. staff to welcome A.A. members from all over the world.

Archives: Archives finished 2018 with approximately 1,600 requests for information and research, and accessioned over 375 new items. Projects for 2019 include digitizing Bill W.'s personal collection of unpublished correspondence; scanning past trustee correspondence and Conference committee background; and organizing, filing and digitizing historical materials from the 1950s and '60s, originally set aside by Nell Wing. There is also a plan to add new content to the Archives section of the G.S.O. A.A. website, including new digital exhibits, excerpts of audio recordings and the timeline.

Reprint Requests: In 2018, A.A.W.S. granted permission/ did not object to 65 requests to reprint from A.A. literature, and denied permission to 53 requests.

A.A.W.S. Updates

Throughout the year, the A.A.W.S. Board has addressed a number of additional matters. The following provides a brief summary:

International Convention: The board reviewed regular reports and preliminary budget information for the 2020 International Convention in Detroit, Michigan, as provided by Talley Management, our International Convention consultant. No major issues have been reported by Talley Management, and they have been meeting with key vendors, with some remaining vendor contracts in the final stages of negotiation and language review prior to legal

review. Plans continue regarding housing, Al-Anon participation, hospitality, registration and other matters.

Information Technology: The selection and development of a new office-wide enterprise resource planning (ERP) system to update G.S.O.'s software systems, especially accounting, contributions, record-keeping and email, has been underway over the past year. A major project, requiring in-depth training and user acceptance testing throughout the office, the project is on track for full implementation in the early months of 2019.

A.A.W.S. Publications Policy: The board reviewed the A.A.W.S., Inc. Policy on Publication of Literature with respect to A.A.W.S.'s ability to update and revise A.A. pamphlets and books and the Board forwarded a proposed revision of the policy along with background information for review by the trustees' Committee on Literature and the 2019 Conference Literature Committee.

Intellectual Property: With the expansion of digital media, the board has maintained a focus on its intellectual property policies, working with G.S.O.'s Intellectual Property Administrator and, as needed, outside counsel.

Administrative Services: Through a process requesting proposals from a number of vendors, G.S.O. management has been seeking new venues for meetings of the General Service Board/AA Grapevine, Inc./A.A. World Services, Inc. and the General Service Conference, with the possibility of adding an additional venue for meetings and events for 2019 and 2020, including the 2021 and 2022 Conferences.

Additionally, office space and room for expansion at G.S.O. continue to be a challenge. A number of single-person offices have been converted to two-person offices to accommodate, and exploration of additional space in the building continues.

Daily Reflections video project: Following discussion throughout the year of potential video projects, including *Daily Reflections*, a presentation will be made to the 2019 General Service Conference to include a proposed audio/ video strategy that will be more fully discussed by the board.

Service Material: The board discussed responses from the Fellowship to the yellow "Safety Card for A.A. Groups" service material, and an internal group of G.S.O. staff members have been reviewing the card in detail with regular updates to the full A.A.W.S. board.

David Noll, Chairperson

AA Grapevine, Inc.

AA Grapevine, Inc. is one of two affiliate corporations of the General Service Board and the multimedia publisher of Grapevine magazine content, available on various platforms and in a variety of formats. AA Grapevine, Inc. also publishes Spanish-language content in La Viña magazine and its related books, CD and audio formats, as well as Spanish-language web pages on aagrapevine.org.

By charter, the AA Grapevine Board consists of seven to 10 directors. Currently, there are nine directors: two general service trustees, two regional trustees, three non-trustee directors, one Class A trustee and the AA Grapevine publisher.

The purpose of the Grapevine Corporate Board is to serve the A.A. Fellowship in the following ways:

- To oversee the publishing operations of AA Grapevine, Inc.
- To provide sound financial management of the corporation.
- To establish corporate policies and set corporate priorities.
- To engage in the ongoing process of strategic planning.
- To operate in accordance with the principles of A.A. as expressed in the Twelve Steps, Twelve Traditions and Twelve Concepts.

The board strives to engage the Fellowship and to ensure members' awareness of the international journals of Alcoholics Anonymous, Grapevine and La Viña, as tools to help carry the message.

The AA Grapevine Board met in person eight times since the last Conference. The board has three standing committees. The Nominating and Governance Committee, chaired by Mark Everett, is responsible for facilitating all facets in the selection of candidates for board openings and selecting a general service trustee. Since there were no Grapevine Board openings this year, that committee focused instead on updates to the AA Grapevine Directors Handbook and the Employee Handbook. The Finance and Budget Committee, chaired by Ginger Rhoades Bell, provided oversight for the budget process.

The Outreach Committee, chaired by Tommi Hanley, served as a planning committee for the annual outreach and communication of AA Grapevine, Inc. Three additional ad hoc committees were formed for 2018–19. The Strategic Planning ad hoc committee, chaired by Josh Eggleston, was responsible for driving the development and providing oversight to the implementation of the AA Grapevine strategic plan. The Search ad hoc committee, chaired by Carole Boerner, was formed to fill the publisher vacancy after the departure of Ami Brophy in October of 2018. The Translation ad hoc committee, chaired by Nancy McCarthy, was formed to review and update policies guiding the translation of Grapevine material into Spanish and French.

Grapevine's Editorial Advisory Board, consisting of members with expertise in media, met five times in 2018–19, always by teleconference, and the La Viña Editorial Advisory Board met three times by teleconference during the same period.

Since the last Conference, AA Grapevine, Inc. has produced 12 issues of Grapevine, six issues of La Viña, an annual wall calendar and pocket planner, and three e-books. In response to a 2018 Conference action, La Viña is now being published in full color. In December 2018, Grapevine and La Viña made available for purchase magazine binders that can store up to 12 magazines. Each binder is labeled with a gold foil Grapevine or La Viña stamp.

AA Grapevine, Inc. distributed 103,420 Grapevine and La Viña books, e-books, CDs, and other content-related items, including the translation into Spanish of the GV book *One on One*, featuring a collection of stories about sponsorship. AA Grapevine also produced two new collections of previously published Grapevine stories, *AA in the Military* and *One Big Tent: Atheist and Agnostic AA Members Share Their Experience, Strength and Hope*; reprinted 10 titles; and completed translation of the book *Emotional Sobriety* into French.

In July 2018, La Viña started the La Viña Story Archive Project, the first archive of original stories of recovery written by members of the Hispanic A.A. community and published in La Viña magazine. The expected completion date is spring 2019.

Grapevine's average monthly print circulation was 66,857 in fiscal year 2018 (this is more than budget by 4,535 and less than 2017 by 2,392). Grapevine Online (GVO) averaged 3,390 subscribers in 2018. The average bimonthly circulation of La Viña was 9,635 (this is 447 greater than budget and 361 under 2017 levels).

Complete and audited financial details for 2018 are included in the Conference Manual and Conference *Final Report*. Here is an overview:

- Grapevine ended 2018 with net loss of $153,500 against budgeted net loss of $271,313. The loss was primarily due to costs incurred as a result of leadership transition.
- Gross profit for the magazine and subscription products reached $1,911,513. Gross profit on the magazine was ahead of budget by $140,236.
- Gross profit on books and related items was $562,436.
- Overhead costs were budgeted at $2,042,590 versus an actual of $2,065,013.

La Viña is published by AA Grapevine, Inc., with the shortfall between revenue and expenses made up by the General Service Board as a service to the Fellowship. La Viña had an average circulation of 9,635 per issue. Total income for the magazine for 2018 was $80,375 with expenses at $229,202. The net difference between revenue and expenses for 2018 was $148,467, or $2,658 more than was budgeted.

AA Grapevine maintains a balance in the Reserve Fund to fund its unfulfilled subscription liability. The balance at December 31, 2018 was $1,943,500, while the actual subscription liability as of that date was $1,533,440. The subscription liability fund is maintained so that in the event the magazine discontinued publication, subscribers could be repaid for those portions of their subscriptions left unfulfilled.

The aagrapevine.org website is regularly updated to better serve the Fellowship and to engage a wider and more diverse audience. Month-end December 2018 reports indicate that an average of 38,861 unique visitors go to an average of 3.6 pages on the website each month.

The 2018 Carry the Message outreach effort encouraged the Fellowship to support those in need by sponsoring subscriptions, with a combined Grapevine and La Viña subscription count of 176 being fulfilled directly through the Grapevine office.

The audio page on aagrapevine.org includes instructions for members on how to record stories up to seven minutes long, with two members' audio stories offered online as samples. Over 1,000 audio stories have been received for Grapevine and are being archived, with 100-plus more for La Viña.

Grapevine continues to produce a complimentary Grapevine Daily Quote online, featuring excerpts drawn from the archives of classic Grapevine literature. Selections are posted daily on aagrapevine.org and may be requested on an opt-in basis for daily email delivery. Subscriptions number 44,912 as of December 2018. The La Viña Weekly Quote, a weekly complimentary quote in Spanish that is extracted from classic Grapevine Literature and the La Viña Book *Lo mejor de La Viña* (*The Best of La Viña*), is posted on the La Viña web pages on an opt-in basis for email delivery to 1,468 subscribers. The La Viña Weekly Quote is also distributed via SMS on an opt-in basis to 2,327 subscribers.

Grapevine and La Viña subscribers are committed to the print magazine as an invaluable Twelfth Step tool, as well as for their own personal recovery. At the same time, Grapevine's online offerings continue to attract new subscribers, with few conversions from print. AAgrapevine.org has become the organization's principal connection with the majority of subscribers. Approximately 33% of Grapevine's online subscribers opt for both print and online magazines. The Grapevine Online subscription provides unlimited access to previously unpublished stories, Audio Grapevine, the GV Story Archive and the current online issues of both Grapevine and La Viña. Grapevine's audio magazine has been incorporated into the GV App available for iOS and Android devices.

In response to an Advisory Action from the 2018 Conference and with the cooperation of A.A.W.S., Grapevine has launched efforts into outside sales. A.A.W.S. customers have been contacted and informed of the availability for purchase of AA Grapevine books and related products. The efforts of the Grapevine board and management team continue to broaden awareness of the magazines, books, audio offerings and website to carry the message through service outreach efforts. The Grapevine board is always looking for ways to expand these efforts. To this end, in 2018 AA Grapevine undertook a Fellowship Feedback project both in English and Spanish, to find out the desires of the Fellowship. Over 4,000 responses were received, from both subscribers and non-subscribers. This valuable input will help guide AA Grapevine, Inc. in their determination of future direction.

2019 is the 75th anniversary of AA Grapevine. In recognition of this, Grapevine has developed a Toolkit, a comprehensive package of recovery tools, for both Grapevine and La Viña, aimed at helping groups build the connections needed to reach other groups and the still-suffering alcoholic.

AA Grapevine continues to have an extremely cooperative relationship with A.A.W.S. at both the board and staff level. This is resulting in efficiencies in operations for both corporations, as well as expanded outreach opportunities for the Grapevine, as seen with our outside sales efforts.

The AA Grapevine Board and management team are committed to self-support and to AA Grapevine, Inc.'s continued financial vitality. The board's focus on financial health as demonstrated throughout 2018 will continue in 2019. To this end the board will:

- Continue to seek opportunities for internal cost reduction through operational review.
- Continue to work closely with A.A.W.S. to identify revenue opportunities and operational efficiencies.
- Work to improve Grapevine/La Viña customer service processes.
- Redesign the website and store to provide a more positive customer experience.
- Review and incorporate results of the Fellowship Feedback.

As a mirror of the membership, Grapevine both reflects and belongs to the Fellowship. For 75 years Grapevine has conveyed the "Voices of A.A." as a tool for many in recovery, evolving over time and reliably carrying the message to anyone who reaches out for the hand of A.A. With the ongoing support of the Fellowship, it will continue to do so well into the future.

Cate Wittig, Chairperson

■ Finance Report

The Finance report, which is summarized and condensed here, was given on Monday afternoon by David Morris, treasurer of the General Service Board and chairperson of the trustees' Finance and Budgetary Committee, covering the finances of the General Service Board, A.A.W.S., the Grapevine and La Viña. The full report, accompanying slides and detailed notes are not included in this publication, but are available upon request. For more details on A.A. finances and the audited consolidated financial statements upon which the financial report is based, please see the financial section of this Report, which begins on page 105, as well as the report from the trustees' Finance and Budgetary Committee (page 77). A question and answer session for all Conference members followed this Finance report.

Good afternoon. My name is David Morris and I am a Class A trustee and treasurer of the General Service Board. It is again my privilege to deliver this year's Treasurer's report to the 69th General Service Conference of Alcoholics Anonymous.

Through this report, often referred to as "Finance Around the Picnic Table," a phrase coined at the 59th Conference, our goal is to help you become familiar with A.A.'s financial position so that you can communicate clearly to your areas. As always, what we need is better communication about what finance really means when members talk about "the numbers." Enhancing our collective understanding of our finances is one way to improve the service structure, and clear and concise communication is the key. Although our finances continue to grow more complex, remember that Corporate Poverty is more a state of mind, rather than the size of our bank account. "Too much money — and we argue over perilous wealth and lose sight of our primary purpose of carrying the message. Too little — and we risk losing the ability to carry the message at all."

The accompanying charts provide a look at some highlights of the Fellowship's finances for 2018.

Self-support: First, 28,314 Groups contributed $6,720,287, a decrease of 805 groups, or 2.8%, and $39,328, or 0.6%, from 2017, which had 29,219 Groups contributing $6,759,615. Second, 5,169 individuals contributed a record $819,280, up $10,481, or 1.3%, compared to the 6,088 individuals, who contributed $808,799 in 2017. Third, total contributions from all sources were

$8,385,009 in 2018, down $24,443, or 0.3%, from $8,409,452 in 2017. Actual 2018 contributions were 2.3% greater than the budget of $8,200,000.

Specifically, the chart below lists the sources from whom we received Seventh Tradition contributions, showing both the dollar amount and the unique number of contributors.

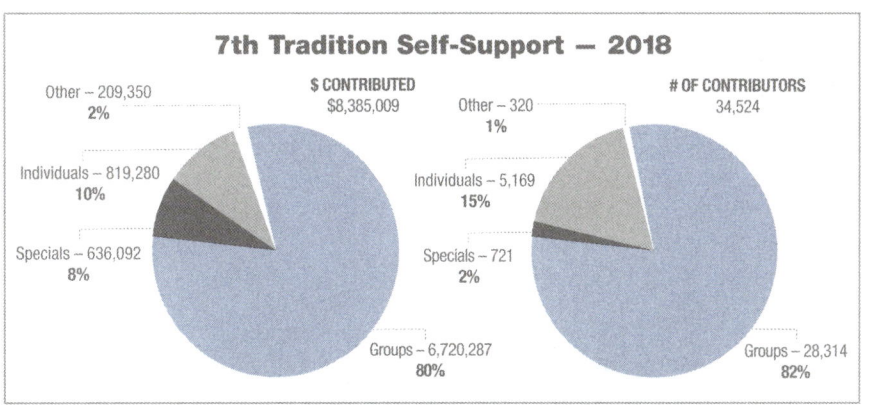

In 2018, total contributions were $8,385,009 with 82,229 contributions received and processed from 34,524 unique contributors. The left pie chart shows the relative dollar significance of each source of our Seventh Tradition:

- Groups contributed $6,720,287, or 80.1% (2017 – $6,759,615 or 80.4%),
- A.A. Entities *not* Groups (e.g., conferences, areas, intergroups) contributed $636,092, or 7.6% (2017 – $660,493 or 7.9%),
- Individuals contributed $819,280, or 9.8% (2017 – $808,799 or 9.6%).

The right pie chart shows the number of unique contributors: Groups – 28,314, or 82.0%; A.A. Entities *not* Groups – 721, or 2.1%; Individuals – 5,169, or 15.0%.

Of the 28,314 total groups contributing in 2018, the majority of support comes in the form of small donations from a very large number of groups (see chart below left). Specifically, 27,364 Groups, or 96.6%, of the 28,314 Groups contributed between $1 and $999, totaling $5,073,330, or 75.5%, of the $6,720,287. Over 50% of the Groups contributed between $100 to $499 totaling $3,127,284, or 46.5% of the $6,720,287. The average Group contribution was $237.35 per group.

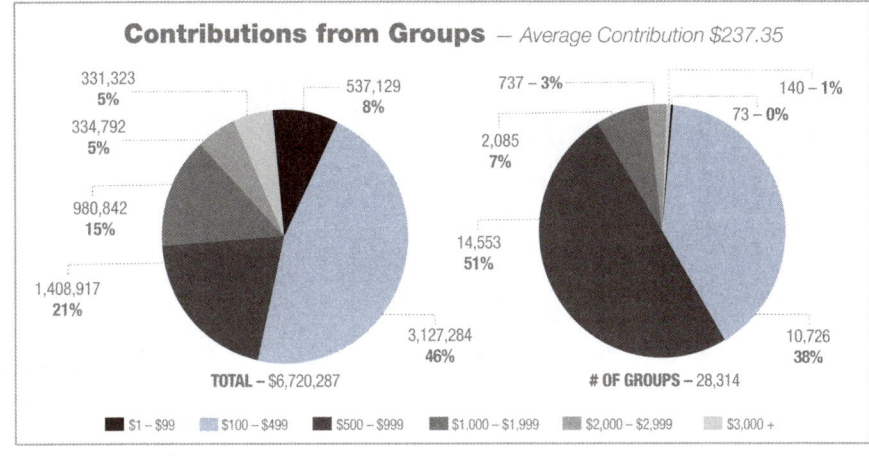

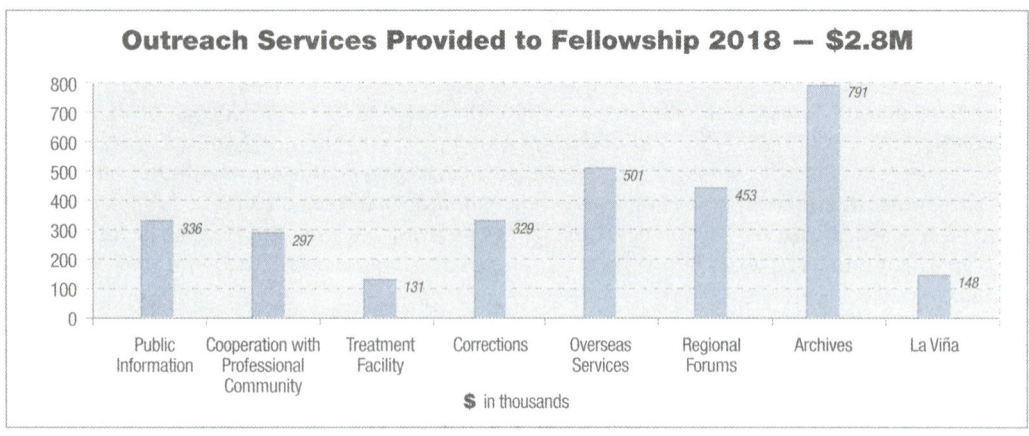

Outreach Services Provided to Fellowship 2018 — $2.8M

Category	$ in thousands
Public Information	336
Cooperation with Professional Community	297
Treatment Facility	131
Corrections	329
Overseas Services	501
Regional Forums	453
Archives	791
La Viña	148

Additionally, due to the extraordinary hard work of our finance and contribution teams, for the first time we can now break down the Seventh Tradition contributions between Groups that have consistently contributed during the past six years and Groups that have made less frequent contributions during the past six years. In 2018, 17,257 groups, or 60.1%, contributed $5,031,270 with each of these groups contributing some amount consistently during the last six years. There were 11,057 groups, or 39.1%, contributed $1,689,017 on a less frequent basis during the six years.

Similarly, the 5,169 contributions from Individuals totaling $819,280 received in 2018 into various dollar ranges. It shows that the majority of the 7th Tradition were small donations from a large number of Individuals. 93.2% of the Individuals contributed between $1 to $499, totaling 40.2% of the dollars. The average contribution was $158.50 per individual.

One particular area of growth regarding Seventh Tradition contributions has been in online contributions. Since the online contribution function's inception in June 2010, online contributions have grown from 1,063 contributions totaling $86,718, or 1.38%, in 2010 to 12,330 contributions totaling $880,311, or 10.59%, in 2018 of total contributions received.

Services: When it comes to services provided to the Fellowship and their related costs, $11,426,835 was expended in 2018 covering the following service activities at G.S.O.: group services, public information, cooperation with the professional community, treatment facilities, corrections, overseas services (literature assistance) and loners, archives, General Service Conference, Regional Forums, World Service Meeting, International Convention, trustees' and directors' activities, nominating and supporting services, which include the direct costs of administration, finance, human resources, information technology, rent, and all other indirect overhead. When these 2018 costs of $11,426,835 are matched up with the 2017 Seventh Tradition contributions of $8,385,009, there is a resulting shortfall of $3,041,826. This shortfall is covered by an excess of publishing profits.

An expressed desire of many in the Fellowship has been to provide financial reporting for La Viña along with the above services provided to the Fellowship. Therefore, for our unaudited reporting, the $148,467 expense for La Viña is noted in the chart (located above) not as an actual operating expense of G.S.O., but rather to show its relative significance as a service activity supported by the General Service Board.

Publishing: A.A.W.S. publishing activities for 2018 show gross sales of $14,235,594, up 2.4% from 2017. Although gross publishing revenue increased, 2018 net profit decreased to $3,436,507, down $135,510, or 3.8%, from $3,572,017 in 2017 due to higher publishing related expenses. The number of orders processed were 26,789 in 2018, up from 25,422 in 2017, an increase of 1,367, or 5.4%. Approximately 82.7% of all 2018 sales were to intergroups, central offices, groups and individuals, compared to 77.4% in 2017.

The difference or shortfall between Seventh Tradition contributions and the cost of services provided to the Fellowship is covered through these A.A.W.S. publishing profits, resulting in a net profit of $394,681.

Grapevine/La Viña: For 2018, the total of all types of Grapevine subscriptions was 72,300, down from 75,329 in 2017. Further, print subscriptions were 66,857 in 2018, down from to 69,249 in 2017. Online and app subscriptions were down to 5,443, from 2017, a decrease of 10.5%.

As many in the Fellowship know, Grapevine's only source of revenue is through the sale of magazines and

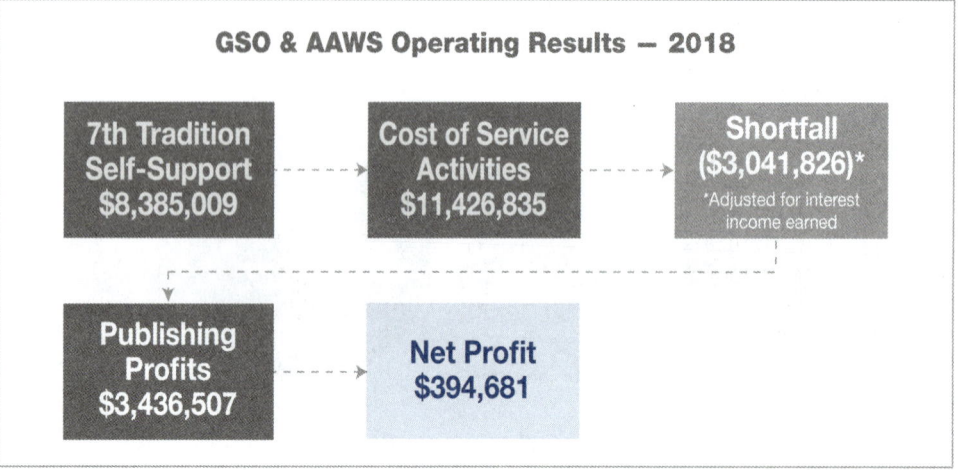

GSO & AAWS Operating Results — 2018

- 7th Tradition Self-Support $8,385,009
- Cost of Service Activities $11,426,835
- Shortfall ($3,041,826)* *Adjusted for interest income earned
- Publishing Profits $3,436,507
- Net Profit $394,681

other content-related materials. Since it cannot advertise or promote its products, the natural attrition or decline in annually sold print materials makes it difficult without the full and complete support of the Fellowship to maintain a constant level of subscription business. That is why it is so necessary for Grapevine to undertake initiatives such as the Subscription Challenge, "Carry the Message with the Subscription Gift Certificates," "Grow Your Grapevine," "4 Seasons of Service," and the automatic option for the purchase of a subscription to the Grapevine included in the registration form to the 2020 International Convention. Magazines function on the ongoing need for renewal by existing subscribers and acquisition of new subscribers to succeed, making Involvement of the entire Fellowship necessary for success.

For La Viña, the difference between revenues earned and the related costs of this service activity continues to be covered through a transfer from the General Service Board's General Fund as La Viña is considered a service to the Fellowship per the General Service Conference. For 2018, gross profit from the sale of magazines and related items was $80,735. After deducting the costs and expenses of $229,202, the result was a net shortfall between revenue and expenses of $148,467.

Pension and Retiree Medical Plans: In 1965, A.A. established a traditional Defined Benefit Pension Program for its employees. This plan will continue to exist until the last eligible employee who is covered retires and then eventually passes away in 40 to 50 years. However, to cap this exposure, A.A. transitioned from a Defined Benefit Plan to a Defined Contribution Plan for all new A.A.W.S. and Grapevine employees hired subsequent to January 1, 2013. Over the very long term, this change will cap the pension plan obligations and reduce ongoing costs. Defined benefit pension costs are funded out of A.A.W.S. and Grapevine current operations and now account for about 7.6% of operating expenses, down from 12% in 2013.

G.S.O./Grapevine Contributions to the Reserve Fund: By Conference action, the "Prudent Operating Reserve" is defined as an amount equal to the preceding year's combined operating expenses of A.A. World Services, AA Grapevine and the General Fund of the General Service Board. At December 31, 2018, the Reserve Fund stood at $15,752,618, representing 9.7 months of combined operating expenses.

To pay its bills and fund its obligations, A.A.W.S. has only two sources of money: contributions and literature sales. At the end of each year, any cash beyond that needed to pay bills on time is transferred to the Reserve Fund. For 2017, G.S.O. was able to contribute and transfer $1,400,000 to the Reserve Fund in early 2018 as a result of 2017 operating profits of $1,758,839. For 2016, G.S.O. was able to contribute and transfer $1,200,000 to the Reserve Fund in early 2017 as a result of 2016 operating profits of $1,453,218.

Grapevine (which has only one source of income: subscriptions/literature sales) has had very positive operating results during the last six years that have allowed contributions totaling $800,000 to the Reserve Fund. Most recently, Grapevine contributed $40,000 from its 2016 earnings in early 2017 and $240,000 from its 2015 earnings in early 2016. Since 1978 Grapevine has contributed aggregated cumulative funds of $1,373,200 against aggregated cumulative withdrawals of $1,447,300.

2020 International Convention: The 2020 International Convention is estimating 47,500 attendees at an advanced registration fee of $115 per person and registration fee of $140 after April 15, 2020. This will generate revenues of $5,583,218; the costs of hosting the event are expected to be $5,518,520, resulting in a budgeted profit of 64,698, or 1.2% of revenues.

New Auditors in 2018: As previously announced at the 68th General Service Conference, we retained the auditing and accounting firm of Marks Paneth LLP to become our independent auditors, replacing Owen J. Flanagan & Company, LLP. As part of that change, we further decided to upgrade the level of audit assurance work being conducted for each quarterly review of our financial results from a compilation review to a "limited review." Under generally accepted auditing and assurance standards, a "limited review" report will provide the General Service Board with a higher level of assurance than a "compilation report" as to the quality of the financial information being produced each quarter by management. This change has no effect on the annual audit of our financial statements and the level of assurance that we obtain from an audit. Also, our audited 2018 financial statements reflect the required adoption of new accounting presentation standards, changing our income and functional expense statements, creating significant differences between the two.

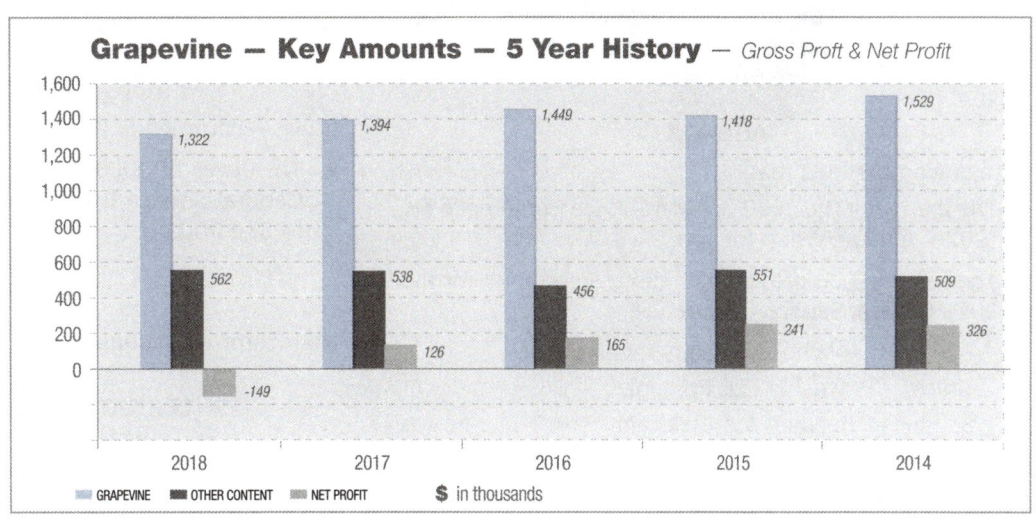

Grapevine — Key Amounts — 5 Year History — *Gross Proft & Net Profit*

$ in thousands

GRAPEVINE   OTHER CONTENT   NET PROFIT

■ Advisory Actions

Conference Advisory Actions represent recommendations made by the standing committees and approved by the Conference body as a whole or recommendations discussed and voted on by all Conference members during general sessions. The group conscience of the Fellowship in the United States and Canada was expressed in the following Advisory Actions, which the General Service Board accepted in its legally required annual meeting following the 2019 Conference.

FLOOR ACTIONS

It was recommended that:

1 The proposed floor action that "A draft Fourth Edition of the Spanish Big Book, *Alcohólicos Anonimos,* be developed and a progress report be brought to the 2020 General Service Conference" be committed to the trustees' Literature Committee.

2 The proposed floor action that "The pamphlet 'A.A. for the Black and African-American Alcoholic' be updated and a progress report and/or a draft be presented to the 2020 General Service Conference" be committed to the trustees' Literature Committee.

3 The "A.A.W.S. Policy on Publication of Literature: Updating Pamphlets and Other A.A. Materials" be recommitted to the trustees' Literature Committee with an updated proposed policy to be brought back to the 70th General Service Conference.

AGENDA

It was recommended that:

4 The theme for the 2020 General Service Conference be: "2020: A Clear Vision for You."

5 The following be presentation/discussion topics for the 2020 General Service Conference:

   Recovery — Who Is Missing in Our Rooms?
   Unity — Practicing Our Principles
   Service — Keeping A.A. Relevant

6 The workshop topic for the 2020 General Service Conference be:

   Attraction Through Action

ARCHIVES*

7 The 1940s home movie of the co-founders and their wives be added to the Archives video "Markings on the Journey" at an estimated cost of $5,000.

COOPERATION WITH THE PROFESSIONAL COMMUNITY

It was recommended that:

8 The text "They may help arrange hospitalization" be removed from the section "What can you expect from A.A.?" in the pamphlet "Alcoholics Anonymous in Your Community."

CORRECTIONS

No recommendations.

FINANCE

It was recommended that:

9 The level of $5,000 for individual bequests to the General Service Board from A.A. members be raised to $10,000.

GRAPEVINE

No recommendations.

INTERNATIONAL CONVENTIONS/ REGIONAL FORUMS*

It was recommended that:

10 An anonymity-protected photograph of the flag ceremony be taken at the 2020 International Convention.

*Members serve on this committee as a secondary committee assignment.

11 An anonymity-protected Internet broadcast of the 2020 International Convention Opening Flag Ceremony be approved.

12 Anonymity-protected video footage with highlights of the 2020 International Convention be produced for maintaining archival footage of the Convention, as well as for sharing the spirit and enthusiasm of the 2020 International Convention.

LITERATURE

It was recommended that:

13 The pamphlet "Questions and Answers on Sponsorship" be revised to add the following text regarding anonymity:

1. Under the section, "What does a sponsor do and not do?" (p. 13), after the current bullet "Impresses upon the newcomer the importance of all our Traditions," add a new bullet with the following language:

    Emphasizes the relevance and spiritual value of anonymity, both on a person-to-person basis, as well as at the public level, including social media. (For more information, see the pamphlet "Understanding Anonymity.")

2. Under the section, "How can a sponsor explain the A.A. program?" (p. 15), add a sixth paragraph:

    Many sponsors discuss the significance of anonymity at a personal level and public level early on. Anonymity at a personal level provides protection for all members from the identification as alcoholics, a safeguard often of special importance to newcomers. At the public level of press, radio, films, and other media technologies, such as the Internet, anonymity stresses the equality in the Fellowship of all members by putting the brakes on those who might otherwise exploit their A.A. affiliation to achieve recognition, power or personal gain. The sponsor is quick to point out the benefit of anonymity at this public level. Sponsors may provide examples from their own experience of maintaining public anonymity.

14 The trustees' Literature Committee update the pamphlet "The Twelve Steps Illustrated" and bring back a progress report or draft pamphlet to the 2020 General Service Conference.

15 The trustees' Literature Committee update the pamphlet "The Twelve Concepts Illustrated" and bring back a progress report or draft pamphlet to the 2020 General Service Conference.

POLICY/ADMISSIONS

It was recommended that:

16 To allow time for discussion, the "Process for Polling the General Service Conference between Annual Meetings" which currently reads:

Timing

In keeping with the G.S.B. Bylaws, Conference members will be given two weeks from the time the poll is emailed to respond with their vote. Dates for all votes and motions will be included with the poll, using a form similar to the "Timeline for Polling Conference Between Meetings." All times listed are Eastern Time.

The original poll will be emailed by 2 p.m., and voting will open that day and remain open for two weeks.

Voting will close at 2 p.m. two weeks after the poll was emailed. By 5 p.m. on the day the poll results are due, Conference members will be notified of the results by email. A request for any minority opinion will be included with the poll results.

Be replaced with:

Timing

In keeping with the G.S.B. Bylaws, Conference members will be given two weeks from the time the poll is emailed to respond with their vote. Dates for all votes and motions will be included with the poll, using a form similar to the "Timeline for Polling Conference Between Meetings." All times listed are Eastern Time.

The original poll will be emailed by 2 p.m., and discussion will open that day and remain open for **one week. Voting will commence on day seven at 2 p.m. after discussion closes**.

Voting will close at 2 p.m. two weeks after the poll was emailed. By 5 p.m. on the day the poll results are due, Conference members will be notified of the results by email. A request for any minority opinion will be included with the poll results.

PUBLIC INFORMATION

It was recommended that:

17 The trustees' Committee on Public Information develop a plan to produce video shorts based on current A.A. pamphlets that provide information about A.A. to the public and that a report be brought back to the 2020 Conference Committee on Public Information.

18 The video PSA "My World" be discontinued.

19 The "Policy on Actors Portraying A.A. Members or Potential A.A. Members in Videos Produced by the General Service Board or its Affiliates" be reaffirmed.

20 Two PSAs be developed at a cost not to exceed $50,000 for each PSA, and that if full-face characters are shown, to include an "actor portrayal" disclaimer on screen.

21 The text addressing anonymity and safety be included in the pamphlet "Understanding Anonymity" as follows:

Q. Is it okay to tell someone if I witness or experience inappropriate behavior that happens either during or outside meeting times? Can I alert the proper authorities if there is criminal behavior?

A. Groups strive to provide as safe an environment as possible in which members can focus on sobriety, and, while anonymity is central to that purpose, it is not intended to be a cloak protecting inappropriate or criminal behavior. Saying something about inappropriate behavior or calling the proper authorities does not go against any A.A. Traditions and is meant to preserve the safety of all members.

22 The wording of the last sentence in the section titled "How A.A. Members Maintain Sobriety" in the flyer "A.A. at a Glance" be changed from:

Sobriety is maintained through sharing experience, strength and hope at group meetings and through the suggested Twelve Steps for recovery from alcoholism.

to:

Sobriety is maintained through sharing experience, strength and hope at group meetings and through the **Twelve Steps of Alcoholics Anonymous, which are suggested as a program of recovery.**

23 A progress report on the usefulness and effectiveness of the A.A.W.S. YouTube channel be brought back to the 2020 Conference Committee on Public Information.

24 All current video PSA titles be updated for search optimization purposes.

25 A.A. World Services, Inc. and AA Grapevine, Inc. apply for "LegitScript" certification to qualify for Google Ad Words/Grants.

26 A.A. World Services, Inc. apply for Google AdWords/Grants, for the purpose of providing information about A.A. to the public.

27 A.A. World Services, Inc. implement Google AdWords/Grants for the purpose of providing information about A.A. to the public and that a report be brought back to the 2020 Conference Committee on Public Information.

REPORT AND CHARTER

No recommendations.

TREATMENT AND ACCESSIBILITIES

It was recommended that:

28 Ashley's story (an A.A. member who is Deaf) be added to the pamphlet "Access to A.A.: Members Share on Overcoming Barriers" and that the video version of the pamphlet be updated to reflect this change.

29 The pamphlet "A.A. for the Older Alcoholic – Never Too Late" be updated with a revised introduction; current and inclusive stories; reference to online A.A.; and an updated "How Do I Find A.A.?" section. The committee requested that a progress report or draft pamphlet be brought back to the 2020 Conference Committee on Treatment and Accessibilities.

30 The trustees' Committee on Cooperation with the Professional Community/Treatment and Accessibilities develop anonymity-protected audio interviews with military professionals about their experience with A.A. as a resource for posting online.

TRUSTEES

It was recommended that:

31 The following slate of trustees of the General Service Board be elected at the annual meeting of the members of the General Service Board in May 2019 following presentation at the 2019 General Service Conference for disapproval if any:

Class A

Leslie S. Backus	Peter Luongo, Ph.D.,
Hon. Christine Carpenter	LCSW-C
Michele Grinberg, J.D.	Nancy McCarthy
Sister Judith Ann Karam,	Al J. Mooney, M.D.,
CSA, FACHE	FAAFP, FASAM

Class B

Thomas Ardolf	Francis Gilroy
Cathy Beckham	Patricia LaNauze
Carole Boerner	Jan Lembke
Beau Bush	David Noll
James Dean	Newton Pritchett
Mark Everett	Ginger Rhoades Bell
Kathi Fowler	Cate Wittig

32 The following slate of officers of the General Service Board be elected at the annual meeting of the members of the General Service Board in May 2019 following presentation at the 2019 General Service Conference for disapproval if any:

Chairperson	Michele Grinberg, J.D.
First vice-chairperson	Nancy McCarthy
Second vice-chairperson	Newton Pritchett
Treasurer	Leslie S. Backus
Secretary	Ginger Rhoades Bell
Assistant treasurer	Bob Slotterback*
Assistant secretary	Mary Cumings*

*G.S.O. employees

33 The following slate of directors be elected at the annual meeting of the members of the A.A. World Services Corporate Board in May 2019 following presentation at the 2019 General Service Conference for disapproval if any:

Beau Bush	Homer Moeller
Cathy Beckham	David Noll
Mary Cumings*	Gregory Tobin*
Deborah Koltai	Carolyn Walsh
Jan Lembke	

*G.S.O. employees

34 The following slate of directors be elected at the annual meeting of the members of the AA Grapevine Corporate Board in May 2019 following presentation at the 2019 General Service Conference for disapproval if any:

Carole Boerner	Tommi Hanley
Josh Eggleston	Nancy McCarthy
Mark Everett	Ginger Rhoades Bell
Ino Fernandez	Albin Zezula*
Kathi Fowler	

*AA Grapevine employee

▪ Committee Considerations

An Advisory Action of the 1990 General Service Conference states: "Items discussed, but no action taken or recommendation made, as well as committee recommendations which are not adopted, be included in a separate section of the Final Report." *Listed by committee, such items are included here "in their entirety" per Advisory Action of the 2018 General Service Conference.*

AGENDA

Committee Considerations:

- The committee discussed the report of the trustees' Committee on the General Service Conference and encourages Conference committee chairs to communicate with their committee both before and after the Board weekend conference calls with their corresponding trustees' committee chairs. The committee noted that this may help to ensure all Conference committee members are fully informed.

- The committee reviewed the 2019 General Service Conference evaluation form and noted that improvements were implemented from the 68th G.S.C. Evaluation suggestions.

- The committee reviewed the summary of the 2018 General Service Conference evaluations. The committee suggests that Conference members be given the option to select the Conference Manual format and that the online version of the evaluation form be formatted such that it can be continually updated during Conference week.

- The committee reviewed the report on the Implementation and Effectiveness of the Conference Agenda Process from the trustees' Committee on the General Service Conference, which included sharing from the 2019 Conference committee chairs. The com-

mittee noted that the January conference call portion of the plan was implemented and request reporting of the 2019 participant survey results to the 2020 Conference Agenda Committee.

- The committee reviewed the sharing results of the 2019 survey of Conference committee chairs.

ARCHIVES*

Committee Considerations:

- The committee reviewed the revised Archives Workbook and newly released Archives Service Piece "Archives Checklist: A quick guide for local A.A. archivists" and expressed satisfaction with the content. The committee suggested that the use of gender-specific language be avoided, when possible, in future printings of the Archives Workbook.

- The committee appreciates the work of the trustees' Committee on Archives in exploring the feasibility of including in the A.A.W.S. Literature catalog all reproductions of archival materials being distributed by the Archives department upon request. However, the committee expressed concerns about pursuing this suggestion, noting that overexposure of these items would increase the workload of the Archives staff and could trivialize the archival materials.

*Members serve on this committee as a secondary committee assignment.

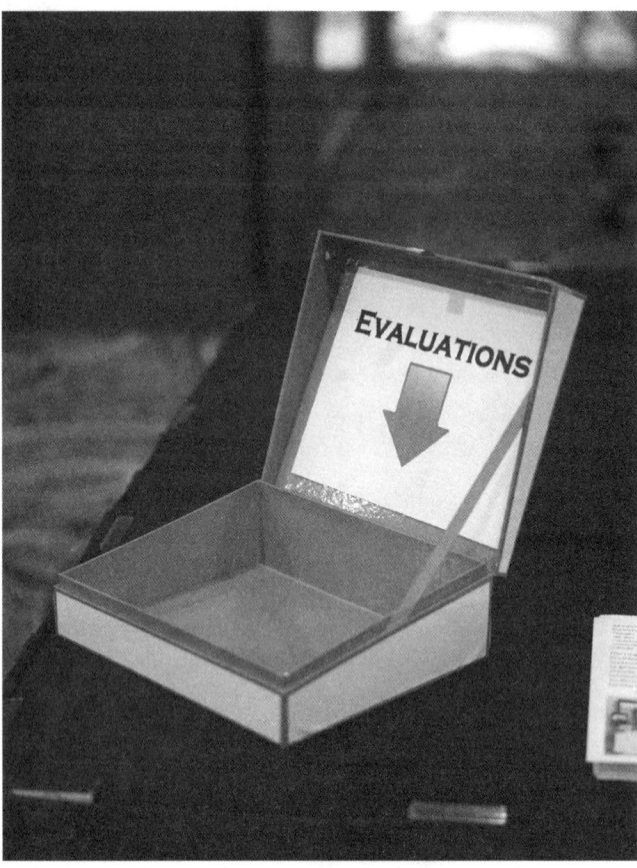

CORRECTIONS

Committee Considerations:

- The committee considered a request for a review of all corrections-related literature in order to make the language more modern and inclusive and agreed to take no action. The committee noted that there was not a widely expressed need to warrant a change in the language currently used in A.A. literature for corrections. The committee also noted the absence of suitable language alternatives that could be used across all areas.

- The committee considered a request that the General Service Office establish and help maintain a database of Correctional facilities in each service area in the U.S. and Canada and the status of meetings held therein, and took no action. The committee noted the merits of the goal but considered that the diverse experiences and needs in different areas would be better served by a tool, or resource, that would help areas develop their own database tailored to their needs. The committee requested that the staff on the corrections desk ask for shared experience from A.A. members involved in corrections service for tools currently being used to create local databases with correctional facility meeting information, the status of the meetings, contacts, possible needs, and any other relevant information, and that the information be considered for a possible service piece or added to the Corrections Workbook, as appropriate.

- The committee expressed appreciation for the hard work accomplished by the trustees' Committee on Corrections and encouraged the continued communication between the chairs of the trustees' and Conference committees on Corrections throughout the year.

- The committee reviewed the Corrections Kit and Workbook and noted that many of the pamphlets used in correction service work have staples. The committee shared that a growing number of correctional facilities will not allow materials with staples into their facilities. The committee requested that the Publishing Department give priority to pamphlets used in corrections service for publication without staples, including, but not limited to, "The Twelve Traditions Illustrated," "The Twelve Steps Illustrated," "Many Paths to Spirituality," "Is A.A. for Me?," "This Is A.A.," "Frequently Asked Questions About A.A.," "Do you think you're different?," "Too Young?" and "Women in A.A."

COOPERATION WITH THE PROFESSIONAL COMMUNITY

Committee Considerations:

- The committee discussed the progress on implementing a static LinkedIn page and felt that the overall goal of the 2018 Advisory Action on creating a LinkedIn page had not yet been achieved. The committee agreed that the wording suggested for the LinkedIn page did not adequately describe Alcoholics Anonymous. The presence of a LinkedIn page describing Alcoholics Anonymous would be a valuable tool to aid local C.P.C. committee work in the U.S. and Canada to inform professionals about A.A. The committee requested that the trustees' Committee on Cooperation with the Professional Community/Treatment and Accessibilities revisit the plan for implementing a LinkedIn page, taking into consideration the following suggestions:

  » Add a disclaimer explaining that the "promoted" content on the LinkedIn page is not affiliated with Alcoholics Anonymous.

  » Include information from current A.A. literature about what A.A. does and does not do that can be useful to professionals who work with alcoholics.

  » Add a concise description of Alcoholics Anonymous that is based on the Conference-approved literature intended for professionals that was reviewed at the October 2018 trustees' meeting.

  » Add a link to aa.org and a link to the information for professionals' page.

  » Add a link to the *About A.A.* newsletter.

  » Include a schedule of C.P.C. exhibits at national level events that are coordinated through the General Service Office.

  » Annually provide a report tracking the A.A. LinkedIn page, including visits to aa.org from the LinkedIn page for review by the Conference Committee on C.P.C.

- The committee requested that the trustees' committee review the pamphlet "A.A. in Your Community" with a focus on what professionals can expect from A.A. and

A.A. members and bring a report back to the 2020 Conference Committee on C.P.C.

- The committee reviewed the C.P.C. Kit and Workbook and noted their value to local C.P.C. committees and suggested that a section be added where local experiences can be noted.

FINANCE

Committee Considerations:

- The committee reviewed and discussed area contributions for delegate expenses for the Conference and took no action.
- The committee reviewed area contributions for delegate expenses, discussed the costs of the Conference and suggested that the trustees' Finance and Budgetary Committee provide a detailed breakdown of Conference expenses be included as background when delegate expenses are reviewed every two years, beginning in 2021.
- The committee requested that additional information regarding statistical information on delegate fees and contribution limits be available as background when reviewed every two years, beginning in 2021.
- The committee reviewed and discussed the Conference-approved maximum annual contribution of $5,000 to the General Service Board from an individual A.A. member and took no action.
- The committee reviewed the Self-Support Packet and suggested the following changes:
  » In the Finance Guidelines mirror the language on how to make a contribution from the end of "The A.A. Group Treasurer" pamphlet.
  » Include the regular contribution envelope in the packet.
  » Revise the back of the Self-Support card as suggested, to reflect the following:
    ▪ Move "What is the value of your sobriety?" under the title.
    ▪ Move last bullet under "Some facts" to be first: "Your contributions help ensure the future of our Fellowship worldwide."
    ▪ Rephrase the first bullet under "Some facts" to read: "Historically, less than half of all A.A. groups contribute to the General Service Office" and make it the second bullet.
    ▪ Remove second bullet regarding "Costs of services…" from "Some facts."
    ▪ Rephrase the third bullet under "Some facts" to read: "Gross profit from literature sales make up for the shortfall in contributions," or something similar to emphasize being more self-supporting.
    ▪ Remove the titles "Personal thoughts" and "Some facts."
    ▪ Include contribution information from the end of "The A.A. Group Treasurer" pamphlet.

GRAPEVINE

Committee Considerations:

- The committee considered a request to remove the Alcoholism at Large section from AA Grapevine and took no action. The committee affirmed Grapevine and La Viña's editorial freedom, as expressed in the Grapevine Charter that states: "to prepare, edit, print and publish…written material concerning generally the subject of alcoholism and related matters and dealing with various means, methods, techniques and procedures available or proposed for the treatment, relief, rehabilitation and recovery of persons suffering from or potentially subject to alcoholism."
- The committee requested that the disclaimer for the Alcoholism at Large section be printed more prominently and visibly.
- The committee agreed to forward to the AA Grapevine Corporate Board the suggestion that Grapevine produce in the year 2020 or later:

  1. The Early Days of AA (working title)
     Classic stories previously published in Grapevine by members from the 1930s, '40s and '50s about what A.A. was like in its earliest days.
  2. Getting Involved in General Service (working title)
     Inspiring stories previously published in Grapevine by A.A. members who have been involved in general service.
  3. Surrender and Hope (working title) (La Viña book)
     Stories by Spanish-speaking A.A. members, previously published in La Viña, about how they came to surrender and join A.A. for a new life.

- The committee reviewed the progress report on the AA Grapevine Workbook revisions and looks forward to reviewing a progress report or draft at the next Conference. The committee also forwarded suggestions to the Grapevine office including expanding shared experience and how to use GV/LV as a recovery tool.
- The committee reviewed the AA Grapevine Fellowship

Survey and summary and noted the actions the Grapevine Board and staff have taken on the findings. The committee looks forward to a progress report at the next Conference on further actions taken.

INTERNATIONAL CONVENTIONS/ REGIONAL FORUMS*

Committee Considerations:

- The committee discussed ways of encouraging interest in Regional and Local Forums and attracting first time attendees and suggested:
  - » Compiling notes from the first timer sharing at a Forum for later distribution to encourage members to attend a future Forum;
  - » Consider developing a Regional Forum app;
  - » Consider developing a micro-site in addition to surface mail for distributing the Regional Forum flyers;
  - » Increase awareness at the local level, including "intentional" outreach to different populations (e.g., young people, Spanish-speaking communities, Deaf and Hard-of-Hearing);
  - » Encourage local welcome committees to create "Save the Date" flyers;
  - » Consider inviting A.A.W.S./AA Grapevine directors to "non-service" A.A. events to increase awareness of regional forums;
  - » Place information about Regional Forums in the AA Grapevine and La Viña.

LITERATURE

Committee Considerations:

- The committee reviewed the request for the development of a Fifth Edition of the book *Alcoholics Anonymous,* which would include a section of stories comprised of individuals who got sober under the age of 25 and took no action, noting that A.A. is inclusive, never exclusive. If a Fifth Edition of *Alcoholics Anonymous* is to be developed, the committee suggested that stories be gathered from as broad a cross-section of the Fellowship as possible, including from those who got sober under age 25.

- The committee reviewed the progress report on the development of a pamphlet for Spanish-speaking women and looks forward to reviewing a progress report or draft pamphlet at the 2020 General Service Conference.

- The committee reviewed the progress report on the development of a pamphlet based upon A.A.'s Three Legacies and looks forward to reviewing a progress report or draft pamphlet at the 2020 General Service Conference.

- The committee reviewed the progress report on the comprehensive update to the video "Your A.A. General Service Office, the Grapevine and the General Service Structure." The committee looks forward to reviewing a progress report or draft revised video at the 2020 General Service Conference.

- The committee reviewed a progress report for the pamphlet "The Twelve Traditions Illustrated" and suggested an emphasis on the importance of anonymity on social media perhaps by adding an image of the Anonymity in the Digital Age poster as well as the following text:

  > To quote Bill W.'s writing on page 15 from *The Language of the Heart,* "...it should be the privilege, even the right, of each individual or group to handle anonymity as they wish." However, when dealing with social media, personal anonymity as well as the group's anonymity may be easily compromised. We must be careful when using social media to not use full names and/or photos of A.A. members in a way that would identify them or others as A.A. members.

The committee looks forward to reviewing a progress report or revised draft pamphlet at the 2020 General Service Conference.

- The committee reviewed a progress report on the revision of the pamphlet "Too Young?" The committee looks forward to reviewing a draft revised pamphlet and/or samples of other potential formats of the pamphlet at the 2020 General Service Conference.

- The committee reviewed a progress report on the revision of the pamphlet "Young People and A.A." The committee looks forward to reviewing a revised draft pamphlet at the 2020 General Service Conference.

- The committee reviewed a progress report for language on safety and A.A. for inclusion in the booklet *Living Sober* and the pamphlet "Questions and Answers on Sponsorship" and clarified that the language is meant to focus on safety at the group level.

- The committee suggested that the trustees' Committee on Literature develop a Literature Committee Workbook and provide a progress report to the 2020 General Service Conference.

- The committee considered a request to add information regarding safety to the pamphlet "The A.A. Group" and took no action. The committee noted that the pamphlet already addresses safety.

- The committee discussed the draft of the proposed revision to A.A. World Services' "Policy on Publication of Literature: Updating Pamphlets and Other A.A. Materials" and supports the proposed policy and its intended impact to support more effectively carrying the A.A. message.

In keeping with Concept Eight, which states in part, "The Trustees of the General Service Board act in two primary capacities: (a) with respect to the larger matters of overall policy and finance, they are the principle planners and administrators..." the committee expressed support for G.S.O.'s publishing professionals and their efforts working on behalf of A.A.

In keeping with Concept One, which states in part, "The final responsibility and the ultimate authority for A.A.

---

*Members serve on this committee as a secondary committee assignment.

world services should always reside in the collective conscience of our whole Fellowship," the committee recognized the importance and the sensitivity of maintaining the integrity of the Conference process for developing and updating literature to best reflect A.A.'s collective experience, strength and hope.

The committee requested that the final version of the complete text of A.A. World Services' "Policy on Publication of Literature: Updating Pamphlets and Other A.A. Materials" be included as background for future General Service Conference committees.

- The committee reviewed the matrix of A.A. recovery literature and suggested that the trustees' Literature Committee consider an update to the pamphlet "Is A.A. for Me?" The committee noted that the pamphlet has not been updated since 1989.

POLICY/ADMISSIONS

Committee Considerations:

- In reviewing the report from G.S.O.'s general manager on site selection for the General Service Conference, the committee noted the change of dates for the 71st G.S.C. that will take place in 2021 and that it had been necessary for the general manager to move forward and contract for the hotel for the 72nd General Service Conference prior to the selection of dates by the Conference Policy/Admissions Committee.

The 71st General Service Conference will take place April 18–24, 2021 in Brooklyn, New York, and the 72nd General Service Conference will take place April 24–30, 2022 in Brooklyn, New York.

- In order to provide additional flexibility to the General Service Office management in contracting the most cost-effective and appropriate venues for the General Service Conference, the committee agreed to select three proposed dates for the 73rd and 74th General Service Conferences. The committee selected the following dates in order of preference for the 73rd General Service Conference: April 23–29, 2023; April 30–May 6, 2023 and April 16–22, 2023. The committee selected the following dates in order of preference for the 74th General Service Conference: April 14–20, 2024; April 28–May 4, 2024 and May 5–11, 2024. The committee noted that these proposed Conference dates do not conflict with any significant holidays. The committee asks that all Conference members be notified of the final dates for the 73rd and 74th General Service Conferences as soon as they are finalized by G.S.O. management.

- The committee reviewed the report from G.S.O.'s general manager on site selection of the General Service Conference and looks forward to a progress report for review by the 2020 General Service Conference.

- The committee considered a process for how a Conference committee could review, discuss, and act on proposed agenda items not forwarded to a Conference committee and appreciates the trustees' Committee on the General Service Conference's work on developing a process thus far. The committee noted the inclusion of a rationale on items not forwarded that are listed on the grid of proposed agenda items. The committee requested that the trustees' Committee on the General Service Conference continue developing the process outlined in their report and provide a report to the 2020 General Service Conference that includes more information regarding the distribution of background and the January conference call between the trustee committee chair and the corresponding Conference committee.

- The committee requested that the trustees' Committee on the General Service Conference develop a process for approving qualified representatives from other A.A. service structures to observe the U.S. and Canada General Service Conference that allows for these observers to be presented for General Service Conference consideration prior to the General Service Conference week for review by the 2020 General Service Conference.

- The committee discussed a request to "develop a procedure to deal with special requests/agenda items" and took no action. The committee noted that Concept Three and the Conference Charter provide adequate guidance and flexibility for dealing with agenda items that are outside of the usual process.

- The committee discussed reconsidering the 1986 Advisory Action regarding a simple majority vote by the full Conference and took no action. The committee asked that implementation of this 1986 advisory action resume with the 69th General Service Conference Final Report:

  If a committee recommendation does not receive the two-thirds vote required to become a Conference Advisory Action, but has a majority of votes, it automatically becomes a suggestion and will be duly noted in the Conference Report.

- The committee noted that the trustees' General Service Conference Committee scheduled a Presentation/Discussion on the Equitable Distribution of the Workload of Conference Committees at the 69th General Service Conference. The committee looks forward to receiving a plan or progress report on this important process for review by the 2020 General Service Conference from the trustees' Committee on the General Service Conference.

PUBLIC INFORMATION

Committee Considerations:

- The committee reviewed and accepted the 2018 annual report from the trustees' Public Information Committee regarding aa.org and aagrapevine.org.

- The committee suggested that the A.A.W.S. Publishing Department update all A.A. pamphlet covers to prominently display the G.S.O. website "aa.org."

- The committee also suggested that it may be helpful to include "www.aagrapevine.org" on the cover of A.A. pamphlets.

- The committee reviewed and accepted the 2018 report from the trustees' Public Information Committee on the Usefulness and Relevance of Public Service Announcements.

- The committee reviewed and accepted the information on centralized distribution, tracking and evaluation of the public service announcement "Changes."

- The committee suggested that the trustees' Committee on Public Information explore online platforms as a possible additional media outlet for future public service announcement distribution.

- The committee suggested that the "how to find A.A." section of all existing PSAs be edited to include current terminologies that describe how people search for A.A.

- The committee reviewed the contents of P.I. Kit and Workbook, and asked that the contents of P.I. Kit and Workbook continue to be updated with current and relevant information for P.I. committees.

REPORT AND CHARTER

Committee Considerations:

- The committee accepted a report from the Publishing Department outlining the General Service Office process for timely and accurate preparation and publication of *The A.A. Service Manual, 2020–2022 Edition* and the 2019 General Service Conference *Final Report.*

- The committee reviewed the progress report from the A.A.W.S. Publishing Department on the redesign of *The A.A. Service Manual* and forwarded their comments to the Publishing Department.

- The committee considered the A.A. Directories (Canada, Eastern U.S., and Western U.S.) especially in light of the new ERP system and the Meeting Guide app, and requested that the General Service Office explore alternative methods of accessing and distributing the contact information contained in the A.A. Directories (Canada, Eastern U.S., and Western U.S.). The committee requested that a report be brought back to the 2020 Report and Charter Conference Committee.

- The committee agreed with the suggestion from G.S.O. management that a new level of privacy was needed in the General Service Conference Final Report for Conference members' personal information, and that as of 2019:

  » The roster section for Area Delegates include only each person's name, city, state or province.

  » The bios of trustees and nontrustee directors include only each person's name, city, state or province.

  » No email addresses for delegates, trustees or nontrustee directors will be included.

TREATMENT & ACCESSIBILITIES

Committee Considerations:

- The committee considered revising the pamphlet "Bridging the Gap Between Treatment and A.A. Through Contact Programs" to include related corrections activities and agreed with the concept. The committee requested that the trustees' Committee on Cooperation with the Professional Community/Treatment and Accessibilities consult with the trustees' Committee on Corrections to review all treatment and corrections committee literature from G.S.O. related to bridging the gap and temporary contact activities with the following in mind:

  » How treatment and corrections material can be updated for currency and inclusion;

  » How this material could be combined;

  » What material might be discontinued;

  » How the combined material might be broadened to encompass the full range of possibilities in which a temporary contact might be useful.

  The committee requested that a report be brought to the 2020 Conference Treatment and Accessibilities committee.

- The committee reviewed a draft Remote Communities Kit and agreed that there is a need for this new material. The committee suggested that before the Kit is made available that a guideline or workbook be developed for inclusion. The guideline or workbook might use a locally produced current Remote Communities workbook as an example.

  The committee also suggested that the guideline or workbook include a list of available material, with details, including the intended audience, and suggestions for when, why and how it might be used.

  The committee forwarded a list of additional pamphlets and service material to be considered for inclusion in the Kit. The committee suggested that the trustees' committee not include paper copies of the pamphlets in the Kit but provide a list of material by category and purpose, linked to encourage digital use.

  The committee noted the availability and relevance of past articles in Grapevine, *Box 4-5-9*, and *About A.A.*, and requested that the trustees' Committee on Cooperation with the Professional Community/Treatment and Accessibilities and staff work with AA Grapevine to make past Remote Communities articles from Grapevine available for those involved in Remote Communities service.

- The committee reviewed the Treatment Committees Kit and Workbook and forwarded a list of suggestions to the trustees' Committee on Cooperation with the Professional Community/Treatment and Accessibilities.

- The committee reviewed the Accessibilities Kit and Workbook and forwarded a list of suggestions to the trustees' Committee on Cooperation with the Professional Community/Treatment and Accessibilities.

TRUSTEES

Committee Considerations:

- The committee reviewed the resumes and approved

as eligible for election all Class B trustee candidates for Northeast regional trustee, Southwest regional trustee, and trustee-at-large/Canada.

- The committee reviewed the drafted procedures for a partial or complete reorganization of the General Service Board, the A.A. World Services Board and AA Grapevine Board. The committee agreed that the procedure needed additional specificity, offered suggestions, and requested that the trustees' Committee on Nominating bring back a revised plan to the 2020 Conference Committee on Trustees.

Recommendations Not Resulting in Conference Advisory Actions

CORRECTIONS

- The Scope of the Conference Committee on Corrections, which currently reads: "The purpose of the committee will be to encourage A.A. members to assume responsibility to carry the message to alcoholics who cannot, of their own free will, seek A.A. help"

Be revised, to read:

The purpose of the committee will be to encourage A.A. members to assume responsibility to carry the message to alcoholics who cannot seek A.A. help **outside the walls.**

LITERATURE

- A draft Fifth Edition of *Alcoholics Anonymous* be developed and a progress report be brought to the 2020 Conference Literature Committee, keeping in mind the 1995 Advisory Action that:

The first 164 pages of the Big Book, *Alcoholics Anonymous,* the Preface, the Forewords, "The Doctor's Opinion," "Dr. Bob's Nightmare," and the Appendices remain as is.

- Text be added to the foreword of the book *Twelve Steps and Twelve Traditions* as follows (Bold text reflects addition):

A.A.'s Twelve Steps are a group of principles, spiritual in their nature, which, if practiced as a way of life, can expel the obsession to drink and enable the sufferer to become happily and usefully whole.

A.A.'s Twelve Traditions apply to the life of the Fellowship itself. They outline the means by which A.A. maintains its unity and relates itself to the world about it, the way it lives and grows.

A.A.'s Twelve Concepts for World Service are an interpretation of A.A.'s world service structure. The Concepts provide guidelines for carrying the message to thousands of suffering alcoholics yet to come. They aim to record the "why" of our service structure. They may be found in *The A.A. Service Manual combined with Twelve Concepts for World Service.*

- The phrase "Nonalcoholics may attend open meetings as observers" be added as the final sentence to the "Open Meeting" side of the Primary Purpose (Blue) Card. The card will read as follows (Bold text reflects addition):

THIS IS AN OPEN MEETING OF ALCOHOLICS ANONYMOUS

This is an open meeting of Alcoholics Anonymous. We are glad you are all here — especially newcomers. In keeping with our singleness of purpose and our Third Tradition which states that "The only requirement for A.A. membership is a desire to stop drinking," we ask that all who participate confine their discussion to their problems with alcohol. **Nonalcoholics may attend open meetings as observers.**

Floor Actions Not Resulting in Conference Advisory Actions

- Production of *The Language of the Heart* in Spanish as an audiobook be prioritized by AA Grapevine, Inc. and a timeline for production be reported at the 70th General Service Conference. **(Not approved)**

- The pamphlet "The 'God' Word" be added as one of the pamphlets used in Corrections service for possible publication without staples. **(Conference declined to consider)**

- In order to illustrate the importance of the committee recommendations that achieve simple majority but not substantial unanimity (i.e., a vote of two-thirds), that such "simple majority suggestions" be prominently included in the Conference *Final Report.* **(Not approved)**

- The "Alcoholism at Large" section be removed from the AA Grapevine. **(Conference declined to consider)**

■ Workshop Summary

This year, the trustees' Committee on the General Service Conference approved the use of a new format to facilitate workshops at the 69th GSC with the intent to get "big and bold discussion ideas" related to the overarching topic that the Conference approved. The format was conducted using variations of Liberating Structures as follows:

Having been asked ahead of time to come up with "big and bold discussion topics," participants were given 3x5 index cards on which to write their ideas. Once this was complete, they were asked to walk around the room and exchange cards with each person they saw, but they were not to read the card. This exercise is called "Mill and Pass." Music was played as everyone milled and passed for 30 seconds. When the music ended, participants were asked to read the card in their hand and score it from 1 to 5 (with 5 being the highest), then raise it in the air when finished. When all hands were raised, the music began again and the mill-and-pass process was repeated four more times. After scoring of the fifth round, participants totaled the scores on the card in their hand.

In the next phase, "25/5 Crowdsourcing," the facilitator asked for and recorded topics with a score of 25, then with a score of 24, and so on. The process was repeated until the five most highly scored topics were identified and recorded. The facilitator then asked if anyone was holding a card with a topic they felt strongly needed to be discussed or if they'd written one they felt strongly needed to be discussed. The highest-ranked card in this category became the sixth discussion topic. (The idea here was to include a "minority opinion" topic.)

The third phase utilized "Open Space" technology, the intent of which is to enable everybody to address those issues that are important to them. Six stations were set up in the room to facilitate the discussion of the six big and bold topics. The four principles of Open Space were posted on an easel:

i. Whoever comes to the Open Space are the right people

ii. Whenever the discussion starts is the right time

iii. When it's over, it's over

iv. Whatever happens is the only thing that could have happened

Also posted were the three parts of Open Space's one law — the Law of Two Feet:

i. Go and attend whichever session you want

ii. If you find you're not learning or contributing, use your two feet!

iii. If you wish to participate in more than one discussion topic, use your two feet!

The authors of each of the six topics were asked to be "conveners." (Authors could decline, at which point a volunteer was asked to come forward.) The conveners were tasked with writing their discussion topic clearly on a Post-

It flip chart and recording the ideas being generated. They were then given five minutes to distill the key points with their discussion groups, and six minutes to report their findings to the full session.

In session A, the top discussion topics were as follows:

1. *The A.A. Service Manual/Twelve Concepts for World Service* and attracting members to service

2. How to be more inclusive of young people

3. Rigidity in A.A.

4. Service sponsorship

5. How to be more inclusive of seniors/ aging Baby Boomers

6. Singleness of purpose

Topic A-1: *The A.A. Service Manual*

Participants noted that *The A.A. Service Manual* itself could be "boring" and make for "difficult reading," and mentioned that use of the "Twelve Concepts Illustrated" pamphlet might be a more effective tool to teach members about service and using the Concepts. Incorporating a "Concept of the month" into the group meeting format (or even starting a Concept meeting) could help members understand the principles of service; some commented that it was important to tie in the Concepts and the Traditions when speaking about service. "Meet and eat" workshops on the manual and service more broadly might facilitate greater understanding and encourage members to get involved. One participant suggested bringing the diagram "Service Structure Inside the A.A. Group" (page S27 of the manual) to one's home group and utilizing it to explain how service should work at the group level.

Topic A-2: How to include young people

Workshop participants were eager to do outreach in this area, making comments such as "Don't wait for them to come to you" or even "to be invited." Ideas included creating YPAA committees at the area level and, more generally, actively seeking opportunities to attend and participate in YPAA events. They added that underpinning these efforts must be an acceptance of young people's lifestyles — including embracing technology and even social media — and a willingness to really hear their stories and to "let them be young." Participants felt it was on A.A. members to "look for ways to work together anytime, anywhere, and however young people want to."

Topic A-3: Rigidity in A.A.

Participants first identified examples of this phenomenon from their own experience, including the use of literature (the Big Book, even the service manual) as a "weapon"; "forcing" recitation of the Lord's Prayer (and using the "God" word); sponsoring "like a drill sergeant"; and pressuring newcomers to identify as an alcoholic. They noted that comments like "This is how we've always done it" typifies this rigid attitude and is often used to rationalize it. Participants recognized that "challenging old ideas" and moving toward greater open-mindedness could be difficult. They suggested holding "flexibility workshops" and being "an agent of change" oneself when encountering rigidity. Participants added that change comes with "democratic thought and action." Along the way, though, they believed it would be necessary to be willing to meet people where they were — to "value difference," even "to listen without an opinion." It was noted that it was critical to "trust the process" and to have compassion and empathy throughout.

Topic A-4: Service Sponsorship

An attitude of humility seemed to underlie comments from participants, who noted it was important to share information, not opinions ("Use tools and tell the truth!"), and that service sponsors don't have all the answers ("I don't know but I'll find out" is often the best answer to a question from a sponsee). In addition, it was noted that service sponsors should have sponsors themselves. Specific ideas around raising awareness about service sponsorship included making it a meeting topic; hosting workshops; creating a service piece; and simply inviting people to serve. One participant mentioned group-to-group sponsorship as well. "Keep it fun" was a recurrent theme.

Topic A-5: How to be more inclusive of seniors/ aging Baby Boomers

"Show respect and patience," noted participants about making seniors feel welcome at meetings. Also important, they said, was to be aware of accessibility issues, especially with respect to hearing (sounds are distracting, and noise can make sharing hard to hear) and vision (have large-print literature on hand). Softer chairs are also appropriate. Be aware, too, that anonymity may be especially important with this population. Regarding outreach, participants suggested hosting virtual meetings; starting senior specialty meetings; and going into senior and assisted living facilities, although this may require overcoming facility resistance to A.A. meetings. Getting seniors involved in P.I./C.P.C. committees (or other service areas) might encourage greater participation. "Start small but smart" characterized participants' outreach strategies.

Topic A-6: Singleness of Purpose

While acknowledging the importance of the Third Tradition, participants also noted that A.A. is "inclusive, never exclusive." Some felt it was critical to direct addicts to N.A. — "If someone is truly not an alcoholic, we might be killing them by not sending them somewhere else" — and that education about the difference between open and closed meetings might help. That said, there was also an emphasis on flexibility: on the importance of accepting cross addictions; on helping addicts hear the solution; and on being open to talk about other drugs. Reaching out to professionals to inform them about other programs (and not criticizing other programs) and other C.P.C. work could raise awareness around A.A.'s singleness of purpose and help addicts find the right program for them. Inclusion of remote communities was also discussed.

Session B chose the following topics:

1. Safety in A.A.
2. Primary purpose
3. Good meeting leadership
4. Singleness of purpose
5. Inclusion
6. Encouraging attitude of service
7. Importance and support of Grapevine and La Viña

Topic B-1: Safety in A.A.

Some in the group believed that safety is the responsibility of groups and the sponsors, and that it is an issue that needs to be addressed. One participant went so far as to say, "silence could mean death." To that end, they said, members need to be willing to report crimes to the police and should be supportive of those who want to do so; criminal activity is not protected by the Traditions. Participants spoke of "truth talk" — of not using terms like "13th stepping" when referring to sexual predatory behavior. Suggestions to surface (and hopefully mitigate) the issue included conducting a group inventory; developing a policy through group conscience; using safety as a meeting topic; having a volunteer read from the service piece on safety; and holding area- or district-level workshops on the subject. At the same time, it was noted, discretion must be used when dealing with problematic individuals: Are they growing up in A.A. and changing for the better, or are they "repeat offenders"? The group acknowledged the challenge: On the one hand, one must "beware of overreacting," and on the other hand, "staying silent will allow the situation to get worse." Making things more complicated, are there emotional or mental issues at play?

Suggested safety measures included "sticking together" as a group when leaving meetings; service positions (such as greeter) that support safety; and single-gender meetings. Participants agreed that underlining any discussion, policy, activity or action regarding safety should be a thorough understanding of anonymity and unity.

Topic B-2: Primary purpose

Some participants felt it was important to read the Preamble, the Traditions and the blue meeting card (defining open and closed meetings). For newcomers, they added, it's important to ensure there is a newcomers packet and a meeting list, and to emphasize sponsorship. Allow newcomers time and the opportunity to understand, said one participant: "Don't tell them they are wrong or berate them for not understanding." To stay focused on A.A.'s primary purpose, some responded, remind everyone to confine their sharing to problems related to alcohol, and pull people aside discreetly when necessary to explain our primary purpose. To make meetings attractive to all, be willing to change things; encourage people to question long-timers of the group; and allow anyone to serve. (On a related note came the comment, "Stop hoarding service positions; rotation is key!") To facilitate greater participation by all, ideas included using secret Facebook pages for information; arranging steering committee meetings (with food); picking up newcomers; and doing fun things outside meetings. Perhaps most importantly, participants said, be an example: Be "enthusiastic," "patient" and "tolerant," and "show gratitude."

Topic B-3: Good meeting leadership

The group first identified things that were "not good," such as the failure to follow a meeting format (including time limits not being enforced). Participants explained that following the meeting format provides a sense of continuity, as do strong, regu-larly scheduled business meetings. Group leaders and G.S.R.s should "understand their delegated authority and responsibility"; to that end, workshops on leading meetings could be held at the district and area level, with attendance being required for meeting chairs. To ensure "responsibility with accountability to those we serve," written documents — including meeting formats, chairperson guidelines and instructions for meeting treasurers (who should also submit written reports) — should be available in the meeting binder. All members — especially home group and long-term members, as well as newcomers — should be encouraged to serve. One member shared about a group that invites relative newcomers to lead meetings with their sponsors alongside as co-chairs, to facilitate learning and encourage service. Group inventories were also strongly recommended; groups/district/areas might also consider workshops on the pamphlet "The A.A. Group."

Topic B-4: Singleness of purpose in the context of the opioid crisis

In this session, participants covered much of the same ground covered in Topic A-6 (Singleness of purpose) — especially the importance of flexibility, of outreach to the professional community, of education about open and closed meetings — with some additional and more specific recommendations. For example, one thought was to offer a court "orientation," i.e., a session to educate judges about where to send those with opioid addictions. In addition, the service piece "Sharing Experience on Coping with Influx of New Members" may be helpful for meetings overwhelmed with addict newcomers; groups may want to address the issue at business meetings. The value of good leadership and effective chairs was mentioned. Ideas for additional guidance included assigning a temporary sponsor; encouraging questions before and after meetings; and having greeters who are knowledgeable about twelve-step programs. An overall attitude of humility — "Don't lead those who are not sure that they are members"; "We are not experts on everything" — should prevail. "Remember," several participants said, "the newcomer may not know what they are," so "welcome them until they decide where they belong."

Topic B-5: Inclusion

At its core, participants noted, inclusion is based on the Third Tradition. We have compassion and tolerance for all and exclude no one — "it's not 'political correctness' to be inclusive." (It was pointed out that exclusion can equal death.) To that end, participants noted members could be more inclusive with respect to gender identification (LGBTQIA), race, ethnicity and accessibility, and more tolerant of atheist/agnostic viewpoints. Inclusion could be moved forward by employing gender-neutral language and developing racial sensitivity, as well as conducting group inventories to discuss these issues. One member cautioned against "treating those with little or fragile faith as if they just need to change their minds." Participants noted that it's helpful to get to know "where newcomers are 'coming from'" by asking them questions — and to get their phone numbers, rather than expecting them to call you. Groups could hold newcomer "orientations" that include a "briefing" on appropriate meeting behavior "so they're not embarrassed by doing or saying something considered inappropriate." This might also be an opportunity to let the newcomer know that predatory behavior ("Don't call it 13th stepping!") is not acceptable. A pervasive theme was the necessity of breaking down "rigid group practices" that may have the unintended consequence of excluding others. Remember that "rotation is key," and, "just like at Conference, [to] sit in different seats with different people at your home group" to create a welcoming atmosphere. The presence of greeters could help, too. Finally, participants said, notice who's *not* in the room: Reach out to remote communities; call members you haven't seen in a while.

Topic B-6: Encouraging attitude of service

Members came up with ideas to broaden the notion of service, such as having a volunteer write a thank-you note to a speaker; in addition, groups could create new service roles such as "safety liaison." It was also suggested that all "non-service" jobs should be acknowledged and appreciated, and that members should be reminded that it is "an honor to serve." To encourage greater participation in traditional service, participants advised sharing about what service has done for you when chairing or in topic meetings, as well as arranging outside service-related activities and inviting others, especially newcomers, to come. Again, the principle of rotation and allowing anyone to serve were discussed as central to encouraging participation in service. Follow-through is important as well: Participants mentioned supporting G.S.R.s (perhaps offering G.S.R. "schools"). Finally, it was agreed that a welcoming posture — an attitude of gratitude and a willingness to be flexible — can make service attractive.

Topic B-7: Importance and support of Grapevine and La Viña

Participants all felt that Grapevine and La Viña are valuable recovery tools and that they ought to be more widely read and used to carry the message. Participants noted that Grapevine/La Viña should be mentioned in every piece of A.A.W.S. literature. In order to broaden awareness of Grapevine/La Viña, participants had many suggestions, including starting a literature meeting where Grapevine stories or AAGV books are read ("buy a box or two of books for the meeting to read!"); having the meeting chair play a Grapevine story audio to set up a meeting topic (or, alternatively, simply using a Grapevine book or story as a topic); and, quite simply, having copies of Grapevine/La Viña available at meetings. One member pointed out that because 77% of Grapevine/La Viña subscribers learn about the magazines in their home groups, all groups should consider electing Grapevine/La Viña reps. Participants had many ideas for GVRs and LVRs, such as stressing the importance of obtaining a subscription for the group; announcing projects like Carry the Message, the subscription challenge, etc.; facilitating the sale of Grapevine books (and announcing new ones) at the meeting; and reading a joke from the new book at announcement time. It was noted that information about becoming a rep should be made more available. Beyond the group level, intergroup committees could support Grapevine/La Viña, and the immediate past delegate could become the area Grapevine chair. More members need to be educated — about what Grapevine offers, such as audio for blind members; about how to use the magazines as recovery tools; about the fact that Grapevine and La Viña magazines cannot be Conference-approved but that the subjects of their books are; and that the Seventh Tradition does not fund Grapevine/La Viña. Finally, individuals, groups, districts and areas can all support Grapevine/La Viña by gifting subscriptions to other members and/or donating them to prisons and treatment centers by passing the "purple can." Sales could be encouraged through creation and implementation of a stand-up card with a QR code. Participants also mentioned hosting workshops on how to write and submit a story. Interestingly, this topic was the "minority" topic, yet it was the most widely discussed in the report-out session.

As the Conference week progressed, members continued to discuss the workshop process and the resulting topics in the hallways and meeting rooms. A gallery of all the groups' Post-Its was displayed in the back of the main Conference room, and delegates took snapshots of them to inform their local reporting. It was interesting to note that as Conference members went to speak at the microphones during the rest of the week, some spoke about developing "big and bold" ideas. At the closing brunch, several rotating trustees shared about these ideas in their farewell talks. One of the trustees thoughtfully questioned whether participants had really discussed big and bold ideas in the workshop or if they had simply discussed standard A.A. workshop topics. The trustee challenged everyone to continue to think about impactful ideas that could make positive changes as we look toward the future of Alcoholics Anonymous.

■ The Visit to G.S.O. — *Welcome all!*

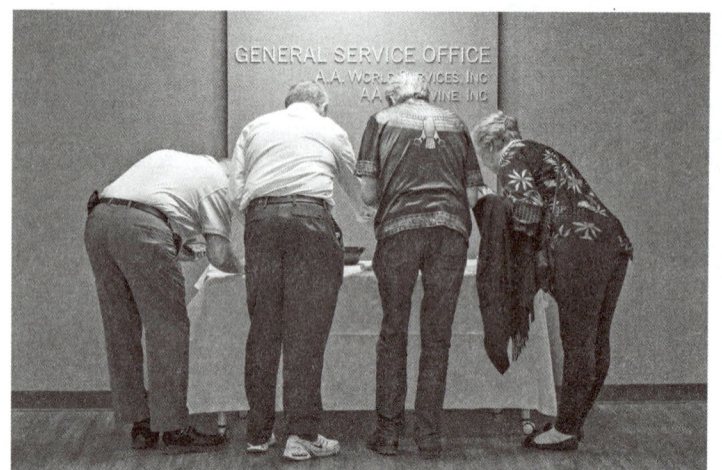

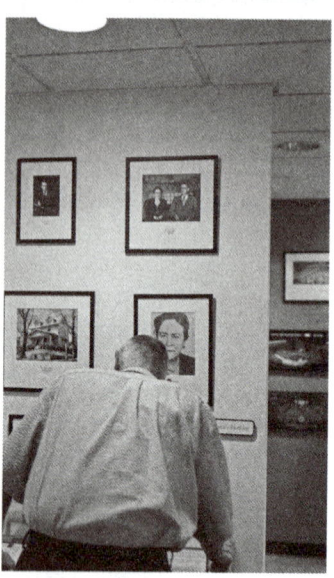

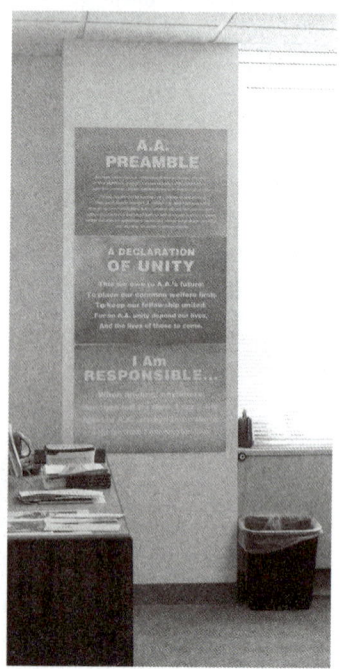

■ Area Service Highlights — Panel 69 Delegates

(Only first-term delegates give Area Highlights. Per 2018 Conference Advisory Action, these highlights are presented "in their entirety.")

Alabama/N.W. Florida: Area 1 encompasses all of Alabama and the panhandle of Florida, and consists of 24 districts with one area-wide Spanish-speaking district. Our assembly meets quarterly, with a pre-Conference assembly each April or March, depending on when Auburn has their A Day game, because we meet in Auburn, Alabama. We have great rates on our rooms, so, naturally, in a college football town, when hotels can charge 400 percent more per night, it's written in our contract that we work around the football schedule. We gladly do it, because we alcoholics are happy to save money every chance we get. During assemblies we have workshops, committee meetings and an area service meeting. All of these are closed meetings. We have an Ask-It-Basket that past delegates sit on. These are great, because you can always get answers to questions such as "What should we do if a drunk comes to our meeting?" or "What should our group do about crosstalking, or someone who only talks about themselves?" We have a hospitality room that serves snacks, drinks and coffee throughout the whole weekend. We're self-supporting, except for the times when someone brings a new sponsee who hasn't learned to practice honesty yet. We have an area convention every other year, but, being alcoholics, we're skipping this year and should have one again in 2020. Despite the few small issues that we have sometimes, as other areas do, we love each other and have fun because of the common solution we all agree on. We actively carry a message of hope to those who may be just as hopeless as I once was, and this is truly an honor. — *Kevin Hawkins*

Arkansas: Area 4 encompasses the entire state of Arkansas, which is 53,179 square miles, with a population of approximately three million people. Area 4 is mostly rural and is comprised of more than 4,500 A.A. members in 262 groups and 13 districts. District 13 is a Spanish linguistic district that serves the entire state with 14 groups and provides translation for its members during our assemblies and convention. In accordance with our Area 4 Structure & Guidelines, area assemblies are a Saturday-and-Sunday event held quarterly, starting in January, at a fixed central location. On Saturday, we offer a Tradition and Concept panel, reports from area officers and D.C.M.s, an Ask-It-Basket panel, committee meetings and an open A.A. speaker meeting. On Sunday, our D.C.M. meeting is held at 7 a.m. and is followed by orientation for G.S.R.s, committee reports, a workshop and the business meeting. Past delegates, delegate, alternate delegate, area officers, D.C.M.s and G.S.R.s are voting members of the assembly. We have ten permanent committees that meet and report at each assembly. These committees consist of past delegates, area officers, D.C.M.s and G.S.R.s. The chairperson for each committee is appointed by the area chair and area co-chair. All of our committees are very active.

Committees and area officers present workshops to groups and districts and assist district committees as needed. Eleven districts hold their service meetings quarterly, a month before the quarterly area assembly. Two districts hold their service meetings monthly. I am humbled by and grateful for the honor to serve Area 4 Arkansas as its Panel 69 delegate. — *Brad Moore*

British Columbia/Yukon: Area 79 includes the Yukon Territory, most of British Columbia and one small section of Washington State. At 1,431,210 square kilometers (approximately 889,000 miles), it is the second largest delegate area in the U.S./Canada structure. Area 79 has 48 districts, including some that are equal in size to the states of Mississippi and Maryland combined. From the southernmost tip of British Columbia to the northernmost tip of the Yukon Territory is a staggering 2,540 km, or 1,587 miles. I am somewhat biased, but I think British Columbia and the Yukon contain some of the most beautiful geography in the world. We have the Pacific Ocean on our west coast, as well as mountain ranges, rivers and lakes equal to none. Our area events, January and July quarterlies, April Pre-Conference Assembly and October Voting Assembly are held in various districts within Area 79, so travel can be extensive. We most often travel by car, which for some includes ferry travel, and some districts (especially in the north) can only be easily reached by plane. The members of Alcoholics Anonymous are represented in our area by over 820 groups. Our General Service Committee (G.S.C.) has 14 members who also sit on the Area Committee and who serve as area officers. We have three area-specific standing committees. First, we have a Remote Communities Committee, and its mission statement in part is "to assist those who are unable to make it to regular face-to-face meetings on a consistent basis." The second is our Website Committee, whose responsibility is to oversee a team of web volunteers who keep our events and meeting listings up to date and who are also responsible for posting our Conference background materials on a secure password-protected site, among other things. The third is our "Grassroots" Committee, and for Panel 69, this is under the umbrella of our Remote Communities Committee. "Grassroots" is our area newsletter, and it is published quarterly after our area events and contains the minutes and reports for those events. — *Gail Patterson*

California (Central): Area 93 is made up of 23 active districts — 16 English-speaking and seven overlying Hispanic districts. There are 948 active groups and approximately 29,000 A.A. members. The geographical makeup of our area begins in the Hollywood Hills at Mulholland Drive, with our southern border touching our mother area, Area 5, which "gave birth" to our area some short 19 years ago. The border goes northeast through the Antelope Valley to the foot of the Owens Valley, and then west across the southern end of the Sierra Nevada Mountains. It runs across the San Joaquin Valley and farther west to the Pacific Coast. Finally, it heads down the coast, south past Santa Barbara and then east to the southern end of the San Fernando Valley. We have 15 committees. Our Seniors in Sobriety Committee, now entering its second full panel, continues to mature and participate in events outside our area. We continue to look at better serving remote regions with an ad hoc committee and have aspirations of utilizing technology to make area events (such as committee meetings and possibly assemblies) available to those remotely situated members. Our C.P.C. Committee participates in events such as California state-wide corrections association fairs, and our Accessibilities Committee — fresh off establishing a Bridging the Gap database — continues to grow and maintain that database to help connect those leaving facilities to get to their first meetings. We have also been participating in the Hispanic women's workshops held in our state for the last three years, sending liaisons to carry our ideas and bring back information. At the end of last year, our assembly approved the purchase of computer systems for all our officer positions. I consider this move a great step in assisting our trusted servants who serve the area. The diversity in landscape as well as our members makes Area 93 what it is. We are here to help bring A.A. to our neighborhoods and people, to carry our message and to be of service to our slice of the great state of California. — *Jeff Gulack*

California (Northern Coastal): Area 6 has an A.A. population of 60,721, with 23 districts (five of them Spanish-speaking) and 151 subdistricts, altogether serving 2,126 groups. We are a fully Spanish/English bilingual area, with all official communications in both languages. In addition to our four annual assemblies, we have a monthly area committee meeting, and our eight area officers ensure that all districts are visited monthly. This level of communication enables the effective transmission of information up and down our service triangle and enhances our unity as a Fellowship. This past year we were privileged to host the Pacific Regional Forum, welcoming 918 participants (including 634 first-timers and 160 Spanish speakers); the third annual Hispanic Women's Workshop, with participation nationally and internationally; and our area's first Foro Hispano. We also provided accurate information to our groups and districts on the options available to them with respect to organizational structure and the legal and tax ramifications of those decisions. We continue to deepen our connection with other service committees in our area that predate the general service structure. Our area also continues to grapple with how to keep pace with technological innovation, and an ad hoc committee formed to consider the situation has recommended we form a standing technology committee. From the Redwoods to Monterey Bay by way of the Golden Gate, our area is as diverse as the communities that give it strength, and if you're looking for a particular type of meeting, chances are you'll find it in C.N.C.A. — *Teddy Basham-Witherington*

California (Southern): Area 5, though small geographically, serves approximately 2,500 meetings and 35,000 members, has two official languages (Spanish and English) and offers Korean- and Russian-language meetings. Facilitating Twelfth Step work are 15 standing committees: Archives, Audio Visual, Cooperation with the Elder Community, Cooperation with the Professional Community, Corrections, Finance, Grapevine & La Viña, Guidelines & Policies, Literature, Public Information, Registration, "SCAAN" (the area newsletter), Translation, Treatment Facilities and Website (facilitated by a paid webmaster). These committees provided archive exhibits; carried the message to senior citizens and professionals; staffed a booth at the Los Angeles County Fair with English and Spanish speakers;

maintained relationships with law enforcement, enabling visits with literature to incarcerating facilities of those arrested under the influence; maintained a contact-on-release program; and encouraged subscriptions to La Viña and Grapevine. Area 5 has five ad hoc committees: Accessibilities, Cooperation with the Young, Hispanic Women, Interpretation and Local Forum. Three committees reach remote communities and two facilitate overcoming language barriers. — *Thomas Sells*

Colorado: Area 10 encompasses the state of Colorado and has approximately 20,000 A.A. members. Currently, our area is comprised of 832 groups in 30 geographic districts and two Spanish linguistic districts that split the state geographically. Each year we hold three area assemblies (in March, July and November), a corrections conference and a state convention. The 2019 Area 10 State Convention will be at the beautiful Keystone Resort August 30 to September 1. Historically, districts have bid to host assemblies in our area. Due to the size of our area assemblies, we have found it difficult to find venues to accommodate us. We are now coming to the end of a three-year experiment to see if holding our spring assemblies at a fixed location would alleviate problems. We will be having discussions with our groups at the assemblies to see if we want to make the process permanent or expand it to our other two assemblies each year. We will also be considering a proposal from one of our districts to create a temporary area-wide Bridging the Gap Committee to serve both Corrections and Treatment. Currently, central offices and intergroups serve the treatment community, and the area Corrections Committee serves prisons and jails. Last year we decided

to expand the duties of our web chair and create a Technology Committee. Included within the purview of the committee will be the maintenance of our webpage, www.coloradoaa.org; our online repository of information; all of our electronic equipment, including computers used by various members of our area committee; transmitters and headsets used by our Translations Committee; and our leased software. Finally, our Finance Committee has been busy preparing guidelines for our area committee chairs on budget guidelines. The intent is to have standardized guidelines for preparing budgets for officers and chairs, including making use of historical precedence on standardized budgeting and expense forms. Additionally, the committee was asked to develop guidelines as to what expenses are and what expenses are not normally eligible to be reimbursed. — *Scott Meiklejohn*

Connecticut: Area 11, incorporated as a 501(c)3 in 2003 as the Area 11 General Service Committee, is comprised of 167 of the 169 cities and towns of Connecticut. The Fellowship carries A.A.'s message to our estimated membership of 33,000 alcoholics through 1,400 groups hosting 1,900 meetings, seven days a week, divided among ten districts — nine geographic and one linguistic. In recent years several districts have investigated redistricting or restructuring to help the 55 D.C.M.s communicate more effectively with their G.S.R.s. Area 11 hosts three yearly assemblies: pre-Conference, spring and fall. Between them are six regular area business meetings, four area sharing sessions and many service committee meetings of members who work tirelessly to carry the message of A.A. throughout the state. These service committees work endlessly to assist and communicate with the membership and the general public what A.A. is and all that we have to offer. In February 2018, we had the pleasure of hosting the 27th Northeast Regional A.A. Service Assembly (N.E.R.A.A.S.A.), which had the highest attendance to date. A move of our area office, archives and committee meeting space from our former location in Meriden to our new home in Southington happened in 2018. With all this service, fun can certainly be had in Area 11 by attending our five sober events, such as the Area 11 Convention. For 2018, the convention introduced the "Home Group Celebration" to help foster the spirit of unity. Each home group was encouraged to submit a colorful banner, have a minimum of eight attendees pre-register, and write a letter of gratitude (the winning submission was read from the podium at the Saturday night main meeting). This created so much enthusiasm and success that attendance at the 2018 convention skyrocketed past the attendance numbers for the previous decade. It has been an honor to be in service with the dedicated membership of Area 11. I am grateful for this opportunity to give back to them. — *John Dussault*

District of Columbia: I'm honored to represent Area 13, the capital of North America's United States and an area as rich in culture as it is in A.A. history. Area 13 includes the District of Columbia and Maryland's two most populous counties, a region whose residents are some of the most ethnically diverse in our country. This is reflected throughout our almost 800 listed groups as well as our many, many unlisted meetings. We continue to reach out to and visit these meetings, sharing highlights of area service and encouraging members to join us at our many events, including yearly assemblies, annual gratitude breakfast (currently in its 33rd year), annual mini-conference (now in its 46th year) and, in odd calendar years, our area inventory. Currently we have 11 English- and three Spanish-speaking districts. I am proud to report that of these 14 only three remain without a district committee member (D.C.M.). This is a huge accomplishment, given that just two panels ago we had only five active districts — two English and our three ever active, engaged and fully represented Spanish-speaking districts. We have much to learn from our Hispanic and Latino members. With consistent area-level representation and contributions from almost 70 percent of their registered groups last year, they serve as an example to us all. Last year many A.A.s of all ages came together to host the 15th Eastern Area Convention of Young People in A.A. (E.A.C.Y.P.P.A.). Out of this achievement came the District of Columbia, Maryland and Virginia Young People in A.A. (D.M.V.Y.P.A.A.) service committee, which has recently started providing reports of their progress at our assemblies. This year we look forward to concluding what has been a four-year process of thoroughly revising our handbook and conducting our first joint service workshop with the sole intergroup in our area. While some nonalcoholics may choose to identify our nation's capital by its political climate, we prefer to stay close to our abundant spirit of service and adhere to our principles — "to place our common welfare first; to keep our fellowship united." Our lives depend on it. Thank you for allowing me to serve. — *Michelle García*

Florida (North): Greetings from the northern part of sunny Florida. Area 14 has over 800 groups and 31 districts, including a linguistic district for our Spanish-speaking members. Our geographical area covers the northern half of Florida except the western tip of the Panhandle, south to Orlando and the Space Coast. We keep a high focus on the General Service Conference process and agenda items. Background material is distributed digitally, and several years ago we began to hold pre-Conference workshops in the districts ahead of our April assembly. In April, all workshops focus on the agenda items, and end with an informed sense of the assembly for our delegate. We take preparing our delegate for Conference very seriously. The area hosts four two-day assemblies each year. The weekend includes four administrative committees that oversee finances, website, assembly operations and district boundaries. Nine service coordinators lead educational workshops at assembly and around the districts. Our goal is to increase the enthusiasm and participation of our members by being highly inclusive, and there is now a scholarship fund to financially assist voting members in attending assembly. We have created a "First Timer" handout for new members at assembly, and often publish a newsletter to encourage interest in assembly. We have created a 13-minute DVD about the Traditions and currently support "Me plus One" — a self-support message introduced by one of our members. It encourages contributions in different ways to make up for those who cannot contribute. We have *A.A. Service Manual* workshops around the area, some with members using Skype to participate. In Area 14 we are not shy about celebrating service every day! — *Annette Dahl*

Florida (South Florida/Bahamas/Virgin Islands/Antigua/ St. Maarten/Cayman Islands): Area 15 covers South Florida and the Caribbean Islands, from Pasco to Monroe Counties, with over 2,728 groups. We have 109 D.C.M.s, 52 alternate D.C.M.s, 1,354 G.S.R.s and 430 alternate G.S.R.s who work with Area 15 groups and membership. The area is divided into 19 districts and two Spanish linguistics districts, with an additional five linguistic subdistricts that are working within the local regions. The areas affected by the hurricanes last year are slowly recovering; thank you for your assistance and prayers. The Area 15 assemblies are three-day events held four times a year, with the participation of over 400 members. They offer Concepts, *A.A. Service Manual*, Traditions and area committee workshops. In April, we conduct two-day pre-Conference workshops featuring Conference agenda presentations, report-backs from committees and feedback from the Fellowship. The area provides ASL and simultaneous Spanish interpretation during our assembly business meetings. The southern region is seeking members to assist in the translation of the pamphlet "Is A.A. for Me?" into Creole. Districts find new and innovative ways of sharing the message through bill-

The bell used to indicate the start of each general session.

boards, airport and movie theatre displays. In July, we will host the Florida State Convention in Doral with an expected participation of over 2,000. In the past year we voted to create an Outreach Committee to provide the Area Committee an opportunity to work with all districts, sharing their experience and assisting with service workshops throughout Area 15. — *Shirley Parrado*

Hawaii: Hawai`i Area 17 has around 5,300 members, 300 groups and 14 districts on six islands. The Pacific Ocean separates us from each other and from the rest of A.A., so it takes a lot of group contributions for us to participate in all levels of service. This year we will gather for three assemblies — Orientation, Inform the Delegate, and Budget — and three committee meetings. In 2020, we will hold four assemblies — Inventory, Inform the Delegate, Budget and Election — and three committee meetings. For decades, we have had A.A. members living in the remote communities of Hana, Lana`i and Moloka`i. Once a month, our young and young-at-heart members travel by boat, plane, car or motorcycle for a meeting, a potluck, beach day or campout, and lots of A.A. fun. Not all our districts are small, though. Kihei has so many meetings that the main street through town is called "The Road of Happy Destiny." Kaua'i District hosts a Gratitude Luncheon where they gather with long timers, and with those outside the fellowship who help alcoholics. You might recall the lava flowing on the island of Hawai`i last year. While dealing with this ongoing hardship, our members in Puna showed us going to any length can mean staying put and doing your best. Puna District hosted our June committee meeting, and a workshop where standing committee chairs and AA members discussed ways to improve outreach. Area committee chairs help to connect our members and districts with AA resources and with each other. It is an ongoing challenge, and always worth the effort.

Throughout Hawaii, AA members take our message to correctional facilities, treatment centers, and places where our seniors live. We have meetings in beach parks, where many a drunken person has wandered over, heard our message of hope and learned to live sober. Last but not least, this November, come to Oahu and join us in Waikiki for our 58th Annual Hawaii Convention. — *Coleen Ashworth*

Illinois (Chicago): Area 19 has approximately 2,800 registered weekly meetings and 20 districts. Four of those are linguistic — three Spanish and one Polish. We have eight standing committees and seven special committees. The Chicago Area Service Committee meets every odd month. Our area service office currently has seven paid employees and myriad volunteers. The office and area are operating this year on a $750,000 budget. Our bookstore has an extensive inventory not only of Conference-approved literature but also of area-approved non-A.A. literature and "drunk junk" such as jewelry, coins, bookmarks and coffee mugs. We are about to go live with our new website, with improved search and directions for meetings and a full on-line bookstore. We have a very active Corrections Committee that works regularly with neighboring areas to carry the message to inmates and help "bridge the gap" to those who upon release will return to Area 19. Our Archives Committee has just about finished up their book project on the beginning of A.A. in the Chicagoland area. The book is in the final editing stage and hopefully will be ready for sale to the Fellowship this year. This year marks the 80th anniversary of the first A.A meeting in Chicago. We celebrate this yearly by hosting the "All Chicago Open" meeting event in September. We host the Illinois State Conference every third year in a rotation with Areas 20 and 21. We are in the process of forming our committee to host in 2020. In addition, our Committee on Conferences is looking to bring back our area Second City Round-Up as a one-day event. In an attempt to get more participation at our area committees and to help those who have trouble getting to our downtown Chicago office for an evening committee meeting, we will be going live this year with audio and visual conferencing for committees through technology by Zoom. This will enable members to participate from a remote location and will hopefully allow for greater participation and therefore the ability to better carry the message as we move forward in our attempt to help the still-suffering alcoholic. — *Brian M. Tenenbaum*

Illinois (Southern): As I visit some of the nearly 470 A.A. groups in the 15 districts of Area 21, I think of how blessed I am to call this part of America my home. Our area is very large and covers roughly two-thirds of our state, reaching from north of Peoria to the border with Kentucky. We have four area assemblies a year, hosted by different districts. And through the work of our committees and the effort of our members, A.A.'s life-giving message travels those long distances every day. Our love for alcoholics transcends the difficulties of carrying the message to rural communities, and not long ago we had the joy of seeing an inactive district spring to life again! Interest in sponsorship, the Big Book and service continues to increase, and Area 21 has responded by organizing service workshops, weekend conferences and, more recently, a pre-Conference workshop. Our area contains nearly two-thirds of the prisons in our state, and our ears are not deaf to the cries of our incarcerated brothers and sisters. Our Corrections Committee reaches out to them with meetings and literature, and we're grateful for the much-needed literature provided by our Chicago and northern Illinois areas. Our area Technology Committee is focused on finding and implementing new ways to carry the message with our Traditions firmly in mind. Area 21 cooperates with neighboring areas on shared conferences, and we're thrilled to see our young people on fire with excitement about A.A.'s 2030 International Convention in nearby St. Louis, Missouri. As I travel the vast prairielands to the north and down through the beautiful Shawnee Forest where I live, I'm struck by the warmth and compassion of my fellow A.A. members. The heart of A.A. beats strongly here in the Heartland, and each day I see the miracle of hope in the eyes of a newcomer who comes in out of the cold, sits down to a cup of coffee, and is warmed by the love we have for them as they listen to our stories of hope and recovery. — *Bobby Davis*

Indiana (Northern): Area 22 is the northern half of Indiana. Area 22 accounts for five of the ten largest cities in Indiana. My home city of Muncie comes in at the 11th largest. Area 22 consist of 48 districts. Each district has an odd number in our area. In those districts we host over 600 registered groups. Area 22 holds four assemblies each year, in February, May, August and November. We divide our area into four quadrants and have a structured rotation for each assembly to encourage participation for those who might not be able to travel the greater distances. A fifth assembly is added in even-numbered years, in October, for elections. The Election Assembly is always held centrally to encourage the most participation. Area 22 holds two D.C.M. conferences every year. The first, in March, is solely dedicated to preparing our delegate for the General Service Conference. Each committee reviews their specific Conference agenda items and offers its group conscience to the delegate. The second D.C.M. conference has been used in various ways, from a G.S.R/D.C.M. college/school or a general sharing session to my personal favorite — "dissecting" a piece of service literature. The Indiana State Convention alternates between our two areas; odd years are in the north. The 2019 convention marks the second time for Area 22 that we have been able to pay and register online. In 2019 we added a "Delegate's Calendar" page to our website in an effort to eliminate questions as to when I, as delegate, am available to make an appearance and help anyone understand the definition of the word *ignorant* — which means "not knowing something I just learned five minutes ago." From conventions to district meetings and website accessibility to one-on-one availability, all this is an attempt to assist and educate new and returning members in their journey, while encouraging enthusiastic contributions to service from the local level to as far as anyone would like to humble themselves. — *Brad Albright*

Iowa: Area 24 is the southernmost state in the West Central Region. Iowa is predominately rural, with four major cities/metropolitan areas: Des Moines, Sioux City, the Quad Cities and Dubuque. Area 24 has 23 districts and over 650 listed groups. Making a meeting can be quite the task, requiring a drive of 15-30 miles or more to a town "nearby." We hold five area functions throughout the year, including a spring assembly in June and a fall assembly in October. The host district is chosen through a bidding process and voted on by those in attendance at the assembly or one of the other service events. At these two assemblies we hold a G.S.R. sharing session, a D.C.M. sharing session, and an area officer and chair sharing session. The area chairs hold workshops on both Friday and Saturday nights, in addition to a speaker with entertainment to follow and, of course, fellowship. Area business is conducted throughout the day on Saturdays with many of the past delegates, G.S.R.s, D.C.M.s, area officers and chairs all present. It is not uncommon to have most districts represented. We end the weekend together on Sunday with a spiritual speaker. Area 24 also holds three additional meetings in Marshalltown, which is centrally located for ease of participation from the entire area. On the Saturday of the January Area 24 service weekend, newly elected G.S.R.s, D.C.M.s, area officers and chairs are welcomed in odd years, and in even years various workshops and presentations are held. The area committee business meeting is held on the Sunday. At the meeting in March, also a two day event, we discuss the General Service Conference agenda items on Saturday, followed by a business meeting on Sunday. The one-day event held in August gathers past delegates, area officers, chairs and D.C.M.s. Area 24 can be found on the Internet at www.aa-iowa.org. If you are ever in the great state of Iowa, we would be glad to have you. — *Dan Geels*

Louisiana: It's an honor to be representing Area 27 here at the General Service Conference. Upon my election, I became the keeper of the delegate's sweatshirt that identifies me as the "Head Sick." Area 27 encompasses the state of Louisiana and consists of 24 districts, one of which is a statewide Spanish linguistic district. We have 507 registered groups and roughly 12,000 members. We hold four assemblies per year, as well as a state convention that rotates around Louisiana. Our area assembly is currently held in Alexandria, a city more centrally located so that more may participate. We have a pre-Conference assembly in April, where we review Conference agenda items to give feedback to our delegate. Every other year, our area conducts an inventory normally facilitated by the Southeast Regional trustee. At our regular assemblies, the G.S.R.s and D.C.M.s attend workshops and sharing sessions and participate on our area standing committees: Archives, C.P.C., Corrections, Grapevine, P.I., State Convention, Treatment, Website, and Budget & Finance. We are pleased to report that we've entered our second year with an active Accessibilities Committee. Our archives continue to be digitized, and the Archives Committee is busy taping oral histories from Louisiana oldtimers. Our C.P.C. Committee works with G.S.O. to staff national conventions in New Orleans, while our P.I., Treatment and Corrections Committees stay busy helping district committees throughout the state. In September of this year, Area 27 will host a corrections conference that we hope will become an annual event. We are also planning to hold the 2022 Southeast Regional Forum in New Orleans. Lots of planning is already underway, and the committee is chaired by one of our esteemed past delegates. It is a privilege to serve A.A. as the Panel 69 delegate from Area 27. — *Sue Tart*

Massachusetts (Eastern): Area 30 is home to around 2,500 meetings across ten counties, from the southeast in Nantucket, north to Essex County and west to Worcester County — which includes Sturbridge, where Area 30 and Area 31 (western Massachusetts) will be hosting N.E.R.D., the Northeast Regional Delegates Weekend, in March 2020. In November of this year, Area 30 and Area 31 will be hosting the 56th Annual Massachusetts State A.A. Convention. We have 26 geographical districts plus one Spanish district, which is a linguistic district. Area 30 is home to Boston Central Service, which opened in 1945 and served most of New England at that time. We also have one Spanish intergroup and four other intergroups serving Worcester, Cape Cod and the Islands. We hold monthly area meetings in Belmont, gathering the area officers, D.C.M.s, Conference committees, standing committees and liaisons from Boston Central Service, Worcester Intergroup and several Y.P.A.A. committees, including the Boston Host Committee for I.C.Y.P.A.A. 2019! We have five assemblies a year, which include budget assembly, a pre-Conference and a post-Conference assembly. Our assemblies are hosted by a different district on a rotating basis. We have translation and hearing-assist equipment at all of our assemblies and area meetings. We have a Finance Committee made up of the eight area officers and the committee chairs and their alternates. We meet at least three times a year to prepare the budget for the following year. Our website, aaemass.org, now has a Spanish link. In 2021 we will be hosting N.E.R.F., the Northeast Regional Forum (just trying to keep our past delegates busy). Oh... did I mention that I.C.Y.P.A.A. is coming to Boston this year? — *Jean Kerivan*

Michigan (Central): Area 32 is in service to 1,100 registered Alcoholics Anonymous meetings. We have 14 districts in an area spanning 300 miles north to south and up to 125 miles east to west (at its widest point). We service an area spanning from Adrian to Alpena, including a portion of Michigan's thumb. We hold bimonthly area assemblies in our various districts. The districts volunteer to hold our area assemblies on a rotating schedule. We may meet in our southernmost district one month, and then in two months meet in our northernmost district. Regardless of where we meet, we have great representation from our groups all over the central portion of the state of Michigan. At our area assemblies we have 14 active service committees that meet and report to the assembly as a whole. We have a general service information meeting to provide members with information and education on various items within the service structure and to share ideas and opinions on A.A.'s welfare. We are truly blessed to have many past delegates and a past East Central Regional trustee attend our area assemblies on a regular basis to share their experience and guidance in service. Every quarter we meet with Areas 33 and 34 at a statewide service meeting that provides collaboration in the areas of C.P.C., Corrections and Grapevine, as well as other service opportunities that arise within our state. We also provide combined efforts on planning the state convention and our Michigan Mock Conference, which helps our delegates fully prepare for their service at the annual General Service Conference. Personally, I have a large legacy to uphold in my service position. In the district in which I reside (District 2, Area 32), I am the fifth delegate to serve the General Service Conference: Preceding me were Alvin Teshka, Panel 11; Harland Sercombe, Panel 41; Larry Sanford, Panel 57 and Mike Kimling, Panel 59. I have been blessed to know four of these five men personally in my sobriety and service journey, and they have paved the road for which I am truly humbled to be traveling. — *Lori Conant*

Michigan (Southeast): We in Area 33 are small geographically as compared to other Michigan A.A. areas — but we are large in heart! We are totally excited for the 2020 International Convention and the opportunity to welcome the world to the Motor City! Our momentum is increasing as we prepare to host Alcoholics Anonymous from around the globe. Comprised of five counties, 24 districts, one Spanish-speaking district and 1,007 groups, we are culturally diverse, from the rural countryside to the urban center of Detroit, and we show true grit. Our commitment to our primary purpose brings us together in unity, allowing us to meet each month for our area assembly and business meeting. In addition to conducting business, we offer a monthly G.S.R. orientation and service manual study, as

well as our committee meetings of D.C.M.s and our 14 standing committee chairs. We encourage member interaction during our area assemblies and special events. For example, our service fair highlights our standing committees and provides small-table discussion revolving around basic service issues. Our area "buddy program" is designed to welcome the G.S.R. newcomer to the assembly and to support G.S.R. retention. Our Detroit event Service Beyond the Group fosters district sponsorship within our area for inactive or underactive districts. Through humility and a respect for member contribution in the basket, we have identified two areas for paid outside services: 1) tax preparation — to ensure accurate and timely submissions; and 2) website design and management — taking us into the future and allowing us to meet the challenge of a changing environment. Come join Area 33 as the world celebrates unity in this glorious Fellowship we know as Alcoholics Anonymous. Detroit is truly excited to say "Welcome" to each of you in 2020! — *Cynthia Bars*

Heard at a meeting

Sponsor screaming to sponsee: "How can you be so stupid? Haven't I taught you everything I know?"

—*From* Take Me to Your Sponsor, *AA Grapevine's new book of jokes and cartoons*

Minnesota (Southern): Area 36 is made up of the southern half of Minnesota, starting just south of St. Cloud and south, east and west, respectively, to the Iowa, Wisconsin and South Dakota borders. We are one of eight areas that make up the West Central Region. Area 36 is made up of roughly 960 registered groups and 27 districts, one of which is a Spanish-speaking linguistic district that hosts its own Spanish service conference once a year. We host a service conference called the Recovery, Unity and Service Conference in January. Its theme mirrors the theme of the General Service Conference each year. We have four area committee meetings and three area assemblies, one of which is combined with the Delegate's Workshop. We also host our yearly Trusted Servant Leadership Training, where we train our G.S.R.s, D.C.M.s, committee chairs and area officers. Area 36 supports its archivist, webmaster and Corrections Committee chair to attend A.A.'s national workshops. We work in cooperation with Area 35 (northern Minnesota) specifically with respect to corrections and treatment to better serve Minnesota. Our Corrections Committee is actively working with correctional facilities to attend their "transition fairs" so we can reach the incarcerated A.A. member who is being released within six

Heard at the Conference

"Blessed are the brief."

—*Jonathan Smith, Southwest Texas*

months. They are also working to update their temporary contact database to make it more user-friendly. Our Public Information Committee facilitates an information booth in the Education Building at the Minnesota State Fair, where districts step up and take days to serve. Area 35 takes a weekend there as well. Our Structure Committee, which is made up of our alternate D.C.M.s, is updating the Area 36 bylaws and the Area 36 Trusted Servant Guidelines. And this last year we passed a budget to include ASL interpretation on Saturday evening at the Recovery, Unity and Service Conference, as well as for our three assemblies and Delegate's Workshop so that everyone has a voice there. — *Missy Patterson*

Missouri (Eastern): Area 38 covers 32,000 square miles of the state of Missouri in its eastern half. Our area serves about 610 registered groups with approximately 9,668 members. With a recent redistricting that turned what was three metropolitan districts into four, we now have 24 geographical districts. Half of these districts are in the metropolitan St. Louis area and the other half are rural districts. Two of these districts are not very active at area level, but we are working hard to change that. We also have one Spanish-speaking linguistic district, which is statewide, extending into the western half of the state, Area 39. We hold four assemblies a year, one for every season. Recently, we have begun to move our assemblies around our area and have changed the spring and fall assemblies into two-day meetings. This has been very successful, especially in bringing new people into general service. We are grateful to have many of our past delegates attending assemblies. All of Area 38's ten standing committees continue to be very active. Our Corrections Committee was energized by having the first National Corrections Conference in our area several years ago. We also had the first National A.A. Technology Workshop in St. Louis, and our Technology Committee is busy with many projects. At our spring assembly we have a Mock Conference to prepare the delegate for the G.S.C. We have instituted a workshop program in which the area offers to hold two workshops a year for districts and one for any group. In all, Area 38 has an enthusiastic and well-prepared group of trusted servants and I am grateful to serve as its delegate. — *Gene Marshall*

Missouri (Western): Area 39 covers approximately 35,000 square miles, with 230 groups and 17 districts, with one designated as a bilingual district. There are two central offices in Area 39, with one located in Kansas City and the other in Springfield. Our area is made up of three larger metropolitan cities, small towns and many rural townships. The Area 39 assembly meets four times yearly for an entire weekend. Saturday morning includes separate G.S.R. and D.C.M. meetings. Through this experience the members have much time to share their experience, strength and hope. The area committees are structured to match those of our General Service Conference and meet during the afternoon. Saturday evening at the assembly is designated for workshops followed by area officer reports and past delegate comments. On Sunday morning the Area 39 business of Alcoholics Anonymous is conducted,

beginning with area committee reports and concluding with agenda item discussions and vote. In conjunction with Area 38 (eastern Missouri), we host the Missouri State Convention. Our area convention, Colors of Fall in the Ozarks, is held every fall in Branson. Our area Institutions Forum is held yearly, bringing together professionals in the community to share with us their needs in understanding how A.A. and the professional can better work together to help the alcoholic who still suffers. Another major event hosted every other year by Area 39 is The Many Faces of Grapevine, which helps districts, groups and members understand the history and stay informed regarding the many services provided by Grapevine. I am filled with a deep sense of gratitude for being allowed to serve at the 69th General Service Conference. — *Jennifer Donovan*

Montana: Area 40 may be the largest geographical area in the Lower 48. There are 14 districts, all of which are active in one way or another in general service. These districts have a total of nearly 300 groups that host daily meetings to bring the message of A.A. and hope to the still-suffering alcoholic, whether they live on the plains and among the coulees of the east side or in the mountains and valleys of the west. We meet twice a year for a roundup where there are speakers, workshops and other forms of fellowship that usually involve ice cream. The location of these roundups rotates between the six largest cities in the area. In the spring and fall, we have our area assemblies, where we conduct the business of Area 40 and prepare for and review the work of the General Service Conference. Until recently we held our area assembly in Lewistown, where it

was equally inconvenient for everyone. We have temporarily moved to Great Falls, where it is only inconvenient to most of us. We have a subcommittee that is researching on how to make attendance at assembly more attractive and accessible to all. In the past year we have created a formal position for a Bridging the Gap coordinator at the area level. We felt there were missed opportunities when individuals transitioning from treatment and correctional facilities were asking for help to attend A.A meetings. By creating this position, we hope that we can provide assistance in a uniform and predictable way. This position has a committee and reports through the Treatment and Accessibilities Committee. It is a non-rotating position, as are the webmaster and archivist in Area 40. This fall we will be performing our area inventory at the assembly as well as hosting the West Central Regional trustee. The past inventory brought about some positive changes to the way we do business at our assemblies. We look forward to identifying other opportunities for improvement and growth. In March 2020, District 11 will host the West Central Regional A.A. Service Conference in Billings and in September 2021, District 81 will be hosting the West Central Regional Forum in Missoula. That covers most of what is happening in Montana, most of which makes up Area 40. — *Paul Lamb*

Nevada: Area 42 spans from Fort Bidwell, California, which is snuggled in the mountainous region of the Oregon-Nevada-California border, all the way to the Colorado River city of Laughlin, Nevada, which is in the sandy setting of the Mojave Desert. Area 42 has 664 active groups among 22 districts, two of which have significant Hispanic and Native American presences. Area 42 is the only area in the A.A. delegate structure that has been divided into two general service parts: the Southern Area General Service Committee and the Northern Area General Service Committee. Each of these committees meets four times a year; the whole of Area 42 meets two times a year for our area assembly, held in the historic silver mining town of Tonopah, Nevada. In February I attended an old-timers panel, where it was clear that A.A. is alive and well in Area 42: Forty-seven attendees had over 30 years of sobriety, and collectively there were over 2,000 years of sobriety in the room. The next day I facilitated a group inventory for S.W.A.C.Y.P.A.A., the Southwestern Area Conference of Young People in A.A. Eighteen members showed up to reflect on their committee's purpose and progress. The group inventory resulted in members' conviction that if they have a "legitimate reason," they can throw a conference anywhere. Young people in Area 42 found a need for a state Y.P.A.A. conference; they petitioned the area, and Area 42 agreed we need a Y.P.A.A. conference. Thus, N.A.C.Y.P.A.A. (Nevada Area Conference for Young People in A.A.) was created. The first conference will be held in 2020. This is the first year that Area 42 is creating the 13 Conference committees in our area. Usually the delegate picks between six to ten agenda items and the area body goes over them during our roundtables and at Tonopah. This year each Conference committee will review all the agenda items and will present them to the

delegate for review. For an area that has many remote and diverse communities, we find a way for A.A. to reach these communities, remembering that recovery begins when one alcoholic talks with another, sharing experience, strength and hope. — *Rhonda Fairchild*

New Jersey (Northern): Eighty years ago in Area 44, Bill W. dictated the Big Book to Ruth Hock at 17 William Street in Newark, New Jersey. Today, one can attend meetings along with the 39,400 members at one of our 1,360 groups. The groups are organized into 32 geographic districts and two Spanish linguistic districts that are clustered in six sections to carry the message and make Twelfth Step work possible. Many of our districts host days of sharing, holiday alkathons and Traditions workshops. The districts work closely with our seven standing and 14 special committees, including Website, Translation, Newsletter, Remote Communities and Technology. Our Technology Committee is in the process of rolling out Office 365 and Sharepoint for our officers, committees, districts and G.S.R.s. Our version of "March Madness" is holding six pre-Conference reports in our geographic sections and two in our Spanish districts, all in the month of March, to prepare our delegate for the Conference. Our section coordinators work with the D.C.M.s in their sections to arrange a delegate post-Conference report in June to review the full actions of the

Conference and to arrange a G.S.R./D.C.M. workshop for new G.S.R.s and D.C.M.s. The group conscience of the area is obtained from our four assemblies annually, including a mini-conference assembly in April just before the Conference. In February, our G.S.R. Midwinter Luncheon is held, with presentations by a Class A and a Class B trustee, to honor the G.S.R.s of our groups. At the end of September, the area hosts a three-day convention with a banquet, alkathons, speakers and a Grapevine play, which is a musical parody that promotes the use of Grapevine and La Viña as recovery tools. When I was two months sober, I won a ticket to that convention and started doing service work, and service became a cornerstone of my sobriety. I am grateful and honored to serve my area and A.A. — *Jeff Bernknopf*

New York (Central): Area 47, Central New York, is about 130 miles wide, stretching from Canada down into Pennsylvania. We're one of four areas in New York. "Fun facts" about our area include, but are not limited to, the following: There are 675 active groups across 64 districts. That includes 23 groups that registered last year. Some districts meet independently, and some meet as clusters. The full area assembly meets 11 times a year. A typical agenda includes meetings of the ten standing committees, a panel or workshop, officer and chair reports, reviewing a Concept, and old and new business. The assemblies in March and April are spent discussing Conference agenda items and discerning the area's group conscience. The assembly is held in a different location each month. This allows local A.A. members to come see what the area is all about or to buy literature when it's held in their town. The month we don't hold an area assembly we have a day of sharing or a weekend-long convention. This is when the General Service Conference report-back is given, and there are multiple other panels and speakers. And, yes, meeting every month *does* come up for debate with some frequency. We've started a new annual D.C.M. summit to better support our D.C.M.s. This provides a forum to share questions, issues and solutions to better serve the districts and to discuss what makes good leadership in A.A. Our area website is a great resource for spreading the word about upcoming events, posting meeting lists, understanding accessibility needs, and signing up for Bridging the Gap or corrections work. This August, the Empire State Convention of Young People in A.A. will be held in our area. Our young people will be hosting this event in Rochester, and they expect 800 people or more. Their enthusiasm and love of service is infectious and fills me with hope for the healthy present and future of A.A. in Area 47. — *Barb Chambers*

New York (Southeast): Area 49, southeastern New York ("SENY"), is comprised of 1,991 A.A. groups from 104 districts. In addition to the five boroughs of New York City, G.S.O., Bill's last drink and 182 Clinton Street, we are home to seven national wildlife refuges, the Hamptons, Montauk, Fire Island, Stepping Stones, the Catskills, the lower Hudson Valley and countless bars. SENY is comprised of 12 culturally diverse counties and an area-wide Hispanic district. All 13 service entities have their own general services meetings and officers, including a

D.C.M.C. In four of our counties, the county itself serves as the district. We have three robust Y.P.A.A. committees; meetings in English, Spanish, Korean, Polish and Russian; some meetings with ASL translation; meetings for men, women, GLBTQ, and atheist and agnostic members. Our urban, suburban and rural transportation diversities present accessibility opportunities for our members to attend five annual area assemblies and one delegate's day of sharing, all of which rotate throughout SENY. All have Spanish translation, as do our seven annual committee meetings hosted in the Bronx, a central location. Our calendar is on our website, www.aaseny.org. SENY elects five officers, and our area chair appoints the committee chairs, subject to approval by the SENY Committee. We hold an area inventory and revise the SENY Handbook every rotation. Like many other areas, our biggest opportunity for improvement is to increase participation at our assemblies. We're excited to be hosting the Northeast Regional Forum May 31– June 2 and invite you to join us at the G.S.O. road show. — *Jane Ehrich*

North Carolina: I am happy to share that A.A. membership in Area 51 North Carolina is growing, and we are not a glum lot, with an annual state convention, Freedom from Bondage Corrections Conference and many other statewide events to celebrate recovery. There are over 20,000 sober alcoholics in 1,095 regular and 52 corrections groups in our state. Our most exciting news for 2019 is that we are joining forces with Area 62 South Carolina to co-host our biennial Southern States Alcoholics Anonymous Service Assembly, lovingly known as S.S.A.A.S.A., at Lake Junaluska Retreat Center near Asheville, North Carolina, November 8–10. Y'all come join us. And finally, the English teacher in me could not help but create a sonnet using iambic pentameter to share our general service status with you: North Carolina's in a state of grace / From designation Area Fifty-one / With aliens who come from outer space / We surely have a plenitude of fun // Our districts number 39 in all / With three linguistic Spanish in the mix / We've two assemblies in the spring and fall / Committee meets four times a year amidst // At Winter Area Committee, D.C.M.s / Partake in Conference (mock) that is first-rate / Agenda items are discussed and then / Pre-Conferences commence across the state // So "alien" alcoholics in N.C./ Inform their delegate for G.S.C.! — *Katy Patterson*

North Dakota: Area 52 consists of 163 groups in nine districts, with approximately 3,300 members and 49.7 percent contributing to G.S.O. We have one group from Montana and a handful from Minnesota. We hold three area assemblies per year and will be welcoming our regional trustee, Tom A., at our March Assembly this year, which allows our area to benefit greatly from his knowledge, as part of March Assembly weekend is devoted to General Service Conference agenda items. Besides his knowledge, his expertise with ice cream is appreciated. The area, led by the most recent past delegate and assisted by the area committee chairs, hosts two G.S.R./P.I.-C.P.C. schools each year in February in towns not usually able to host larger service assemblies — one in the east and one in the western part of the state — to acquaint newly elected G.S.R.s to the service structure of A.A. using *The A.A. Service Manual* and Area 52 Service Handbook and to encourage their group's participation in district and area service. Area 52 has very active groups and districts, hosting Fellowship events, picnics, dances and roundups. Fargo/Moorhead Intergroup will be putting on the Third Annual A.A. Symposium for professionals, the public and A.A. members, featuring information for professionals, as well as information on how to get involved with P.I./C.P.C. and institutions in order to carry the message to the still-suffering alcoholic. Area 52 will be hosting the 2019 W.C.R.A.A.F. (West Central Regional A.A. Forum) August 16–18 at the Alerus Center in Grand Forks, North Dakota. As an area, we have recently undertaken some redistricting, with less-served district committees/groups being absorbed by their neighboring districts. — *Curt Winmill*

Nova Scotia, Newfoundland/Labrador: Area 82 is divided by large bodies of water, which requires either an eight-hour ferry ride and a three-and-a-half-hour car ride to the airport from either end of Nova Scotia plus a plane trip to travel between the provinces. To reach Labrador requires a few plane trips from most places. To drive from the ferry terminal to the capital city in Newfoundland is also a ten-hour car ride. The very active Remote Communities Committee does a very good job of keeping our members in Labrador feel a part of our area. Every couple of weeks, they make time to have conference calls and discuss the

program in general. Area 82 has 17 districts with 207 groups. The geography of Area 82 makes it very difficult to visit all groups or districts. The upside is that most parts of the area hold roundups or conventions, which gives the delegate a chance to attend and meet with members from a lot of the surrounding districts. Most districts in Area 82 have active committees in P.I., Corrections and Grapevine. The message is being carried throughout the area. The geography of the area does not hinder a great turnout at our annual assembly, no matter in which province it is held. Therefore, I am happy to say that Alcoholics Anonymous is alive and well in Area 82. — *Kirk Stone*

Ohio (Central and Southeast Ohio): Area 53 covers 39 counties in central and southeastern Ohio. The area currently has 765 registered groups, 25 districts and nine standing committees. All but two of the districts have a D.C.M., and all but one of the standing committees are active. The area assembly meets quarterly, and the Area Committee meets the following month to plan the agenda for the next assembly. The second weekend of March we hold a mini-conference to address a subset of the Conference agenda items. We normally have in attendance a G.S.O. Staff member and the regional trustee who give G.S.O. and regional reports and share their stories with us. Our Corrections Committee's "Spare Change Changes Lives" program purchased and donated to incarcerated A.A.s last year 1,285 Big Books and 843 "Twelve and Twelves." The Treatment Committee is re-introducing the Bridging the Gap program. The C.P.C./P.I. Committee is active throughout the area, making presentations and working with professionals. Our Group Services Committee conducts a G.S.R./D.C.M. school in districts on request, and at our annual mini-conference. Last year, the Grapevine Committee conducted a writing workshop that generated several submissions. Beginning with this panel, web administrator is an elected, rotating position. The Web Administration Team is introducing a new website, which is off to an impressive start. If you're interested, you can find it at area53aa.org. We are working to build stronger relationships with the area's Y.P.A.A. groups *y con los grupos hispano hablantes*. Both of these communities are very active, but not participating consistently in the general service structure. Another goal for this panel is to reignite the Accessibilities Committee. Thank you for giving me the opportunity to share these highlights, and I look forward to serving as a member of Panel 69. — *Stephen Shelton*

Ohio (Northeast): Area 54 is home to approximately 1,500 registered groups. Our area covers 20 of Ohio's 88 counties, and there are 62 districts within our boundaries, which also include a Spanish-speaking district. There are eight intergroup/central offices in Area 54. We hold six assemblies each year. In addition, our area hosts a G.S.R. school in February and a D.C.M. college in August. These presentations are available, upon request, to travel to our districts and groups throughout the year. We also hold a Unity Day the third week of May to highlight the cooperative nature of A.A. services. In June we have our annual

Estimates of Groups and Members as of January 1, 2019[1]

	Groups	Members
United States	66,345	1,361,838
Canada	5,091	84,891
Sub-Total	71,436	1,446,729
Correctional facilities	1,607	40,218
Loners, Internationalist, Homers	1	168
Total	73,044	1,487,115
Outside U.S. & Canada[2]	52,308	643,304
Grand Total	125,352	2,130,419

1. *The General Service Office does not keep membership records. The information shown here is based on reports given by groups listed with G.S.O. and does not represent an actual count of those who consider themselves A.A. members.*

2. *We are aware of A.A. activity in approximately 180 countries, including 64 autonomous general service offices in other lands. Annually, we attempt to contact those G.S.O.s and groups that request to be listed in our records. Where current data is lacking, we use an earlier year's figures.*

Open House Picnic, which is spearheaded by an Area 54 district. In November, we commemorate Gratitude Sunday, when we come together to fellowship, enjoy a meal and express our gratitude for this way of life. We host a weekend mini-conference each spring prior to the General Service Conference. Here we review Conference agenda items and provide our delegate with the conscience of the area. There is much activity and opportunity to serve in our area. Area 54 continues to work with our young people in A.A. and has gone another step further: We now have an O.Y.P.A.A. liaison who acts as a link to assist communication and cooperation with our young people's group. Additionally, we have embraced newer technology and can now accept electronic payments for our annual mini-conference. Change can be slow in A.A., and I am glad that Area 54 embraces new and better ways to connect with our members. As I close, I extend my humble thanks to Area 54 Northeast Ohio for allowing me to serve as their Panel 69 delegate. As my journey continues down the service triangle, I look forward to learning more about general service and growing into an ever-deepening appreciation for our Fellowship. — *Shyrl Blair*

Oklahoma: Area 57 covers all of Oklahoma — 69,960 square miles. We have 405 registered A.A. groups with approximately 8,500 members. We have eight districts — four located in metro areas and four in the rural parts of the state. We also have a Spanish subdistrict. Each metro district has a monthly service meeting that does a report on a Tradition, a Concept and a service topic. The four rural districts have area-hosted workshops on service topics. We have four committee meetings and one assembly per year. We have an intergroup office in Oklahoma City and a central service office in Tulsa. Our area office has a paid secretary and displays our archives collection. Fun in the Fellowship is an annual service conference designed to generate interest in all areas of service, with committee workshops and two "schools" — one on being a G.S.R., the other on being a D.C.M. We hold an annual state conference in May, where we have a delegate's report and three days of speakers and service-related workshops. This event draws over 1,000 members from all over the state. We also have a very active Young People in Alcoholics Anonymous (Y.P.A.A.) group that puts on its own Conference, with the purpose of teaching about working on committees and in general service. Each year Area 57 hosts the Southwest Regional Delegates Assembly, preparing incoming delegates for the General Service Conference. I am grateful for the opportunity to be of service to Area 57 and to A.A. as a whole. — *Steve Shuffield*

Ontario (Eastern): Area 83 covers approximately 63,000 square kilometers, from the Québec border in the east to Mississauga in the west, north to Algonquin Park, and south to New York State. District 42 is located in northern New York State, giving our area an international flair. There are approximately 13,500 members with 574 active groups in 25 districts, including eight correctional facility groups. District 16, our linguistic district, serves ten Spanish-speaking groups. Our seven subcommittee chairs, working

with their district counterparts, strive to carry the message of recovery to the alcoholic who still suffers in eastern Ontario. We also have an appointed archivist and webmaster. An ad hoc committee is currently looking into the feasibility of creating a standalone Accessibilities Committee. A second ad hoc committee was formed to review our operating procedures. Our area hosts two assemblies per year, with a pre-Conference assembly in the spring, and seven area committee meetings throughout the two-year term. We are grateful to be part of the Eastern Canada Region and look forward to hosting the Regional Forum in November 2020. Our area is also pleased to participate in C.E.R.A.A.S.A., the biannual Canadian Eastern Region Service Assembly. Area 83 is one of four areas making up the Ontario Delegates Committee, and we will host the biannual committee meeting in February 2020. This meeting is designed to help prepare the delegates to represent their area at the General Service Conference and includes participation from alternate delegates, past delegates and our regional trustee. Our area remains healthy, vibrant and active in general service. I'm truly humbled to serve Area 83 as Panel 69 delegate. — *Rob McArthur*

Ontario (Northwest): Area 85 is northwestern Ontario from Hornepayne on the eastern border west to the Manitoba border. Our southern boundary is the U.S., and we extend north to Hudson Bay. It is an area of 203,251 square miles. To get an idea of its size, Dr. Bob's state of Ohio would fit in 4.5 times and Bill's state of New York would fit in 3.7 times! We have seven districts, of which one has been dark for some years now. We have about 55 groups, of which 17 are in the city of Thunder Bay; the rest are scattered throughout this vast area in small towns with populations well under 10,000, the exception being Kenora, near the Manitoba border. We have an excellent website that is easy to navigate and kept up to date. The area map is phenomenal. Our remote community meetings may be discontinued due to lack of First Nations people attending these videoconference meetings. Four years ago, attendance from the 13 remote communities on board averaged four people per meeting; now it is one person every three or four meetings. It is hard to get volunteers to chair meetings when no one comes. Service is in decline in Area 85. It's difficult to get members involved. Never have there been so many vacant subcommittee positions: We almost didn't have an area treasurer. We need to use technology to allow members from outlying small groups to fill the positions without having to relocate to Thunder Bay. Many of our small-town groups feel a real disconnect with A.A. beyond our meeting rooms. To them, New York may as well be on the moon. That is why we have our spring assemblies hosted by these outlying districts. Members get to see A.A. on an entirely different level, and they get involved. Despite these challenges, which someone said are "opportunities in disguise," the very spirit of A.A. is alive and thriving in Area 85. — *Lorraine Payette*

Pennsylvania (Eastern): Area 59 encompasses the eastern half of Pennsylvania. The Area Committee, nine subcommittees and special servants (e.g., archivist, web servant and tech servant) provide the general service link to approximately 33,000 members and 1,600 home groups in 48 districts – one being a Spanish linguistic district. The Area Committee cooperates with several P.E.N.N.S.C.Y.P.A.A. bid committees, an I.C.Y.P.A.A. bid committee and 11 intergroup associations to help carry the message. Our subcommittees are active with several priorities, including: 1) encouraging more active district support for the Bridging the Gap program; 2) updating digital communications and website; 3) supporting members to participate in National Technology, Corrections and Archives workshops; 4) supporting both AA Grapevine and La Viña; 5) supporting intergroup and Y.P.A.A. Share-A-Day events; and, 6) researching better ways to digitally record our archives. Our service calendar features many events, including a D.C.M. and subcommittee chairperson orientation; the pre-Conference sharing session; two delegate Conference reports and mini-assemblies; area committee service inventory; an area service day; four quarterly area committee business meetings; and our General Service Assembly and Convention. During the past year, area officers and special servants worked to strengthen our communications and inspire more interest in general service by hosting four area forums across the area. These events featured a similar agenda to Regional Forums. Area officers presented member-requested service topics. The forums presented the opportunity for members to become more acquainted with their area servants and the role of general service. We are grateful for a robust service culture in eastern Pennsylvania. — *Ken Dennison*

Pennsylvania (Western): Area 60 of western Pennsylvania stretches from Lake Erie and New York State in the north all the way south to West Virginia and the Mason-Dixon Line between Pennsylvania and Maryland in the south. Our western edge borders Ohio, and the east is home to the Allegheny Mountains, which we share with Area 59. Area 60 is home to the Laurel Highlands, Pittsburgh and Lake Erie regions. Our area has a strong foothold in sobriety, with 44 districts, 850 groups and 10,250 members, with approximately 44 percent of our groups donating to the General Service Office. We also have two intergroups — Pittsburgh and Erie. Area 60 meets six to seven times per year, with four quarterly meetings and three assemblies. Generally, we meet in the Pittsburgh area, but districts do have the opportunity to host area quarterly meetings, and in 2018 we held the third quarterly meeting in Erie, Pennsylvania. We are especially proud of our pre-Conference assembly weekend, where on Friday and Saturday we hold panels and then break off into committees to discuss specific agenda items. On Sunday at the pre-Conference assembly, we get a sense of the meeting on those several agenda items that were discussed in depth, giving the delegate a sense of how the area feels. Also, at our recent weekends we have hosted the trustee-at-large, the Northeast Regional trustee and a Class A trustee. All spent time explaining their roles at G.S.O. We have several standing committees, including a newsletter that is published quarterly, Literature, Grapevine, Archives, Corrections and Treatment. We also have a top-of-the-line website that averages approximately 1,500 unique visitors monthly. Area officers and coordinators attend days of sharing and workshops hosted by districts, and in 2021 we look forward to hosting N.E.R.A.A.S.A. in Pittsburgh, which will be close to transportation and a hop, skip and a jump from Dr. Bob's home in Akron, Ohio. — *Marjorie Stanislaw*

Québec (Northeast): It's with a great pleasure that I introduce Area 89 (northeast Québec) to you. Our area is a vast territory stretching from Louiseville in the west to Blanc-Sablon in the east, and from Chibougamau in the north to Lévis in the south — about 400,000 square kilometers altogether. The nearest district from my place is a 15-minute drive and the farthest is an 11-hour drive each way. Each year we hold two general assemblies and four regional assemblies. We also have seven committees: Archives, Correctional, Public Information, "Le Nordet," Seminars, Publications and Website. For our regional meeting in December, in even years we have a meeting called Welcoming the Newcomers, and in odd years we have our regional inventory. Both meetings run a whole weekend. Our large and beautiful area counts 21 districts. It has 250 groups — 240 French-speaking, five English-speaking, two bilingual, one in Atikamekw and two in the Innu language. There are 280 meetings per week, and we count 3,950 registered members. The Regional Executive Committee meets twice a year with the regional committees of the three other Québec areas. As delegates, we have the responsibility and privilege to be trustees of our bimonthly magazine, *La Vigne*. Eastern Québec has a very well-built website (quite easy to use) and a Seminars Committee. The seminars are given by our past delegates, who share with us their knowledge and experience of our principles and our legacy. Our area also has the honor and privilege to hold a Native convention, held in Pessamit, on the northern shore of the St. Lawrence River. August will mark the 19th year of this convention. We count on an intergroup in Quebec City, where we find various service committees. We also have an administrative assistant who is the "ears" of our area. I am privileged to serve in an area that respects the A.A. principles and Traditions — a very healthy area in action. And it's with gratitude and humility that I represent my friends. I thank them for giving me such an opportunity, and thanks to all of you for what you're doing for A.A. — *Alain Gélinas*

Québec (Southeast): Area 88 covers a large territory south of the St. Lawrence River, from the Eastern Townships to the Magdalene Islands. And we serve six French-speaking groups in the northwest of New Brunswick. We have 18 districts, mostly rural, and a total of 192 groups, with approximately 1,900 registered members. Our largest city is Sherbrooke, with a population of 165,000 including the immediate surroundings. Every other year, we try to fly to the Magdalene Islands to meet with this isolated district and answer to their needs. We hold three area meetings a year plus one annual meeting at the end of September for the election of executives at the area level. We also hold two gratitude dinners in June, one in the western part of the area and one in the eastern part to allow as many as possible to attend. These are organized by the district host with the help of the area executives. It is our way of showing our gratitude to A.A., and the profits of these events are donated to G.S.O. We hold workshops at the districts' demand for their members and we ask them to invite the nearby districts in order to be more efficient and save on expenses. In January of this year, we held a welcome meeting for new people in service. There were six districts and a total of 43 people present. It was appreciated by everyone there. Last year, we held the Eastern Canada Regional Forum in Victoriaville, with an attendance of over 700. Thanks to the help of many volunteers, the weekend was a success. I conclude by expressing my gratitude to A.A. and my area for placing their trust in me. You — meaning all the A.A. members that I have worked with over the years — have made me a better person and A.A. servant. — *Serge Vigneux*

Saskatchewan: Area 91 Saskatchewan just completed its first two-year term of our new committee system, with committee chairs for Archives & Trustees, Treatment & Accessibilities, Corrections, Cooperation with the Professional Community, Grapevine, Literature, Public Information, Finance and Remote Communities. As we move through the growing pains of change in Area 91, our new table officers and committee chairs are eager to build more tools to help carry the message to our members in Saskatchewan. We experienced a great loss in our area, as

our newly elected Grapevine chair, Chico T., passed away unexpectedly at the beginning of February. Chico was an inspiration to us all, as his love for service was visible by the growth in his District 6, and it's with heavy hearts we have to elect a new Grapevine chair at our upcoming March spring assembly in Carlyle, Saskatchewan. Financially, we had a surplus, with an increase in contributions from our groups; for our next year we will continue to carry the message of self-support, contributions and more on our committees. — *Ray McCallum*

Texas (Northeast): Area 65 covers about 70,000 square miles, with the Dallas/Fort Worth metroplex centrally located within our borders. We have 29 districts, five of which serve our Spanish groups. It is estimated that we have around 500 active groups. (And wouldn't it be wonderful if at least 25 percent of those groups had representation at our assemblies?) We start each January off with three orientations for G.S.R.s, D.C.M.s, and anyone interested in learning about our general service structure from top to bottom. Our area committee meetings are generally in February, April, July and October, and are attended by area officers, 12 standing service committee chairs, and D.C.M.s. We have a two-day pre-Conference Spring Area Assembly in March, where members break into mock committees to discuss the final Conference agenda Items. Each mock committee reports back to the assembly body afterward for a collective sense of the area group conscience. I look forward to the extra time we have this year to continue to have discussions about the agenda items and to gather additional feedback from more of our members at the group and district levels before attending the G.S.C. in late May. It will be a challenge to prepare my report for the two-day post-Conference Summer Area Assembly held in mid-June, but I will do the best I can with God's help, and will look forward to other opportunities for myself and my alternate to sharpen our reporting skills as we get invitations to visit our districts throughout the remainder of the year. Our Fall Area Assembly is a three-day event in September, and we combine it with a Conference format, where we invite past delegates, past or current trustees, and a G.S.O. staff member to speak Friday night, Saturday night and Sunday morning. We have found it very helpful to have G.S.R. and D.C.M. sharing sessions at each assembly, offering unified support and a larger pool of experience and solutions. Area 65 is blessed to have up to eight or nine past delegates still

participating and serving in any way they can, whether it be in workshops, our orientations, ad hoc committees or sharing their knowledge or archival information from past panels at the mic during assemblies and area committee meetings. We are really excited about our newly formed Technology Committee, and look forward to their development, expertise and guidance in being more effective in this ever-growing digital world. I thank God for the privilege of serving our Fellowship with each and every one of you during this Conference. — *Tina Palmer*

Texas (Southeast): Area 67 is only 25,406 square miles, but is centered around Houston, the fourth largest city in the U.S. Our area encompasses not only Harris County, the country's third largest county, but also its seven contiguous counties, which have a combined population of nearly seven million. So, while our area is the smallest geographically of Texas's four areas, we have a larger population and therefore traditionally more groups. A recent count indicates we have 693 groups on our rolls. These groups come together to form 18 districts, five of which are linguistic (Spanish-speaking) districts. Our area meets quarterly starting in January with the combined area assembly and SETA Convention, which rotates between Houston, Beaumont and Galveston. This year's convention was held in Galveston and had the theme "Carry the Message to Other Alcoholics" and registered just over 1,600 attendees. The remaining three assemblies have an average attendance of 200 members representing 30 percent of our active groups. This year, area trusted servants will be addressing several items from our recent area inventory, including concerns about how we conduct our two-day assemblies as well as their costs. This will add to an already busy year, as Area 67 will host not only the Texas A.A. State Convention in July but also the Southwest Regional Forum in October and finally the Third Annual National Correctional Facilities Committee (C.F.C.) Conference in November. So, if you find yourself in our area for any reason, I promise you will find amazing A.A. meetings and — regardless of the time of year — humidity. — *Troy Bush-DiDonato*

Utah: Area 69 is made up of the entire state of Utah, more than 84,000 square miles. In December 1944 the first A.A. meeting in Salt Lake City was held. We currently have 11 districts, with one being a Spanish-speaking district. Each district is represented by a D.C.M.C., D.C.M. or M.D.C. There are 516 registered groups and approximately 7,740 members. Of that number of groups, only around 401 groups are active. A lot of Area 69 is rural and remote. District 9 has one group that meets every day and is 461 miles from District 10, our largest district, which has 134 groups within the boundaries of South Salt Lake. In March 1951, Clyde G.'s name was pulled out of the hat to become the first delegate to represent Area 69. Today Area 69 has seven officers, nine standing committee chairs and one non-rotating repository archivist. Each year we hold three area assemblies. At the pre-Conference assembly in the spring, we hold roundtables with the standing chair committees to discuss the agenda items for the upcoming

Conference and inform our delegate of the group conscience of the Utah area. In May at our post-Conference assembly, the delegate gives a report on what actions were taken at the Conference and presents financial reports. At the fall assembly, standing committee roundtables and/or panels are held so members can become better informed about ways to carry the message beyond the group level. In even years, our area elections are held. Area 69 holds two area committee meetings a year to allow the delegate to share current information from G.S.O., to discuss agenda items so the districts can be better informed, and to discuss solutions to ongoing problems and concerns in order to better carry the message. We hold three area workshops a year to provide a forum to discuss the General Service Conference theme and workshop/presentation topics for the current year. This may be done by panel presentations or roundtable discussions. Of our three workshops, one is a Bridging the Gap workshop, where we provide a joint forum for the Corrections and Treatment Committees to share experiences with the Bridging the Gap program and to discuss ways it can be better utilized in our area. All area events are hosted on a rotating basis among the districts and selected one or two years in advance. In the last two years we have been translating our area guidelines, assembly minutes and event flyers into Spanish to better carry the service message to our Spanish-speaking members. — *Matt Dyer*

Virginia: Area 71 covers approximately 40,000 square miles, encompassing 95 counties and 39 independent cities with a population of approximately 8.4 million. Virginia stretches from the beautiful shores of the Atlantic Ocean across the majestic Blue Ridge Mountains to the foothills of the Appalachians and up to the busy metropolitan area of northern Virginia. We have 1,572 listed groups within 44 active districts, of which one was formed last year as a result of a district split. We have 11 standing committees and seven special assignment coordinators, and we meet four times annually. We meet in January to plan the agenda for our spring assembly and again in July to set

the agenda for our fall assembly. We have participation from all corners of the state, with an average attendance of 500 at assemblies. Area events rotate around the state to allow local members to participate and so that no one district has to always bear the long-distance travel. We also have an area convention hosted by a local district and the Archives Annual Open House each spring held at our archives office. The area sponsors two workshops each year, Corrections and P.I./C.P.C., which are hosted by local districts on a rotating basis. We recently began accepting group contributions online through our area website and have formed an ad hoc committee to begin the process of conducting an area inventory. I am both honored and excited to serve on Panel 69 of the General Service Conference. — *Barb Dove*

Washington (Western): Area 72 encompasses the western half of Washington State and was born from an area split many years ago. We have 42 districts, two of which are geographical Spanish-speaking districts, and more than 1,500 groups. Our annual assembly breaks 800 in attendance, with over 400 voting members. We collaborate with neighboring areas to hold the Pacific Northwest Conference (pnc1948.org). We enjoy meaningful and ongoing engagement with our past delegates, who are ex officio members of our area committee. Last year we created a new appointed position dedicated solely to managing our area's translation and interpretation needs. We have an area history book named *Our Stories Disclose*. We are currently writing the third edition of this book. Over the past several years we have also begun to participate in topical national conferences such as the National A.A. Archives Workshop and National A.A. Technology Workshop. I am happy to say that we are doing very well in the western Washington area, and it is such a privilege to serve as delegate. — *Alan Foster*

West Virginia: Our archives tell us that some locals went to Akron, Columbus and Cleveland to get sober. They came back and ordered the Big Book. Then two groups

A sponsor's wish

A sponsor and sponsee are talking in the parking lot of a meeting:

SPONSOR: "I'm happy to be your sponsor. I wish I had one or two more sponsees like you."

SPONSEE: "Gosh, that's nice to hear. I argue with you all the time and mostly refuse to do most of the things you suggest."

SPONSOR: "Yeah, but I still wish I had one or two more like you. The problem is that I have six!"

—*Bob M., Green Valley, AZ, from* Take Me to Your Sponsor

merged, and our first recorded meeting was in Charleston, West Virginia, in 1942. A group later decided to create an "All Purpose Foundation/Institution" that "combined research, education, rehabilitation and doing good." Multiple rules and regulations ensued until huge disagreements stalled the project. A member wrote to the A.A. Foundation and got the "not in line with A.A. experience" response. Sometime later, the Foundation received a card folded in half with the text "Rule #62" on the outside of it. When it was opened it read, "Don't take yourself so damn seriously." Area 73 is the home of Rule #62! This could be a motto for many of our A.A. members. This may also account for the warmth, openness and welcoming vibe to A.A. in West Virginia. Most groups and districts are small. That lets those of us in service get to know each other pretty well. Area 73 has 55 counties, with some meetings in Ohio and Maryland. We have 17 districts (15 active) and seven regions. We have two assemblies and one convention a year, and rotate hosting throughout the state. West Virginia is a gorgeous state with old mountains. Come visit any time. — *Susan Vlajk*

Wisconsin (Southern): Geographically, Area 75 covers southern Wisconsin south of Green Bay, west to La Crosse and the Mississippi River, and south to the Illinois state line. It is diversely populated, with many large cities, small towns and rural communities. We have 955 active registered groups served by 30 districts, including one Spanish-speaking district, which hosted the 18th Wisconsin Hispanic Convention this past October. Five intergroup offices serve Area 75, often "taking the show on the road," displaying literature and various items for sale at conferences, district workshops and events. W.I.C.Y.P.A.A., the Wisconsin Conference of Young People in A.A., is also an active and growing presence in our area. Five assemblies for area business are held annually. January and June assemblies include a G.S.R. school, D.C.M. sharing session and service committee meetings. Our area archives have recently been relocated, and the committee is busy transitioning while welcoming a new non-rotating archivist. The Corrections Committee presents the annual State Corrections Workshop in conjunction with our northern neighbor, Area 74. Treatment, P.I. and C.P.C. committees actively participate in "A.A. at the V.A.," an annual workshop at the Veterans Hospital in Milwaukee. Our Delegate's Workshop, a roundtable discussion held in March, offers the Fellowship an opportunity to review and provide feedback on the upcoming General Service Conference agenda items. The fifth and final assembly takes place at our fall conference. It is devoted to an area inventory in odd-numbered years and to area elections in even years. This year's fall conference (October 18–20 in Milwaukee) will also host the East Central Regional Conference. Program chairs are working with Area 75 members and E.C.R. delegates to create interesting, informative panels and presentations for the event. I am extremely grateful and honored to represent Area 75 as a Panel 69 delegate. Thank you for this opportunity to serve Alcoholics Anonymous. — *Kris Krueger*

■ Trustees' Committees and Staff Reports

ARCHIVES

Trustees' Report: The trustees' Archives Committee was established by the General Service Board and held its first meeting in October 1973. This committee is responsible for developing and implementing the policies that govern the Archives services. The committee makes recommendations to the General Service Board on Archives procedures and budget. Through its group conscience and guided by A.A.'s principles and professional standards, the committee undertakes and upholds its responsibility and authority for the maintenance and use of the Archives.

The committee supports the G.S.O. Archives' commitment to permit access to members of Alcoholics Anonymous and others for research purposes. Since the 2018 General Service Conference, the committee granted permission to 19 researchers for use of archival material. The permission also included access to archival audio recordings, for limited use. Each request is carefully considered through recommendations from the archivist and established Archives policies. The permission to conduct research is granted conditionally on a signed agreement to strictly maintain the anonymity of all members, alive and deceased, including A.A.'s co-founders.

At the committee's meeting in July 2018, the report of the 2018 Conference Committee on Archives was reviewed. The committee was informed that *Our Great Responsibility: A Selection of Bill W.'s General Service Conference Talks, 1951 – 1970,* approved by the 2018 General Service Conference,

was forwarded to G.S.O.'s Publishing Department. They noted the Additional Committee Consideration to add text in appropriate sections of the Archives Workbook that distinguishes archivists from historians and collectors. In addition, it was also suggested to add text clarifying that archivists generally do not purchase items and do not appraise items for monetary value in both the Archives Workbook and Archives service piece, "The A.A. Archives." At the January 2019 meeting, the committee approved the proposed draft texts, which will be added to the next printing of the Archives Workbook and "The A.A. Archives" service piece.

At the October 2018 meeting, the committee considered a proposal from the G.S.O. Archives to make available a selection of five archival photographs to be reproduced and distributed for A.A. use only, following publication of the new book *Our Great Responsibility: A Selection of Bill W.'s General Service Conference Talks, 1951 – 1970.* The committee approved the distribution of the selected photographs, at a suggested contribution of $2.75 each.

The committee continued their discussion on uses of a recently accessioned film — a 1940s home movie of A.A.'s co-founders and their spouses at Stepping Stones — accepted by G.S.O. Archives in 2017. Following a wide-ranging discussion, the committee agreed to the following uses:

- The committee agreed to forward to the 2019 Conference Committee on Archives a request to consider adding the newly accessioned 1940s home movie of the co-founders and their wives to the video "Markings on the Journey."

- The committee approved the distribution of the film as an item available from the G.S.O. Archives at an appropriate contribution, determined by the Archives staff to defray reproduction cost. It was agreed that copies will be distributed in accordance with the G.S.O. Archives Sound and Moving Image Access Policies and Procedures.

Furthermore, the committee broadened the discussion about archival items available to A.A. members and requested that the G.S.O. Archives and A.A.W.S. Board explore the feasibility of including in the A.A.W.S. catalog all archival reproductions currently being distributed.

Earlier last year, the committee discussed a proposal to create a list of questions related to starting or improving local A.A. Archives. The committee requested that the archivist seek sharing from local area and district archivists and bring back a progress report for the committee's discussion. Throughout the year, the committee was kept apprised of the progress of this work and in January 2019, they approved this new G.S.O. Archives material titled, "Archival Checklist: A quick guide for local A.A. Archivists" noting that it will be distributed as service material.

The committee discussed the General Service Board Strategic Plan (updated July 2018) items relevant to this committee. In October 2018, the chair asked that the committee review all Archives Policies and report their questions or thoughts. At the committee's next meeting in January, the chair continued the discussion, requesting that the committee review existing Archives literature and report back at the July 2019 meeting.

In January 2019, the committee considered a proposal to change the statement in the G.S.O. Archives Policy on Loans from "The G.S.O. Archives generally does not accept items on loan" to "The G.S.O. Archives welcomes items on loan that meet our policy for loaned items" and took no action. It was agreed that accepting items on loan presents liability concerns for A.A.W.S., security issues, increased operational costs and other factors. Following the discussion, the committee noted that the G.S.O. Archives policy regarding loaning of, or not accepting items on loan, appears in the "G.S.O. Archives Ownership of Material" statement as well as the "G.S.O. Archives Collection Policy" and discussed creating a separate policy on loans. The G.S.O. archivist will bring a draft policy for discussion at the committee's July 2019 meeting.

The committee also reviewed a report from legal counsel concerning distribution of photocopies of unpublished correspondence entered into the public domain. The counsel's report included a consideration to add the following statement to the G.S.O. Archives Photocopying Policy, "A.A.W.S. in its discretion may refuse to permit photocopying of certain sensitive material." The G.S.O. Archives Photocopying Policy was revised to include the statement recommended by legal counsel.

Throughout the year, the committee was kept apprised of projects executed by the Archives staff, projected goals for the upcoming year, as well as tabulated research inquiries handled by the staff.

Mark Everett, Chairperson

Staff Report: The Archives staff provides resource material and service to A.A. members, researchers and others about A.A. history, responds to worldwide information requests, and offers professional support to local areas, districts or groups interested in researching their history. In 2018, we responded to over 1,500 requests for information, utilizing a combination of unpublished primary sources and published material maintained in the repository. We welcomed new local archivists and committee chairs serving either in the area or district position and furnished each individual with an Archives Workbook, Guidelines and other resources. None of the work reported here would be possible without the help of a diligent team of archivists, working to fulfill the mission and goals of the G.S.O. Archives.

A new and ongoing scanning project instituted in 2018 entailed digitizing co-founder Bill W.'s collection of unpublished correspondence. This vast collection includes Bill's ideas and opinions on scores of subjects related to the Fellowship. These include, for example, letters addressing "criticism" of himself and the Movement, "Finances," his unrelenting endeavor to form a "General Service Conference" and other notable subjects. The collection also holds personal correspondence with notable friends of A.A. including Sister Ignatia, Father Dowling and Dr. Silkworth. Included within the collection are correspondences with Dr. Bob, whose handwritten letters had to be typed prior to scanning. We anticipate this project to be completed by the end of December 2019. The original letters are being preserved for permanent storage in the Archives' secured offsite facility while reference copies are maintained onsite. This digitization project enables Archives staff to efficiently search the digital files and reduces wear on the paper documents.

Archives staff worked on digitizing a small collection of yellowed, fragile newspaper clippings acquired from sources around the country that contain mention of Bill W. during his travels and meetings with groups and members. They also worked on scanning other significant resources, such as 112 back issues of *Loners-Internationalists Meeting (LIM)* bulletin, vital correspondence from past delegates and trustees and other records, thus aiding in the growth of the Archives digital repository. Due to the large volume of materials assessed for future digitization, we hired a part-time scanning position to help with this endeavor.

Archives staff also completed several other projects, including organizing and cataloging foreign pamphlets, services pieces and other printed pieces published by A.A.W.S.; updating the Archives Disaster Plan; performing quality-checks in the entries of the audio catalog, ensuring standardized language and correcting errors; and converting digital recordings of past General Service Board and General Service Conference to an audio preservation format.

The G.S.O. Record Retention Policy is administered by the Archives staff and IT Director with guidance from an accredited Records Manager consultant. During the month of February, Archives staff held several training workshops on Records Management for employees, emphasizing the significance of appropriate maintenance and disposition of all records created or received by the General Service Office.

Archives staff worked on curating a series of new exhibitions in the Archives exhibit area, including a new exhibit highlighting monthly events in A.A. history and another documenting the history of the writing of A.A.'s Twelve Steps, scribed by Bill W. in December 1938. We also curated an exhibit to mark the 80th anniversary of the establishment of the General Service Board (then known as the Alcoholic Foundation) in August 1938. In October, in observance of National Archives Month in the United States, posters were displayed around the offices that highlighted the importance of Archives.

In October 2018, the senior archivist was tasked with a long-term project of organizing and preserving over two cubic feet of materials previously set aside by G.S.O.'s first archivist, Nell Wing, that she marked, "for future microfilming." The materials date from 1956 through the 1960s and include documents originating from activities of the General Service Board, General Service Conference, copies of letters written by Bill and other significant documents.

Archives staff continue to develop the "Archives and History" portal of the G.S.O. website. The A.A. Timeline was updated to include new entries of A.A. events around the world for the year 2017.

On an experimental starting point in May 2018, we began to keep a numerical log of accessioned items, both paper and digital. The log includes items generated internally such as reports and publications that we are responsible for archiving, as well as items received from members. From May through December, over 400 new items were archived.

Michelle Mirza, Archivist

AUDIT

Trustees' Report: The trustees' Audit Committee, formed by the General Service Board in 2003, is composed of a minimum of three and a maximum of five trustees who are appointed by the chair of the General Service Board.

The committee was originally created as a proactive measure to assist the General Service Board in fulfilling its fiduciary obligation of Prudent Corporate Governance. As a result of the recent passage of the New York State Nonprofit Law, the committee now has specific responsibilities that are set forth under the law, some of which are set forth in the last paragraph of this report.

The committee meets at least twice a year with the outside independent auditors and G.S.O. and Grapevine management, separately with the auditor, and in executive session without the auditor.

The Audit Committee reports to the General Service Board and reviews such items as audit process, audit results, internal controls, best accounting practices, and management integrity. The Audit Committee also recommends appointment of the auditors to the Board.

David Morris, Chairperson

COMMUNICATION SERVICES

Staff Report: G.S.O. offers an A.A. website at www.aa.org to serve the Fellowship of Alcoholics Anonymous as a resource for A.A. members; those seeking help from A.A.; professionals working with alcoholics; the media; and the public at large. G.S.O.'s website provides accurate and consistent information about A.A., provides details about services coordinated by G.S.O. and encourages participation of A.A. members, groups and committees in A.A. services and activities.

In addition to the website, a YouTube channel has been created to provide an added platform from which videos can be easily shared with a broader audience. A new website design for aa.org and an A.A.W.S. app are also currently in development.

The Communication Services staff member serves as the liaison for information about G.S.O.'s A.A. website, collecting feedback on design and content from visitors to the website; chairing G.S.O.'s Website Committee, which also has oversight of the A.A.W.S. YouTube channel; and collaborating with G.S.O.'s digital media manager to continually update and improve both the YouTube channel and aa.org. Collected experience regarding local website committees is shared from this desk upon request.

This staff member serves as secretary to the A.A.W.S. Technology/Communication/Services (TCS) Committee and prepares Website Activity Reports for the A.A.W.S. Board and the Conference Committee on Public Information.

The Communication Services staff member attends the annual National A.A. Technology Workshop, first held in August 2014, to provide a forum for individuals to gather, share and seek solutions to technology-related issues faced by local A.A. members, groups and service entities.

Clement Cann

COMPENSATION COMMITTEE

Trustees' Report: The trustees' Compensation Committee, formed in 2006 by the General Service Board, consists of at least four trustees. The committee was created as a proactive measure to assist the General Service Board in fulfilling its fiduciary obligation of Prudent Corporate Governance.

The Compensation Committee reports to the General Service Board and reviews and advises A.A. World Services, Inc. (A.A.W.S.) and AA Grapevine, Inc. (AAGV) on such items as overall compensation philosophies and policies, best compensation practices, and compliance with the IRS for executive compensation for nonprofit organizations.

The committee worked with A.A.W.S. and AAGV to obtain the services of Astron Solutions to conduct analysis of the total compensation for the highest paid executives in each corporation. The committee received the reports and met with Astron Solutions to discuss the results of the analysis. The reports indicated that the total compensation packages of the highest paid executives are within reasonable levels and do not represent excessive compensation.

Ginger Rhoades Bell, Chairperson

CONFERENCE

Trustees' Report: The committee met three times since the 2018 General Service Conference. During that period, the committee considered the Advisory Actions and Additional Committee Considerations pertaining to the General Service Conference and discussed the proposed agenda items pertaining to the 2019 Conference.

The committee reviewed a 2016 report from the General Service Board suggesting that "Before the January [General Service Board] meeting, the entire Conference committee could have a conference call with the corresponding trustees' committee chair and staff secretary to review items submitted as agenda items and to talk about items still being considered by the trustees' committee." The committee reviewed a request from the 2018 Conference Agenda Committee that trustees' committee chairs implement this conference call. The chair of the General Service Board agreed to implementation and the calls were completed in 2019.

The committee discussed an email regarding the ramifications or benefits to one delegate having access to more information than others and agreed that implementation of the conference call prior to the January board meeting with the trustees' committee chair and the Conference committee members removed this potential issue. The committee also commented on the fact that the Conference committee chair is responsible for communicating with their committee throughout the year.

The committee reviewed a request to create a process for area delegate review of proposed agenda items that were not forwarded to a Conference committee. The committee noted that two additional items on its agenda corresponded to this request: a proposal for a two-year process for proposed agenda items; and a proposed Conference agenda item regarding the grid of proposed agenda items not forwarded to a Conference committee.

The chair appointed a subcommittee to consider all three items regarding area delegate review of agenda items. The subcommittee was also asked to consider creation of a workable plan for equitable distribution of the workload of Conference committees by combining and/or creating committees, as well as the consequence of a simple majority vote of the Conference.

The subcommittee reported the following:

First, the committee discussed reimplementing a simple majority vote practice resulting from a 1986 Advisory Action, which has not been performed since 1995. The committee reviewed and agreed to forward to the 2019 Conference Policy and Admissions Committee the 1986 Advisory Action: "If a committee recommendation does not receive the two-thirds vote required to become a Conference Advisory Action, but has a majority of votes, it automatically becomes a suggestion and will be duly noted in the Conference Report." Should the Conference Policy and Admissions Committee reaffirm this process, the trustees asked that the committee provide suggestions regarding appropriate action to be taken when a Conference committee recommendation fails but receives a simple majority vote.

Second, the committee reviewed a preliminary process for how the Conference Agenda Committee could review, discuss and act on proposed agenda items not forwarded to a Conference committee. The committee agreed to forward a final process and workflow diagram to the Conference Policy and Admissions Committee for consideration.

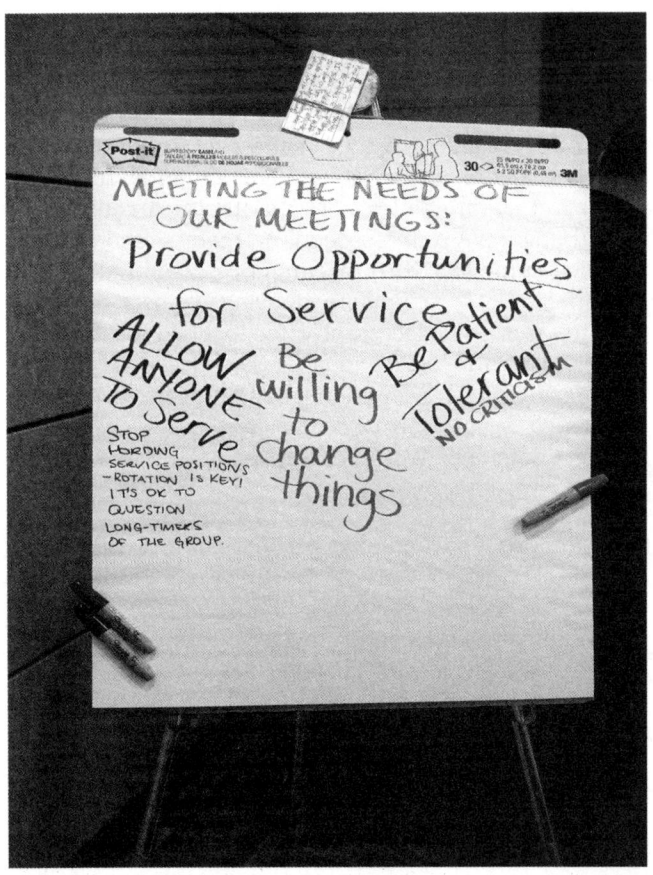

MEETING THE NEEDS OF OUR MEETINGS:
Provide Opportunities for Service
ALLOW ANYONE TO Serve
Be willing to change things
Be Patient & Tolerant
NO CRITICISM
STOP HORDING SERVICE POSITIONS
- ROTATION IS KEY!
IT'S OK TO QUESTION LONG-TIMERS OF THE GROUP.

Finally, the subcommittee believes that a broader discussion is needed on the topic of equitable workload distribution of Conference agenda items. A conversation is requested to include trustees' committee chairs, G.S.O. management and staff, the Conference Agenda Committee chair and delegate chair. The subcommittee introduced four questions that could be used to guide the discussion. The committee requested the Conference coordinator plan to use one of the 69th General Service Conference general sharing sessions for this purpose.

The committee discussed a request to develop an information sheet reflecting experience and guidance on usage of the Conference dashboard. The committee reviewed Conference member sharing about their experience and usage of the Conference dashboard. The staff secretary provided an update that a reorganization of the Conference dashboard is underway using the feedback provided and that a future project is planned to continue revisions to the Conference dashboard. The committee requested staff distribute the newly developed Conference Dashboard Tip Sheet to Conference members.

The committee reviewed the Conference Evaluation Summary and a summary of the in-house Post-Conference Sharing Session. At least one response provided through the new electronic evaluation was not received, and the system will be tested to ensure that all evaluations are collected. The committee agreed to add questions to the evaluation form related to the Conference dashboard, electronic evaluations and the electronic Conference manual.

The committee agreed to remove mention of voting by show of hands from "How the Conference Operates,"

since voting is now being done electronically. The committee further reviewed a proposal to add a "show of hands" to the electronic voting process and agreed to take no action. The committee felt that the Conference member discussions, as well as the minority opinion, provide the understanding of the reasons for a Conference member's vote.

The general manager reported to the committee that the dates for the 69th General Service Conference will be May 19–25, 2019. He explained that, due to an error regarding contract dates with the hotel venue, a poll of all Conference members was conducted to change the dates of the 2019 Conference. The poll was conducted according to the "Process for Polling the General Service Conference" approved at the 2018 Conference. The motion to change the dates from April 21–27, 2019, to May 19–25, 2019, passed. This was followed by a motion to reconsider, which was seconded. The motion to reconsider failed, so the approved dates of the 69th General Service Conference were scheduled for May 19–25, 2019.

The committee reviewed and accepted its preliminary 2019 budget and forwarded it to the trustees' Finance and Budgetary Committee.

The committee reviewed the 2019 General Service Conference week schedule and noted the addition of a presentation on the 2020 International Convention by the International Convention coordinator and a presentation on the A.A.W.S. Audio/Video Strategic Plan.

The committee reviewed a grid of 68 items that have been proposed for placement on the 2019 Conference Agenda that are posted on the Conference dashboard in English, French and Spanish.

The committee considered a proposed agenda item, "That work begin on the development of a fifth edition of the book *Alcoholics Anonymous,*" and the committee agreed to forward it to the trustees' Literature Committee for review at their January 2019 meeting.

The committee considered a proposed agenda item that "All agenda items for censure or reorganization be forwarded directly to the Conference Committee on Trustees" and took no action. The committee agreed that it is important to follow our proposed agenda item process.

The committee considered a proposed agenda item "That the Conference consider establishing a new Conference Committee on CEC" and took no action. The committee noted that the Accessibilities/Remote Communities assignment currently shares collected experience and it was felt there is not a need to create a new Conference committee.

The committee requested that the secretary forward the proposed agenda item's secondary request "That the General Service Office consider the need to develop a service piece and/or service material on CEC" to the trustees' committee on C.P.C/Treatment and Accessibilities for consideration.

The committee considered a proposed agenda item to "Set the publishing schedule of the Conference Final Report at the highest priority to ensure they will be delivered before August 31, as they were in the past" and took no action. It was reported by the Publishing Department that the principal reason for the delayed production of the 2018 Conference Final Report was the workload impact from the many projects generated by the 68th General Service Conference Advisory Actions. The committee was concerned about tying the Conference Final Report production to a specific date. Planning is underway to produce an early electronic "mini" report of Conference actions for Conference members in 2019.

The committee agreed to forward to the 2019 Conference Policy and Admissions Committee a discussion topic pertaining to the process of approving qualified personnel from other service structures to observe the U.S. and Canada General Service Conference.

The committee agreed to forward a proposed agenda item "That the Policy/Admissions Committee develop a procedure to deal with special requests/agenda items," such as inviting General Service Board consultants to attend the General Service Conference as observers, to the Conference Policy and Admissions Committee for consideration.

The committee discussed the proposed agenda item "Consider a request that a staff assignment be created at the General Service Office for a Young People in A.A. (YPAA) Liaison." The committee determined suggestions related to the oversight of the General Service Office are the responsibility of A.A. World Services, Inc. and forwarded the proposed agenda item to that board for consideration.

The committee agreed to forward a proposed agenda item to revise our "Process for Polling the General Service Conference between Annual Meetings" to the Conference Policy and Admissions Committee for consideration.

The committee considered a proposed agenda item "That the General Service Conference should move to a midwestern city in the interest of financial prudence" and took no action. The committee felt there was not a widely expressed need supporting the request. General Service Office management is performing ongoing site selection analysis and a report will be provided to the 2019 Conference Policy and Admissions Committee.

The committee considered a proposed agenda item to "Reconsider the 66th General Service Conference Advisory Action to delete two paragraphs, and add an endnote, from the Concept Eleven essay regarding 'male/female' distinctions, which is the writing of our co-founder, Bill W., in the Twelve Concepts for World Service" and took no action. The committee felt there was not a widely expressed need supporting the request.

The committee considered the proposed agenda item that "The General Service Conference consider ceasing the development of new literature and focus on making all our current literature accessible in all possible formats" and agreed to forward it to the trustees' Literature Committee due to the broad implications of this request.

The committee agreed to forward to the 2019 Conference Agenda Committee the "Report to the Conference on the Implementation and Effectiveness of the Conference Agenda Process." The Conference Agenda Committee requested an annual survey be completed of the communication experience between Conference committee and

trustee chairs, which is included in the report.

The committee received a verbal report from the committee vice chair on three General Service Board Strategic Plan items that are relevant to this committee. The committee asked staff to send a request for sharing to area delegates regarding the different underrepresented populations of suffering alcoholics that the area could focus on carrying the A.A. message to. A progress report will be provided at the July 2019 meeting.

Staff facilitated a random drawing to elect the delegate and trustee replacement voters needed for the 2019 Conference Northeast Regional Trustee elections.

The committee reviewed the report and approved using the "Open Space" format to facilitate the 69th General Service Conference Workshop session.

Richard Purtell, Chairperson

Staff Report: The Conference coordinator is the G.S.O. contact for General Service Conference members. The Conference process continues throughout the year, and the coordinator corresponds regularly with delegates and alternate delegates who cooperate to make the annual Conference responsive to the needs of the Fellowship.

The annual meeting of the General Service Conference, which first met in April 1951, is the closest thing A.A. has to a group conscience in the U.S. and Canada.

A.A. members are encouraged to submit topics through their area structures for consideration by the Conference. Suggested topics may be forwarded to a trustees' committee for consideration and, where appropriate, referred on to a specific Conference committee. Occasionally topics are submitted that fall more appropriately under the purview of either the A.A.W.S. or Grapevine Boards. These items are accordingly forwarded to those boards for their attention.

The Conference coordinator is responsible for:

- Serving as secretary to the Conference Agenda Committee and the trustees' Committee on the General Service Conference;

- Assembling suggestions for the Conference theme, presentations/discussions and workshop topics for review by the Conference Agenda Committee, which then makes selections that are recommended to the Conference for approval;

- Working with the G.S.O. staff and general manager on planning and coordinating each phase of the Conference program, agenda and scheduling;

- Working with the Publishing Department to schedule, assemble and coordinate translation of Conference material;

- Working with the Publishing Department on the summer edition of *Box 4-5-9* and the Conference *Final Report*;

- Cooperating with the IT Services Department to develop and maintain necessary digital platforms for transmission of Conference material to Conference members.

Patrick Claymore

COOPERATION WITH
THE PROFESSIONAL COMMUNITY/TREATMENT
AND ACCESSIBILITIES COMMITTEE

Trustees' Report: The trustees' committees on Cooperation with the Professional Community and Treatment Facilities were combined by action of the General Service Board in April 1998. In August of 2009, the trustees' committee expanded its scope to include service to Special Needs-Accessibilities Committee and oversight of Special Needs literature. The title of the committee was changed to Cooperation with the Professional Community/Treatment/Special Needs-Accessibilities in 2009. In November 2015 "Special Needs" was removed from the committee name and throughout the committee's Composition, Scope and Procedure.

The trustees' Committee on Cooperation with the Professional Community/Treatment and Accessibilities met three times since the 2018 General Service Conference, in addition to numerous teleconferences involving subcommittees throughout that period. The committee undertook the following tasks this past year:

General Service Board Strategic Plan: The committee discussed relevant items in the General Service Board Strategic Plan and noted those activities already in progress, including the review of literature and outreach to professionals serving underrepresented populations within A.A. The committee also agreed to create a schedule for regular review of literature under the committee's purview.

Cooperation with the Professional Community (C.P.C.): The committee reviewed the list of 2018 Conference C.P.C. Committee Advisory Actions and Additional Committee Considerations.

Following the 2018 Advisory Action and Additional Committee Consideration for creating a LinkedIn page, the committee agreed to move forward slowly and mindfully on the development of the LinkedIn page, with realistic expectations about what a LinkedIn "company" page can accomplish.

After the committee reviewed and discussed examples of how A.A. content could display on a LinkedIn page that might carry out the 2018 Conference Advisory Action and Additional Committee Consideration, the secretary was asked to work with a consultant (Impact Collaborative) on the creation of a LinkedIn page, with the findings provided to the trustees' committee at the January 2019 meeting.

The committee reviewed the findings and agreed to respond to the consultant's questions and recommendations involving appearance, style, posting content, implementation and maintenance of a LinkedIn page. The trustees' committee noted the importance of having the Conference C.P.C. Committee discuss the progress on implementation of an A.A.W.S. LinkedIn page and agreed to forward the work of the consultant and the trustees' committee to the Conference C.P.C. Committee.

The committee reviewed a request that LinkedIn be used "only as a link to aa.org with no further content added to LinkedIn" and took no action. The committee felt that an introductory description would be more effective and would align with goals of the 2018 Advisory Action to create a LinkedIn page.

The committee reviewed a request to repeal the General Service Conference decision to approve the use of LinkedIn, and took no action. The committee noted the due diligence of the Conference process and agreed that sufficient time is required to implement the 2018 Advisory Action for a LinkedIn page.

The committee reviewed a request to remove the text "They may help arrange hospitalization" from the section "What can you expect from A.A.?" in the pamphlet "Alcoholics Anonymous in Your Community" and forwarded it to the 2019 Conference Committee on C.P.C. for consideration.

The committee also reviewed a request to incorporate text from the "Blue Card" into the pamphlet "Members of the Clergy Ask About Alcoholics Anonymous" and took no action, noting that the current language in the pamphlet adequately explains the difference between open and closed meetings.

The committee discussed how to best carry the message to those coming to A.A. through court referrals and how to keep court professionals and community corrections professionals informed about what A.A. is and is not. The committee also noted that communications addressed to professionals comprise a different audience from local A.A. committees in the U.S. and Canada. The committee also discussed potential alcoholics coming to A.A. through court referrals and requested that the staff secretary update the A.A. Guidelines on Cooperating with Court, D.W.I. and Similar Programs to better reflect what A.A. is and is not.

The committee reviewed and accepted the 2019 C.P.C. exhibit list and noted the excellent work of the local com-

mittees who made sure that the A.A. booth was always staffed with A.A. members to greet attendees. The secretary updated service pieces "For Chairpersons Staffing an A.A. Exhibit" and "For Volunteers Staffing an A.A. Exhibit" based on shared experience from some General Service Board trustees and A.A. members who volunteer to staff exhibits. Other General Service Board trustees were encouraged to attend those professional conferences from the 2019 exhibit list that are within their local area and field of expertise.

The value of badge-reader technology was discussed as a tool that can support local C.P.C. committee efforts at professional conferences, and this was recently included in the C.P.C. workbook. The committee reviewed a pilot summary on badge-reader technology. The committee agreed to move forward with providing badge readers to the scheduled 2019 exhibits when possible.

Treatment: The committee noted a preliminary plan from the Publishing Department to identify literature used in treatment and corrections settings that would benefit from being staple-free. The committee also noted that the Publishing Department is researching the most feasible options.

The committee reviewed a request to revise the "Bridging the Gap" pamphlet to broaden the focus to include local Bridging the Gap work for correctional facilities and forwarded it to the Conference Committee on Treatment and Accessibilities for consideration.

The committee agreed that adequate information for new committee chairs is provided in the Treatment Workbook, and asked that the welcome letter point out and emphasize this guidance.

Accessibilities: The committee reviewed an Additional Committee Consideration for a service piece for new Accessibilities chairs and took no action. The committee agreed that adequate information on helping new committee chairs to get started is provided in the Accessibilities

Workbook, and asked that the welcome letter point out and emphasize this guidance.

The Subcommittee on Accessibilities — Deaf and Hard-of-Hearing was formed at the July 2018 meeting. The scope was to continue exploring ways to meet the needs of A.A. members who are Deaf and Hard-of-Hearing. The subcommittee reviewed the results of an October 2017 request for shared experience and agreed that the experience from these members highlighted the following:

a. The lack of a clear definition between the topics of Deaf versus Hard-of-Hearing in our literature and service material.

b. The need to develop additional content and language regarding how A.A. performs ASL interpretation services.

c. The need to detail how A.A. as a whole is overcoming access barriers of the Deaf versus Hard-of-Hearing.

d. The need for references to designated seating for meetings and events to support overcoming access barriers for Deaf and Hard-of-Hearing.

e. The need to ensure A.A. members who are Deaf or Hard of Hearing have full access to participation in all Three Legacies of A.A.

The subcommittee also discussed ideas that were gleaned from this sharing. These included:

1. Clarifying and differentiating Deaf versus Hard-of-Hearing in accessibilities literature.

2. Expanding shared experience from members and committees regarding Deaf/Hard-of-Hearing in accessibilities literature.

3. Reviewing registration forms for events hosted by the General Service Board (Regional Forums, International Convention, World Service Meeting, General Service Conference, G.S.B. weekend, etc.) to see if they include questions about accessibility needs.

4. Requesting that all video content have captions for accessibility.

5. Suggesting a revision of the pamphlet "The Twelve Steps Illustrated," and taking a piece of current A.A. literature and simplifying the language in ASL/English.

6. Investigating ways to include more stories from A.A. members who are Deaf/Hard-of-Hearing in AA Grapevine.

7. Providing the new ASL Big Book and *Twelve Steps and Twelve Traditions* in shorter videos that might be helpful for ASL meetings.

8. Creating streaming video around Deaf/Hard-of-Hearing for G.S.O.'s A.A. website; subject ideas include obtaining ASL interpreters, an FAQ, and supporting accessibility.

The full committee approved the subcommittee's recommendations for changes to the following service materials:

- A.A. Guidelines — Accessibility for All Alcoholics
- A.A. Guidelines on Sharing the A.A. Message with the Alcoholic Who Is Deaf
- Serving All Alcoholics
- Accessibilities Workbook
- Accessibilities Checklist

The subcommittee also considered sharing about the need for simplified language literature. The subcommittee wants to ensure that any such simplified language does not lose the powerful meaning of the A.A. message, but lowers the reading level so that it is accessible to more individuals. They reviewed currently available A.A. literature that is simplified and illustrated, and noted that there have been requests for a simplified version of the Big Book, as well as other literature. The subcommittee recommended that the pamphlet "The Twelve Steps Illustrated" be updated with simplified language and illustrations that reflect the meaning of the Steps, and the full committee agreed to forward it to the 2019 Conference Committee on Treatment and Accessibilities.

The subcommittee encouraged the survey respondents to write their stories for Grapevine. The subcommittee recommended that Ashley R.'s story be added to the pamphlet "Access to A.A.: Members Share on Overcoming Barriers," and the full committee agreed to forward it to the 2019 Conference Committee on Treatment and Accessibilities.

The subcommittee asked that registration forms for Regional Forums, Board Weekends, the General Service Conference and the International Convention be reviewed to accommodate participation from all A.A. members, wherever possible.

The Subcommittee on Accessibilities — A.A. in the Armed Services was formed at the July 2018 meeting. The scope was to improve the effectiveness of carrying the A.A. message and improve cooperation with the armed services. The subcommittee noted that veterans and active duty members of the military are two very distinct groups and separate approaches may be needed.

The subcommittee considered all branches of the military (in the U.S., the Air Force, Army, Coast Guard, Marine Corps, Navy, National Guard and Reserves; in Canada, the Canadian Armed Forces), as well as veterans and veteran services.

The subcommittee agreed that activity is needed at the top levels of the military because of the command structure. The subcommittee noted that high-level contacts could pave the way for acceptance of A.A. interaction at the local level. Several informal conversations with military contacts involved with veterans, armed forces and military service organizations were had. These might open the door to armed services publications or A.A. exhibits at national conventions.

The subcommittee considered how A.A. might cooperate with transition offices that help active duty personnel as they move into civilian life, and took no action. It was noted that these offices deal primarily with employment and education, rather than personal transition.

The subcommittee agreed on the importance of local committee activity. C.P.C. committees can reach out to local military facilities such as National Guard units, military hospitals, VFW Posts, armories and military installations. In addition to sharing about A.A. with military professionals, this might open an avenue to distribute A.A. literature to military facilities. Contacting these facilities might become an annual activity.

A request for sharing was sent to committee chairs throughout the U.S. and Canada asking for their experience in cooperation with the armed services. This experience will be collated and may be included in service material such as the C.P.C. and Accessibilities Workbooks or Guidelines. Topics such as initiating contact or starting a meeting on a base can be incorporated into articles for *Box 4-5-9*, Grapevine and *About A.A.*

The subcommittee made several suggestions to update references in service materials to active duty personnel and veterans. The subcommittee reviewed current A.A. literature and suggested an increase in visibility of stories from active duty and veteran A.A. members. The subcommittee recommended that the pamphlet "A.A. for the Older Alcoholic — Never Too Late" be revised to incorporate recent stories, replacing ones that reference the Depression and WWII; to include information about online meetings; and to add information about AA Grapevine and its website.

The subcommittee agreed on the usefulness of creating additional audio content to carry the message to military professionals. The subcommittee modified and accepted a list of potential interview questions for chaplains and medical personnel. These audio clips, 5 to 10 minutes in length, could be used in various places such as G.S.O.'s A.A. website, an app, LinkedIn, the A.A.W.S. YouTube channel, etc. An unedited sample interview was reviewed by the full committee and forwarded to the Conference Committee on Treatment and Accessibilities. The subcommittee also recommended that the A.A.W.S. Board consider posting anonymity-protected audio interviews with military professionals about their experience with

A.A. as informational content for C.P.C. or P.I. use. The subcommittee suggested that audio sharing of A.A. members could come from the existing stories in the pamphlet "A.A. and the Armed Services" published by G.S.O., since they are already Conference-approved. It was suggested that audio stories could come from the new AA Grapevine book *AA in the Military*.

The committee also reviewed a request to develop a Remote Communities Kit and Workbook and requested that the staff secretary compile materials to be considered for a kit. A draft Remote Communities Kit was forwarded to the 2019 Conference Committee on Treatment and Accessibilities for their review.

Nancy McCarthy, Chairperson

Staff Reports:

Cooperation with the Professional Community (C.P.C.)/ Treatment: Experience indicates that many professionals are aware of A.A., yet relatively few know what the A.A. recovery program is and how it differs from other professional resources, including other Twelve Step Fellowships. The staff member on the C.P.C./Treatment assignment, along with an assistant, works to provide accurate information about A.A. and to facilitate communication with those outside A.A. who have direct contact with the still-suffering alcoholic through their professional work.

The C.P.C./Treatment desk responds daily to numerous inquiries from professionals and frequently puts them in touch with local C.P.C. committees who respond to requests and make sure that A.A. is an available resource.

Communication with professionals also occurs through the newsletter *About A.A.*, typically published twice a year, and most recently updated with a modern design. The fall 2018 issue featured an article entitled "A.A for the Older Alcoholic." Currently there are about 13,000 digital and 1,500 print subscribers. Recently, back issues were added to the website (1970–1999) as a resource. C.P.C. chairs and others within the service structure receive the newsletter upon request, and it is available at professional exhibits.

Professional exhibits continue to result in requests for additional A.A. information, as well as personal contacts with local committee members. In 2018 the C.P.C./ Treatment assignment arranged for displays at 31 national or international professional conferences, and plans to exhibit at 35 national conferences in 2019. These national exhibits cover 12 professional categories including Accessibilities, Alcoholism and Addiction, Clergy, Corrections/Court/Legal, Counseling/Social Work, Education, Gerontology, Healthcare, Human Resources/Workplace, Psychiatry, Public Health, and Public Information. At these exhibits, G.S.O. provides the booth space, display and literature; local C.P.C. committees coordinate A.A. volunteers who staff the booth to answer questions and provide literature and contacts.

Local C.P.C./Treatment chairs throughout the U.S. and Canada contact the C.P.C./Treatment desk, which serves as a resource. New area and district chairpersons receive welcome letters and applicable C.P.C./Treatment background material. We encourage committees to send meeting minutes and to share local experiences for possible inclusion in future *Box 4-5-9* articles. Articles are published in *Box 4-5-9* about local C.P.C. activities throughout the year. This creates interest in C.P.C. service work with courts, clergy, doctors, medical students, educators and other professionals.

The C.P.C./Treatment staff member also serves as liaison to several national organizations, such as the National Institute for Alcohol Abuse and Alcoholism (NIAAA) and the Substance Abuse and Mental Health Services Administration (SAMHSA), a branch of the U.S. Department of Health and Human Services.

Diana Lewis

Accessibilities and Remote Communities: The overall purpose of the Accessibilities and Remote Communities staff assignment is to share A.A. and service committee experience and information through literature, activity updates and other communications. Area, district and intergroup committee chairs for Accessibilities and Remote Communities currently receive communications from this assignment, with 314 Accessibilities committees (including 17 Cooperation with the Elder Community committees) and 51 Remote Communities committees listed. The staff member also cooperates with G.S.O.'s Publishing Department on development and updating of accessibilities materials.

New chairs receive welcome letters, workbooks, service-related materials and service kits for their particular position and committee. These materials continue to be shipped via postal mail. At every opportunity these trusted servants are reminded that the vast majority of information that they seek can be read or printed on G.S.O.'s A.A. website (www.aa.org). On the committee web page, anyone can access the majority of committee service-related materials regardless of their position within the committee. In addition, area level chairs receive a list of other area level chairs to share their local experience and activities.

Committee chairs receive updates through articles in *Box 4-5-9* and from the assignment coordinator. These updates may contain ideas, activities, questions and solutions from other committees. These activity updates also contain information about the General Service Office, requests for local sharing, and clarification of areas of potential confusion.

The staff member on this assignment serves as secretary to the Conference Committee on Treatment and Accessibilities, and as co-secretary to the trustees' Committee on Cooperation with the Professional Community/Treatment and Accessibilities.

Rick Walker

CORRECTIONS

Trustees' Report: The trustees' Committee on Corrections recommends to the General Service Board actions that support carrying the A.A. message to alcoholics confined in a variety of correctional settings. Since the 2018 General Service Conference, the trustees' committee has met three times.

In keeping with an Additional Committee Consideration of the 2018 Conference Corrections Committee, the trustees' Committee on Corrections discussed several ways

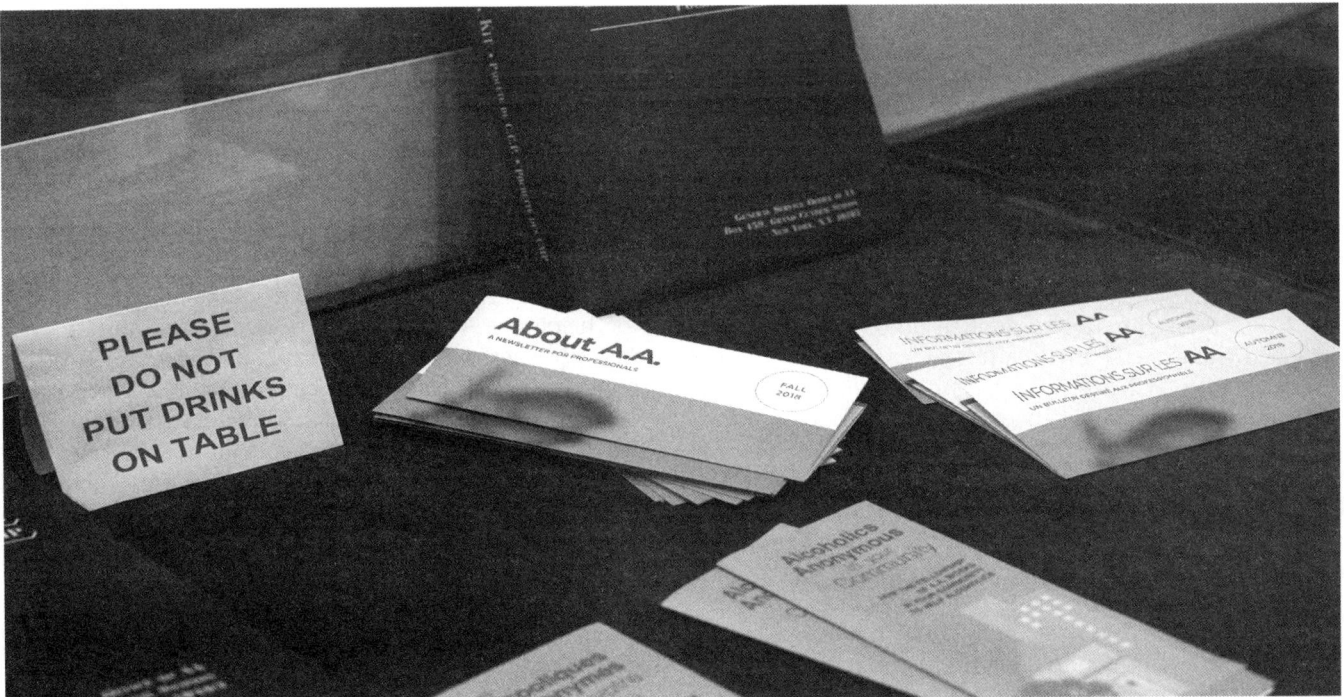

A.A. materials could be utilized in juvenile facilities. The committee noted the short duration of juvenile incarceration and that many receive mental health and community services prior to incarceration. The committee requested the following:

- That the staff secretary gather shared experience from the local corrections committees about successes, challenges, and literature utilized in juvenile facilities that could be included in the juvenile facility section of the Corrections Workbook.
- That the pamphlet "Twelve Traditions Illustrated" (P-55) and selected A.A. Grapevine stories from young people be added to the content of the Youth Prison Recovery Package (YPRP).
- That the staff secretary work with the Publishing Department to identify options to utilize digital A.A. materials in juvenile facilities, including existing videos.

Also in keeping with an Additional Committee Consideration of the 2018 Conference Committee on Corrections, the committee discussed the value of locally coordinated Prelease and Bridging the Gap services and agreed that direct contact with corrections professionals should come from local committees. The committee requested that staff create a draft letter to raise awareness about A.A. volunteers' role in Prelease and Bridging the Gap services. The committee agreed that the intent of the letter (from the Corrections assignment at the General Service Office) is to inform corrections professionals that A.A. services for alcoholics soon to be released from prison are provided by corrections committees in their local areas, and how to contact them. After review, the committee asked a member of the committee to further edit the letter taking into consideration the suggestions provided during the meeting and that a new draft be brought back for review in July 2019.

In keeping with an additional committee consideration from the 2018 Conference Committee on Corrections, the trustees' committee noted the progress of dubbing the video "A New Freedom" in French and Spanish and agreed to add it to the contents of the Corrections Kit. The committee shared that this video can be used to help inmates decide if they might be alcoholics, especially when no A.A. meetings are available in a correctional facility.

The committee also agreed to add the following items to the Corrections Kit:

- DVD and URL of the video "A New Freedom" in English, French, and Spanish.
- Postcard for the AA Grapevine book *Young and Sober*.
- Pamphlet "Experience, Strength and Hope: A.A. for Alcoholics with Mental Health Issues — and Their Sponsors" when available.

The committee also discussed an Additional Committee Consideration from the 2016 Conference Corrections committee suggesting shorter versions of the existing 30-minute video "A New Freedom." One committee member shared how the length of the existing video can compete with the time that an outside volunteer may have in a correctional facility, and the committee agreed on the need for creating varying lengths of the video, recommending that the existing 30-minute video be produced in a 15-minute and three-minute version with an estimated cost not to exceed $12,000. The committee noted that a compilation DVD could be produced that would include the three versions.

The committee discussed an Additional Committee Consideration from the 2018 Conference Committee on Corrections suggesting the creation of a checklist for local corrections committees to inform their A.A. communities of the need for volunteers to carry the message to incarcerated alcoholics in local correctional facilities. The committee noted that suggestions currently exist in the Corrections Workbook, and would welcome additional input from the Conference Committee on Corrections to clarify their suggestion to create this checklist.

The committee appreciated a report on sharing from local committees to help develop a list of frequently asked questions (FAQ) for new chairpersons starting corrections service and reviewed a draft for possible inclusion in the Corrections Kit. The committee noted that the draft included valuable sharing, and the chair appointed a subcommittee of Mark Everett (as chairperson), Carolyn Walsh and Scott Huyghebaert to review content and streamline the draft FAQ sheet. The committee heard a progress report from the subcommittee and expressed their appreciation. A revised draft is being developed by the Publishing Department and the committee looks forward to reviewing it at their July 2019 meeting.

The committee discussed items in the General Service Board Strategic Plan (updated July 2018) that are relevant to the Corrections Committee. The committee reviewed a list of training programs for corrections professionals, academies for corrections personnel, judges, chaplains, corrections organizations, etc., and provided several suggestions for additional resources. The committee also discussed the next steps in the development of a strategy for how to communicate with the different organizations, taking into consideration the General Service Board's Strategic Plan focus on inclusivity. The committee agreed to continue discussion on these items at future committee meetings.

At the January 2019 meeting staff reported that updates to "A.A. Corrections Prerelease Contact Information — For A.A.s on the Inside" (F-163) and "A.A. Corrections Prerelease Contact Information — For A.A.s on the Outside" (F-162) had been forwarded to the Publishing Department for review, editing and development. A final draft is expected to be completed for review in July 2019.

Staff also reported that the Publishing Department has engaged a consultant firm to research and recommend distribution options for e-books and audiobooks to reach consumers, academic and public libraries, and the incarcerated.

The committee agreed to forward to the 2019 Conference Committee on Corrections a request for a review of all corrections-related literature in order to make the language more modern and inclusive for their consideration.

The committee also agreed to forward to the 2019 Conference Committee on Corrections a request that the General Service Office establish and help maintain a database of Correctional Facilities in each service area in the United States and Canada and the status of meetings held therein for their consideration.

The committee reviewed a report provided by the Publishing Department regarding efforts to address requests for staple-free pamphlets for use in corrections and treatment settings. The report provided a preliminary plan to identify literature most often used in corrections and treatment settings, to review current literature distribution practices and to explore costs. The Publishing Department is researching the most feasible options for presentation to the A.A.W.S. Board. The committee suggested that the review may also include the General Service Board's Strategic Plan goal to inventory its materials and services with an eye toward inclusion and acceptance.

Christine Carpenter, Chairperson

Staff Report: The Corrections assignment is responsible for helping A.A. members and local committees carry the A.A. message to incarcerated alcoholics. One of the most gratifying aspects of the assignment is communicating with area and district Corrections, Hospitals and Institutions, and Bridging the Gap committees. As a result of their dedication, in 2018, the assignment answered over 7,000 letters from inmates, along with more than 2,500 emails and 900 phone calls from outside A.A. members involved with corrections work.

Approximately 600 pieces of mail a month arrive from inmates — many requesting free literature, others asking to participate in our Corrections Correspondence Service (C.C.S.) or for help in making contact with A.A., either by asking for a prerelease contact or for a meeting in their facility. Additionally, close to 600 requests from inmates or corrections professionals were forwarded to area corrections committee chairs.

While not everyone who writes to G.S.O. has a problem with alcohol, all letters are answered. If an incarcerated alcoholic requests free literature, he or she may be sent a Big Book, a copy of Grapevine or La Viña, and a selection of pamphlets, and often the booklet *A.A. in Prison: Inmate to Inmate*, with an explanation that the enclosed literature is made possible through the voluntary contributions of A.A. members throughout the United States and Canada. However, this assignment tries to avoid being viewed as the primary source of A.A. literature, since "carrying the A.A. message" in this way is an A.A. service opportunity for local A.A. members.

The Corrections Correspondence Service links A.A. members who are incarcerated with A.A. members on the outside so that both can share their experience, strength and hope. The C.C.S. is coordinated through G.S.O. and is intended for those who have more than six months to serve on a sentence.

Prerelease Contacts help incarcerated alcoholics get acquainted and comfortable in A.A. in the community they are being released to. They are intended to be made three to six months prior to a release date. Requests from inmates are received by G.S.O. and forwarded to the appropriate area corrections chair. In 2018, we forwarded 540 requests.

The assignment sends out a periodic activity report to each of these committee chairs with updated information or requests for shared experience. Last year included a call for male participants in the C.C.S.

G.S.O.'s website has a special section where most Corrections service material can be found, including the video "A New Freedom," along with current and past issues of the newsletter *Sharing from Behind the Walls*.

Many inmates express their gratitude for the hope found in the literature received, as well as for the many dedicated members who take the time to bring an A.A. meeting into the institution or reach out via the C.C.S.

Julio Espaillat

FINANCE AND BUDGETARY

Trustees' Report:
2018 Budget vs. 2018 Actual Results
General Service Office: At last year's Conference, we reviewed the proposed budget for 2018 and reported that the General Service Office (G.S.O.) expected a profit from operations of $501,693. There were no actions of the 68th General Service Conference that required revisions to the budget. For the year 2018, G.S.O. had net income from operations of $394,681, a decrease of $107,319. These results reflect the continued significant and gratifying Seventh Tradition contributions received from the Fellowship, which were $185,009 greater than anticipated in the budget. Additionally, gross sales of publishing activities for 2018 were $14,235,594, $235,594 more than budget. However, operating expenses were approximately $484,391 more than budget.

AA Grapevine: The 2018 Grapevine budget anticipated a net loss of $271,313. Instead, the actual results were significantly better, with the loss being $149,167. Essentially, Grapevine would have broken even, if not for severance payments of $126,303 and related legal expenses. For the year, gross profit from all publishing activities was $132,857 better than budget. Expenses for the year were approximately $21,471 more than budget.

2018 Actual Results vs. 2017 Actual Results
General Service Office: Our revenues come from only two sources: Seventh Tradition contributions from the Fellowship and profits from literature sales.

Contributions of $8,385,009, received from groups and members (including funds received from World Service Meeting countries) were $24,443 less than the $8,409,452 received during 2017. The $8,385,009 in contributions came from 28,314 groups, 5,169 individuals, and 721 service entities. Approximately 41.3% of the 68,478 groups listed with G.S.O., down from the 43.7% of the 66,860 groups listed last year, contributed Seventh Tradition contributions. The decrease in percentage is due to 905 fewer groups contributing in 2018, coupled with an increase of 1,618 groups being listed with G.S.O.

As shown in the Contributions Statistics report included in the Conference material, there were 68,478 groups, some 1,618 more than the 66,860 groups reported last year. It is important to remember, however, that the statistics we use concerning the number of groups, membership and averages are only a reflection of the information we capture on "our systems." We report to you what you report to us.

During 2018, 82,229 contributions were received, with 85% of them being received through the U.S. postal service. This compared to the 85,316 contributions in 2017,

with 87% being received through the mail.

During 2018, we processed 12,330 online contributions totaling $880,311. This represented 15.0% of the transactions processed and 10.6% of the total dollars received. The 2018 amounts compare to 11,492 contributions totaling $802,438 in 2017; 7,425 – $565,884 in 2016; 4,563 – $434,274 in 2015; 3,503 – $343,207 in 2014; 2,989 – $304,313 in 2013; 2,301 – $201,789 in 2012; 1,710 – $152,546 in 2011; and 1,063 – $86,718 in 2010, when the online system first became operational.

The recurring contribution function is an underutilized gem of A.A. Remember that individual members can set up an account to automatically charge their credit card monthly, quarterly or annually. The individual has the option to allow the member to designate his or her home group if so desired or simply designate the contribution for G.S.O.

Beginning in 2002, we commenced recording funds received on behalf of the World Service Meeting International Literature Fund as contributions to G.S.O. Total contributions of $8,385,009 received by G.S.O., reflected in our 2018 financial statements, include $75,690 received to help carry the message around the world from those participating countries. The comparisons with prior years were: 2017 – $70,055; 2016 – $62,885; 2015 – $44,800; and 2014 – $69,578.

Turning to the other major component of our income, gross sales of literature were $14,235,594, an increase of $337,044 from the prior year. During 2018, approximately 902,004 Big Books were sold, compared with 905,080 in 2017; 860,674 in 2016; 780,019 in 2015; and 1,130,500 in 2014. Not included in the 780,019 and 1,130,500 Big Books sold in 2015 and 2014 were sales of 12,749 and 177,888 copies of the 75th Anniversary Edition. The large increase in 2014 units sold and associated reduction in 2015 units sold was a result of large bulk purchases occurring in the third quarter of 2014 prior to the October 1, 2014, price increase. Printing and manufacturing costs and shipping expenses were $4,567,534 in 2018. This resulted in a gross profit from literature sales of $9,452,615, which was $91,002 greater than 2017.

Total recurring operating expenses were $19,736,206 in 2018 compared to $18,059,041. There were three significant increases in our expenses from 2017. As a point of reference, this recurring operating expense number is the expense number that is used in the calculation of the Reserve Fund Ratio. First, employee-related costs were $12,559,726 in 2018, compared to $11,439,549 in 2017. This increase is due to the filling of all open positions that arose from normal turnover and retirements in 2016 and 2017. Actual headcount was up only 1 person at year-end 2018 compared to 2017. Second, contracted services were $1,683,000, compared to $1,331,000 in 2017, due primarily to the ongoing installation of the new Enterprise Resource Planning (ERP) system. Third, the General Service Conference was held in New York City and cost $1,092,163, an increase of $322,000 over 2017 when it was held in Rye.

When the cost and expenses related to our publishing activities are subtracted from the recurring operating expense of $19,736,206, we are left with the costs associated with the services provided to the Fellowship. In 2018, the cost of services provided to the Fellowship was $11,426,835, compared to $10,222,650 in 2017. The 2018 service dollar was spent on the following activities: Group Services – 19.6% (which includes various group contact-type costs in addition to *Box 4-5-9*, A.A. Directories, records and files, contributions processing, and French and Spanish services); Public Information – 2.9%; C.P.C. – 2.6%; Treatment/Accessibilities – 1.1%; Corrections – 2.9%; Overseas Services & Loners – 4.4%; Regional Forums – 4.0%; Archives – 6.9%; General Service Conference – 9.6%; trustees' and directors' activities – 5.2%; Nominating – 2.3%; World Service Meeting – 1.8%.

Seventh Tradition contributions provided 73.4% of the support for these services and 26.6% came from the profits from literature sales. This compares with 82.3% and 17.7% in 2017.

Dividing the total contributions received of $8,385,009 by the 68,478 groups listed gives us an average of about $122.45, down from last year's $125.78, while the cost of services provided to the Fellowship of $11,426,835 amounted to approximately $166.87 (up from $152.90 last year) per group. The shortfall is $44.42 per group.

2019 G.S.O. Budget: Net sales for 2019 are budgeted at $14,775,000, up from $14,020,000 actual. The increase is due to the publication of the new book *Our Great Responsibility*. When this increase in sales is coupled with budgeted Seventh Tradition contributions being essentially equal to 2018 actual and budgeted expenses increasing 1.0%, the result is a budgeted profit of $501,221.

Reserve Fund: At December 31, 2018, the Reserve Fund balance represented approximately 9.7 months of operating expenses, compared to a 2018 budget of 9.7 months. The Reserve Fund was $15,935,331 at December 31, 2018. Recurring operating expenses were $19,736,206.

Grapevine: Gross magazine income for 2018 of $1,977,834 was $66,871 less than the prior year. Total magazine income includes the print magazine, single copies, back issues, digital magazine subscriptions, GV Online, Digital Archives Project subscriptions, the Audio Grapevine and the product of the mobile app. The average paid circulation for print magazines was 66,857 in 2018 down from 69,249 in 2017. Subscriptions for the online & mobile app magazine averaged 5,443 for 2018, compared with 6,080 for 2017.

Gross profit on the magazine of $1,321,696 was $72,259 less than 2017, but $81,201 greater than budget. Gross profit on other content activities of $562,438 were $24,696 more than 2017 actual, and $51,654 greater than budget. Total income, including interest earned, was $1,914,894, which is $36,803 less than 2017, and $143,615 greater than budget.

Costs and expenses for editorial, circulation and business, and administration were $2,064,061. Costs and expenses were $238,492 greater than 2017, and $21,471 more than budget. The Grapevine reported a loss from operations of $149,167, which was $275,295 less than

the 2017 profit of $126,128, but $122,146 better than the budgeted loss of $271,313. Grapevine would have essentially broken even in 2018 had it not had severance payments of $126,303 and related legal expenses.

Grapevine's 2019 budgeted loss of $134,559 is down from the 2018 actual loss of $149,167. This budgeted loss anticipates magazine and other content-related income of $2,065,773 ($181,639 more than the $1,884,134 realized in 2018). Operating expenses are anticipated to be $2,220,332, an increase of $156,271 over 2018 actual of $2,064,061.

Most importantly, it must be pointed out that the 2019 budget is prepared on a different basis from prior year budgets. In prior years, the projections of magazine circulation and revenue were prepared by our third-party circulation consultant, considering only the natural decay rate of magazine renewals. These numbers were not adjusted for any efforts by GV to generate new subscriptions through programs such as "Carry the Message." The 2019 budget has been adjusted to include an additional add-on of 5% to 6% to reflect the anticipated positive impacts of various staff changes and the initiatives being planned in 2019 to increase circulation. The positive additional net subscription revenue of these actions is $91,000.

La Viña: La Viña is the Spanish-language magazine approved by the 1995 General Service Conference. The magazine had a 2018 average circulation of 9,635. This compares with a 2017 average circulation of 9,996; 2016 average circulation of 10,374; a 2015 average of 10,355; and a 2014 average of 10,380.

During 2018, subscription income was $120,520 and direct costs of publishing were $55,177, resulting in a $65,343 gross profit. La Viña also realized approximately $15,392 from the sales of other items, net of costs. Operating expenses associated with these publication activities were $229,202. These include editorial, circulation and administrative costs. The difference of shortfall net between revenues earned from publishing activities versus the costs to produce and distribute was $148,467.

This shortfall of $148,467 is covered by the General Fund of the General Service Board as a service activity to the Fellowship. The 2018 shortfall compares with the 2017 shortfall of $126,440; the 2016 shortfall of $152,082; the 2015 shortfall of $146,377; the 2014 shortfall of $132,026; and the 2013 shortfall of $142,544.

For 2019, the shortfall is budgeted to be approximately $165,838 ($17,371 greater than 2018), with circulation anticipated to be at approximately the same level.

Other Items

A.A.W.S. Self-Support report 2018: The trustees' Finance Committee heard various reports from A.A.W.S. on their self-support efforts during the year. A recurring item was the need to continually remind both groups and individual members of the availability of the online contribution system, in particular that it allows users to make repetitive contributions automatically.

Other Actions:

The trustees' Finance Committee forwarded the Conference Finance Committee's Additional Considerations to A.A.W.S. Set forth below is the detailed report of the A.A.W.S. Ad Hoc Committee on Self-Support.

Add language regarding group-level electronic contributions and passing the "virtual" basket to the section Passing the Basket in the service piece "The A.A. Group Treasurer" and also include such language in the pamphlet "Self-Support: Where Money and Spirituality Mix" and the Guidelines on Finance.

A recommendation was made and passed at the A.A.W.S. Finance Committee Meeting in March to add the following text to the service pamphlet "The A.A. Group Treasurer":

A number of groups have utilized digital payment platforms to provide opportunities for members to make cashless contributions. There are different payment platforms to facilitate this service and it is up to the group to determine which one to use. Experience suggests that the treasurer is a likely choice to handle digital contributions, though some groups add more than one trusted servant to share the responsibilities or create a new service position to inform the group about digital payment options and assist other group members who are interested in contributing this way.

A recommendation was made and passed at the A.A.W.S. Finance Committee Meeting in March to add the following text to the Finance Guidelines:

Question: Some members of our group want to pass a "virtual" basket — to collect Seventh Tradition contributions digitally. How could we do this?

Answer: A number of groups have utilized digital payment platforms as an adjunct to passing the basket in the conventional sense in order to provide opportunities for cashless contributions. There are different payment platforms (such as Venmo, PayPal or others) to facilitate this service, and it is up to the group to determine which one to use. After experimentation with different methodologies, some groups have found that a smartphone app-based payment platform is the most efficient, seamless and minimally disruptive solution for providing a digital contribution. Experience suggests that the treasurer is a likely choice to handle digital contributions, though some groups add more than one trusted servant to share the responsibilities or create a new service position to inform the group about digital payment options and assist other group members who are interested in contributing this way.

A recommendation was made and passed at the A.A.W.S. Finance Committee Meeting in March to send the following draft text to the Conference Finance Committee for the pamphlet "Self-Support: Where Money and Spirituality Mix":

Question: Some members of our group want to pass a "virtual" basket — to collect Seventh Tradition contributions digitally. How could we do this?

Answer: A number of groups have utilized digital payment platforms as an adjunct to passing the basket in the conventional sense in order to provide opportunities for cashless contributions. There are different payment platforms to facilitate this service and it is up to the group to determine which one to use. Some groups have found that a smartphone app-based payment platform is the most efficient, seamless and minimally disruptive solution for providing a digital contribution. Experience suggests that the treasurer is a likely choice to handle digital contributions, though some groups add more than one trusted servant to share the responsibilities or create a new service position to inform the group about digital payment options and assist other group members who are interested in contributing this way.

A memo from the Self-Support Committee was sent to the A.A.W.S. Publishing Department on August 30, 2018, to act on the following Additional Considerations:

- Update illustrative material on the Seventh Tradition Fact Sheet (F-203) to reflect current pamphlet covers and website.

- The Publishing Department has implemented this additional consideration and there is an updated F-203 in print and on the website.

- Update birthday contribution envelopes per member per year statistics.

- Following evaluations from the Publishing Department, it was determined that this was not a cost-effective element since this number changes every year.

- The pamphlets "Self-Support: Where Money and Spirituality Mix" and "The A.A. Group Treasurer" be consistent in print and revision coding on the back.

The Publishing Department reviewed this consideration and the difference has to do with different vendors placing the revision code in different areas. If it is not in the back of the pamphlet, it's in the inside cover of the pamphlet.

The committee discussed developing a method to standardize increases to the limits on individual contributions and bequests to the General Service Board and felt that the consumer price index fluctuates by such small proportions that a change would be costly and not conducive to the Fellowship and took no action.

The Conference Finance Committee also requested the following with regard to AA Grapevine:

- That there be a greater online presence — The ad hoc subcommittee sent a memo to the chair of the T.C.S. committee requesting that as A.A.W.S. redesigns the website, consideration be made to add a statement on the contribution page about the Grapevine as well as a link to the Grapevine page.

- That a fact sheet on the topic of Grapevine be included in the Self-Support Packet — The Grapevine Board is currently working on a draft of the Fact Sheet which will be reviewed at their next board meeting.

- That the General Service Board make available issues of Grapevine for distribution purposes through G.S.O. staff assignments — A.A.W.S. had previously allocated $6,000 for distributing Grapevine issues through service desks.

The committee requested that when A.A.W.S. develops an A.A. app that self-support information be easily accessible. The committee also discussed having access to assignment folders containing literature relevant to the services — The ad hoc subcommittee sent a memo to the chair of the T.C.S. committee requesting that G.S.O. consider research on how A.A. might utilize an app to further increase carrying the message of recovery and self-support, and that when A.A.W.S. develops an A.A. app self-support information be easily accessible.

Two items from the 2017 Conference Finance Committee Additional Considerations are on hold while the new ERP system is being implemented:

- The committee requested that the trustees' Finance Committee consider utilizing the Fellowship New Vision database to provide regular communication to the Fellowship about the spiritual message of Seventh Tradition contributions and the role they play in carrying A.A.'s message, being certain not to convey a solicitation of funds.

- The committee requested that the General Service Office (G.S.O.) consider adding the recurring contributions information to the area quarterly contributions report.

David Morris, Chairperson

GENERAL SHARING SESSION

Trustees' Report: Since the 68th General Service Conference, the General Service Board has held three General Sharing Sessions. In July 2018, the topic was "Love and Tolerance of Others Is Our Code — Philosophy or Practice?" Regional trustee Kathi Fowler presented on the subtopic "Making the Doors Wider in A.A." and G.S.O. staff member Clement Cann presented on the subtopic "Are We Inclusive?"

During the October 2018 board weekend, the sharing session topic was "Rigidity in Alcoholics Anonymous: Our Greatest Danger." G.S.O. staff member Jeff Wine presented on the subtopic "The Essentials of Recovery — Honesty, Willingness and Open-mindedness" and General Service trustee Beau Bush shared on the subtopic "Is Our A.A. Service Manual, like the Big Book, Meant to Be Suggestive Only?"

In January 2019, the sharing session topic was "Social Media — the Colossus of 21st Century Communication." Class A trustee Peter Luongo presented on the subtopic "Unity and Social Media" and G.S.O. staff member Sandra Wilson presented on the subtopic "Anonymity and Social Media."

Complete copies of these presentations are available and may be requested from the staff coordinator at G.S.O.

Newton Pritchett, Chairperson

GRAPEVINE

Office Report: Since the last Conference, AA Grapevine, Inc. has produced 12 issues of Grapevine; six issues of La Viña; two new books and e-books, *AA in the Military* (a collection of stories by members who are serving or who have served in the military) and *One Big Tent* (stories of experience, strength and hope from atheist and agnostic A.A. members); an annual wall calendar; and a pocket planner.

AA Grapevine initiated a Fellowship-wide "Subscription Challenge" for Grapevine in 2018 to encourage members, groups and areas to help support Grapevine. Two states,

A cold wife

I just got off the phone with a friend who lives in North Dakota. She said that since early this morning the snow has been nearly waist-high, and it's still falling. The temperature is 32 below zero, and the north wind is increasing to near gale force. Her husband has done nothing but look through the kitchen window and just stare. She says if it gets much worse, she may have to let the drunken bum in.

—Dick S., Shrewsbury, PA, from Take Me to Your Sponsor

provinces or territories will be recognized: the ones with a) the highest percentage growth in new subscriptions, and b) the greatest increase in new subscriptions overall. Grapevine posted a resource page on its website (www.aagrapevine.org/grapevine-challenge) to help the Fellowship view the progress of the challenge. The winners will be featured in a special section in an issue of Grapevine in 2019.

A Grapevine subscription app was introduced to the Fellowship in 2017. The first phase was for iOS, followed by Android, Microsoft 10 and Amazon Kindle Fire. This year, AAGV, Inc. began working with a new app vendor. Our new platform provides a seamless user interface with more links that allow the reader to navigate anywhere within the magazine from within the table of contents. It also features a new "Audio TOC," which can access all the audio stories from that month's issue by simply clicking on the title.

The AA Grapevine website continued to expand and in 2018 received an average of 32,830 unique visitors each month. In 2018, the Archive team started tagging the Spanish-language stories of La Viña. The tagging process for the GV Story Archive continues to improve the search process. AAGV, Inc. has started its web migration project to Drupal 8, which will make it a more user-friendly, responsive, flexible and integrable platform. AAGV, Inc. started working in coordination with Stikky Media not only to improve the website's traffic and ranking but to also bring prequalified visitors and convert them into lifetime customers.

In 2018, La Viña continued its audience-building effort using short message service (SMS, also referred to as "text"). The community now comprises 2,327 active members. Also in 2018, La Viña received written personal stories submitted from an average of eight to ten story-writing workshops each month. In July 2018 LV initiated the LV Digital Story Archive project, the first archive of Spanish-language recovery stories. Expected completion of LV Digital Story Archive is April 2019.

In 2018, AA Grapevine developed a YouTube channel, which is still in its early stages. Currently, it holds the A.A.W.S. video "Doors," a video produced from a Grapevine Audio Project submission, and several other in-house videos. Grapevine is currently working on ideas to increase the content on their new channel, which will include explainer videos.

In 2018, Grapevine and La Viña magazines continued the Carry the Message project in an effort to inform members and groups about an option to purchase subscription gift certificates for area chairs or local committees to distribute to members in need. Throughout the year, AAGV, Inc. has collaborated with G.S.O.'s Corrections desk to fulfill 176 sponsored Carry the Message subscriptions for inmates.

This year, AA Grapevine continued to produce the Grapevine/La Viña visitor's info packet for all visitors to the G.S.O. office. In 2018, in an effort to increase GV/LV awareness and visibility, Grapevine, Inc. hired an outreach coordinator to develop processes to increase awareness and visibility of GV and LV to the Fellowship.

In 2018, Grapevine and La Viña staff participated in events across the U.S. and Canada, including several locations to celebrate La Viña's annual anniversary and the International Conference of Secular A.A.

Jon Witherspoon, Senior Editor

GROUP SERVICES

Staff Report: To assist groups across the U.S. and Canada, G.S.O. develops service material based on an indicated need, sharing information and experience not found in Conference-approved literature. A seven-page list describes the service items. Examples of service material include: Group Handbooks; G.S.R. and D.C.M. Kits; A.A. Guidelines; Referral List of "Fellowships Similar to A.A."; "Is Your Group Linked to A.A. as a Whole?"; and "Anonymity Online."

Service material is available upon request and differs from Conference-approved literature in that it has not come about through Conference Advisory Action. It is produced when there is an expressed need for readily available information on a specific subject or in a specific format. Service material reflects A.A. group experience as well as specific and timely information that is subject to change.

The group services coordinator:

- Acts as G.S.O.'s liaison to approximately 478 central and intergroup offices in the U.S. and Canada, and coordinates the participation of A.A.W.S. at the annual intergroup/central office seminar, serving on the seminar's Policy and Site-Selection Committees;

- Supervises the updating of G.S.O.'s available service material upon request, and in Spanish and French, whenever possible;

- Serves as a resource to the Publishing Department regarding updating of *The A.A. Service Manual*;

- Collaborates with the special projects manager regarding the three regional A.A. Directories (Canadian, Eastern U.S. and Western U.S.), G.S.O.'s group and service committee records, and intergroup and central office records and lists;

- Serves as secretary to the Conference Committee on Report and Charter;

- As of the 2018 rotation, the group services coordinator serves as liaison to other Twelve Step Fellowships and to Special International Contacts.

Jeff Wine

INTERNATIONAL

Trustees' Report: The trustees' International Committee is responsible for suggesting policies and actions to assure that the A.A. message is available around the world, especially in areas where there is no established service structure. The committee provides shared experience, supports translations of A.A. literature in other languages, and encourages the expansion of regional or Zonal Meetings. The committee is the primary link between the international A.A. community and the U.S./Canada General Service Board of Trustees.

The 2019 Literature Assistance budget of $40,000 will allow A.A. World Services to translate and publish a variety of foreign-language books, pamphlets and reprints. A portion of this expense will be drawn from the International Literature Fund, representing contributions from A.A. groups and structures around the world. A.A.W.S. holds the copyrights on all foreign-language versions of our Conference-approved material and issues licensing agreements for publication and distribution, as requested, to those countries that have an established general service board. When necessary, we translate and publish the material, subject to scheduling by the Publishing Department and approval of the A.A.W.S. Board. The Big Book is currently available in 71 languages, and other literature is available in approximately 106 languages.

World Service Meeting — The 25th World Service Meeting (WSM) was held October 7–11, 2018, in Durban, South Africa, with the theme "Our Twelve Traditions: A.A.'s Future in the Modern World." In attendance were 72 delegates representing 45 countries or linguistic zones, including two countries attending for the first time, Bolivia and Turkey. Representing our General Service Board was first-term delegate Newton Pritchett, trustee-at-large/U.S.,

and second-term delegate Scott Huyghebaert, trustee-at-large/Canada. G.S.O. general manager Greg Tobin and General Service Board of South Africa chair Frank Vandrau presided over the five-day meeting. Staff member Mary Cumings served as WSM coordinator; and staff members Clement Cann, Eva Sanchez and Sandra Wilson acted as committee secretaries. The committee acknowledged with appreciation the extensive work done by the World Service Meeting coordinator Mary Cumings and staff assistant Ayleen Martinez.

It was reported that the World Service Meeting established a World Service Meeting Fund as a way for countries to provide financial assistance to countries that request funding and to support the World Service Meeting. The World Service Meeting Fund will be maintained and administered by A.A. World Services under the purview of the WSM Policy/Admissions/Finance Committee.

The committee noted that the 25th World Service Meeting committee on Policy/Admissions/Finance did not recommend a change to the WSM delegate fee, which is currently set at $1,500 U.S. It was reported that some countries expressed their appreciation for the opportunity to contribute financial support to allow other WSM countries to attend the meeting.

The anonymity-protected digital version of the 25th WSM *Final Report* was posted on www.aa.org in March. The WSM has a significant impact on the unity of A.A. and the effectiveness of our Twelfth Step efforts. The 26th WSM will be held in 2020 in Rye Brook, New York. The committee recommended to the General Service Board that delegates to the Twenty-Sixth World Service Meeting be invited to attend the October 31–November 2, 2020 Board Weekend as guests of the General Service Board of U.S./Canada.

International Trips – The General Service Board and General Service Office respond to many invitations from other countries to attend events including conventions, anniversary celebrations, conferences, board meetings, office visits and service assemblies. Since last year's General Service Conference, trustees and staff members visited Argentina, Czech Republic, Cuba, Germany and Mexico. They also attended the 70th anniversary of A.A. in Finland and the 30th anniversaries of A.A. in Hungary, Latvia and Lithuania. In November, Class A trustee Peter Luongo, trustee-at-large Scott Huyghebaert and G.S.O. staff member Julio Espaillat attended a medical conference hosted by Cuba's Ministry of Health. Tentative international travel for 2019 includes Russia's 31st General Service Conference, Honduras's 47th Conference, Peru's 30th General Service Conference, the 45th Anniversary Convention of A.A. Poland, the 30th Anniversary of A.A. Slovenia and the Zonal Meetings (Asia-Oceania Service Meeting, European Service Meeting, Sub-Saharan Africa Service Meeting and the Meeting of the Americas).

International A.A. Data Map — The committee reviewed the International A.A. Data Map and PowerPoint presentation and approved the International A.A. Data Map. The committee also reviewed the plan for Phase II of the International A.A. Data Map. Noting that FNV is currently the data source for the Data Map and will be replaced by the ERP system, the committee agreed to move forward with Phase II to post the International A.A. Data Map presentation slides (static slides) on aa.org. Prior to posting the slides on the website's "A.A. Around the World" page and on the WSM dashboard, updates will be made to the slides and Publishing will develop accompanying narrative to provide context. The slides will be made available as service material in PDF format on aa.org and the WSM dashboard. The goal of Phase III is to make the International A.A. Data Map available in a live interactive format on the "A.A. Around the World" page on aa.org. Implementation process and timing will be determined by two major related projects: full implementation of the ERP system and the development of the new aa.org website.

Service Material — The committee reviewed and approved the revised "Country-to-Country Sponsorship: Carrying the Message Worldwide" and "International Literature Fund" service material that has been added to aa.org.

The committee reviewed and accepted their preliminary 2019 budget and forwarded it to the trustees' Finance and Budgetary Committee.

The committee discussed the General Service Board Strategic Plan and Process 4.1: "The G.S.B. will develop a plan to embrace more direct sponsorship of other countries, will explore ways to strengthen our relationships with other service structures and ways to make the World Service Meeting more efficient and effective." The committee agreed on exploring ways of linking our Class A trustee professionals (U.S./Canada) with Class As who serve on A.A. general service boards in other countries to exchange experience. The committee noted that the G.S.B. (U.S./Canada) welcomes requests from other countries to attend our General Service Conference (in accordance with our Conference policy/procedures on guest observers). The committee will continue discussion on this agenda item.

We continue to be encouraged and inspired by the international A.A. community and general service boards and offices in other countries, who carry the A.A. message to countless thousands in new regions and across difficult linguistic, cultural and economic barriers.

Scott Huyghebaert, Chairperson

Staff Report: The International desk receives correspondence from groups, individual A.A.s and professionals interested in obtaining information about A.A. in countries outside of the U.S. and Canada. Additionally, the staff member corresponds with 63 international general service offices and/or literature distribution centers.

Correspondence arrives at the International desk in many languages and is answered in the appropriate language, often accompanied by A.A. literature. In order to accomplish this, the staff member on the assignment is assisted by a bilingual (English-Spanish) assistant and outside professional translation services. Where there is a nearby office, we provide that contact information. We emphasize our trust in the fact that these members can maintain sobriety, help others and become independent in their own countries.

The International staff member benefits from the experience of G.S.O. staff, cooperation with the Publishing Department and the support of the trustees' International Committee, which he or she serves as secretary.

Other responsibilities on the assignment are:

- Serving as coordinator for the biennial World Service Meeting (WSM) and maintaining contact with WSM delegates and their offices throughout the year;

- Maintaining close communications with our Publishing Department on requests for new translations of literature and the beginnings of new general service or information offices that may be able to distribute literature to local members and groups;

- Each year, A.A. World Services, Inc. receives requests to translate our literature into foreign languages. The Big Book has now been translated into 70 languages, and additional translations are in progress. Primary in consideration of each request is the need to ensure the integrity and authenticity of A.A.'s message. To that end, the Publishing Department has the responsibility of having each translation checked against the English original. In countries where there is a general service board licensed to publish or distribute A.A. literature, an approved translation is often financed and published there. Where a stable A.A. structure is not yet present, the A.A.W.S. Board undertakes the new publication when funds are available;

- Handling communications related to overseas travel, including the Trip Consultation Team, which considers international invitations, and attendance at Zonal Service Meetings. Our trustees-at-large (U.S. and Canada) are delegates to the Meeting of the Americas (REDELA). Other Zonal Meetings include the Asia-Oceania, European, and Sub-Saharan Africa Service Meetings.

- Working closely with our Records Department to ensure that our International A.A. Directory (for countries outside of the U.S. and Canada), which is published annually, contains updated contact information for G.S.O.s, central and intergroup offices, groups, and foreign contacts around the world.

Eva Sanchez

INTERNATIONAL CONVENTIONS/ A.A. REGIONAL FORUMS

Trustees' Report:
International Conventions — Since the 2018 General Service Conference, the committee has met three times.

The purpose of the trustees' committee as it relates to International Conventions is to work on plans for each forthcoming International Convention. The objectives of the International Convention are:

- To provide opportunities for a rededication of attendees to the primary purpose of A.A.

- To enable attendees to witness the success and growth of the A.A. program around the world.

• To let the world know that A.A. is alive, flourishing and available as a community resource, locally and internationally.

The committee acts and makes recommendations to fulfill the broad purposes of the General Service Board, as those purposes relate to the strengthening of the Fellowship and the advancement of its message, through well-planned International Conventions. The detailed work inherent in putting on the Convention is executed by the Convention coordinator and a professional Convention Consultant.

Following the 2018 General Service Conference recommendation that Indianapolis, Indiana, and St. Louis, Missouri, be considered as possible sites for the International Convention in 2030, a site inspection team visited the two cities in the summer of 2018. Based on the recommendation of the site inspection team, the trustees' Committee on Regional Forums/International Conventions recommended to the General Service Board that St. Louis, Missouri, be the site of the 2030 Alcoholics Anonymous International Convention.

At their July 2018 meeting, the committee reviewed and accepted the 2018 third quarter financial report from the A.A.W.S. Finance Committee, including information on contracts and activities for the 2020 International Convention.

Also at the July 2018 meeting, publishing director David Rosen provided a general description of the 2020 International Convention souvenir book that will be published in English, French and Spanish. The content would include a visual history of A.A. and more.

The committee reviewed the General Service Board policy on discounts and subsidies that has been in effect since it was adopted in 1989, and noted that as contracting for facilities and services for the 2020 International Convention moves forward, this is the policy that will be followed. This policy reads, "Whenever a discount or subsidy is that which would be offered to any other organization of similar size requiring a purchased service or product of similar character and magnitude, for example, convention rates at hotels, it may be accepted. Whenever a discount or subsidy is partly or in total offered because we are Alcoholics Anonymous, it must be declined."

In July the committee reviewed the general guidelines that the Volunteer Committee used at the 2015 Convention in Atlanta, noting the vital role that the committee plays in the success of the Convention. At the October meeting the committee recommended to the General Service Board that Carlyle Wimberly serve as the local Volunteer Welcome Committee chair for the 2020 International Convention.

Also in October, the committee reviewed and accepted the quarterly financial update through September 2018 from the A.A.W.S. Finance Committee regarding contracts and activities for the 2020 International Convention.

The committee reviewed and accepted proposed revisions to the site selection guidelines for the 2035 International Convention. The committee noted that the revisions expanding the bidding timeline to include the full

month of July may increase the number of cities able to participate in the bidding process for 2035.

The committee discussed attendance at A.A. International Conventions and agreed on the importance of early communications and of engaging the A.A. Fellowship. The committee agreed on the benefits of continued discussions of different options that could increase participation at future international conventions.

At the January 2019 meeting the committee reviewed and accepted the quarterly financial update through December 2018 from the A.A.W.S. Finance Committee regarding contracts and activities for the 2020 International Convention.

The committee reviewed the 2020 International Convention budget and held a discussion about setting a registration fee for the 2020 International Convention that takes into consideration a realistic budget, the committee's responsibilities relevant to International Conventions, and the spirit of self-support. The committee recommended to the General Service Board that the 2020 International Convention Advanced Registration fee be $115.00 (USD) per attendee and that the Registration after April 15, 2020 be $140.00 (USD) per attendee.

The committee reviewed and accepted the tentative program titles for the 2020 International Convention and also reviewed a sample of the 2020 International Convention stationery, noting that the stationery will be used by the General Service Office beginning in March 2019.

The committee agreed to forward to the 2019 Conference

Committee on International Conventions/Regional Forums discussion of an anonymity-protected photo of the flag ceremony to be taken at the 2020 International Convention.

The committee discussed background regarding the 2005, 2010 and 2015 broadcast of an anonymity-protected, delayed Internet broadcast of the Convention Flag Ceremony. The committee agreed to forward to the 2019 Conference Committee on International Conventions/Regional Forums the discussion of an anonymity-protected, delayed Internet broadcast of the Convention Flag Ceremony for the 2020 International Convention. The committee also suggested the Conference Committee on International Conventions/Regional Forums consider the production of anonymity-protected videos of other highlights of the convention as a way of sharing the spirit and enthusiasm of the 2020 International Convention with A.A. members.

Additionally, the committee suggested exploring the use of the videos of past International Convention flag ceremonies on aa.org, as a sampler of what you will see at the 2020 International Convention in Detroit. The committee requested that a report on the feasibility of making the videos available be brought to the July 2019 meeting of the committee for consideration.

Regional Forums — Since the 2018 General Service Conference, Regional Forums have been held in the Western Canada, Eastern Canada, Pacific and Southeast Regions; and one local forum was held in Area 08 San Diego Imperial, CA. Almost 2,100 members attended Regional Forums, including over 1,300 first-time attendees. General Service Board participants at the 2018 Forums included 15 trustees, two AA Grapevine directors, two A.A. World Services directors, 10 employees of the General Service Office, and 10 special workers from G.S.O. and Grapevine.

Each Forum was viewed as an opportunity to exchange information among trusted servants, staff and members for the opportunity to relate services to experience, strength and hope, as well as challenges and successes of A.A. members on the frontlines of carrying A.A.'s message to the still-suffering alcoholic. Notable events included a writing workshop at the Pacific Regional Forum providing Spanish-speaking women the opportunity to write and submit their stories to be considered for the pamphlet for Spanish-speaking women alcoholics currently under development, and at the Southeast Regional Forum, a workshop entitled "Who's Not in the Room?" — along with three presentations — sparked meaningful discussions and new ideas on fostering participation in A.A.

The committee reviewed and accepted the Regional/Local Forums Schedule for 2018–2020 Forums. The committee reviewed and accepted the General Service Board participation schedule for 2019 Regional Forums with changes to reflect rotation after the 2019 General Service Conference. The committee also recommended to the General Service Board that the request for a Local Forum in 2019, to be hosted by Area 05 Southern California, be approved.

The following Regional Forums are scheduled for 2019:

2018		
Northeast	May 31–June 2	Tarrytown, NY
East Central	July 12–14	Detroit, MI
West Central	August 16–18	Grand Forks, ND
Southwest	October 11–13	Houston, TX

The committee reviewed and accepted the summaries of the evaluation questionnaires for the 2018 Western Canada, Eastern Canada and Pacific Regional Forums. The questionnaires along with a summary of remarks have been included as background for the 2019 Conference Committee on International Conventions/Regional Forums.

The committee reviewed a progress report regarding the production of an anonymity-protected video of a virtual forum and looks forward to updates as the project continues.

The committee reviewed the Special Forums Information Packet and Timeline. The committee suggested collecting "shared experience" reflecting different approaches to Special Forums (e.g., remote communities) and adding such information to the packet. The committee also discussed the importance of "getting the word out," suggesting that the A.A.W.S. app may be useful, in addition to encouraging area delegates to disseminate information regarding Special Forums.

The committee recommended that the General Service Board include a line item in the trustees' IC/RF Committee budget for 2019 to accommodate an expense of up to $10,000 to give free AA Grapevine Complete subscriptions to the first 50 first-time Forum attendees at each of the four Regional Forums in 2019.

The committee discussed relevant items in the General Service Board Strategic Plan (updated July 2018). The chair appointed a subcommittee charged with inventorying all Regional Forum and International Convention materials to ensure the inclusive nature of the Third Tradition is reflected in all communications related to Regional Forums and International Conventions. It was requested that the subcommittee prepare a report for the July 2019 trustees' committee meeting.

Leslie Backus, Chairperson

Staff Reports:
International Convention — The International Convention assignment entails coordinating every aspect of the processes and plans involved in producing the A.A. International Convention, held every five years. Working with four committees — Trustees, Conference, G.S.O. Planning and Welcome — the International Convention coordinator is responsible for making sure that the Convention comes together as a wonderful opportunity for A.A. members to celebrate gratitude and sobriety. In addition, the International Convention coordinator and alternate coordinated the A.A. meetings held during

Al-Anon's International Convention over the July 4, 2018, weekend in Baltimore, Maryland.

Plans proceed for the 2020 International Convention, which will be held July 2–5, 2020, in Detroit, Michigan. The Convention theme, chosen from suggestions sent in by the Fellowship, is "Love and Tolerance Is Our Code."

Throughout the Convention week, more than 4,000 local A.A.s coordinated by the Detroit Welcome Committee will greet visitors from around the world. The Convention will kick off with a "Party in the Park," with dances and celebrations flowing from Hart Plaza to the Cobo Center and back out to the Hart Plaza.

During the day on Friday and Saturday, the Convention Center will be packed with workshops, panels, regional meetings, topic meetings and marathons. Approximately 750 speakers will participate in over 200 meetings. Friday night, Saturday night and Sunday morning all attendees will come together for the Big Meetings in the Ford Field stadium, a comfortable walk from the Convention Center.

The traditional flag ceremony of nations in attendance will take place at the Friday night meeting in the stadium, and on Saturday night oldtimers chosen from the hat will share about their years of experience, strength and hope in Alcoholics Anonymous.

Information about the Convention is available on G.S.O.'s website and will be updated as additional information becomes available. Registration and housing information will be mailed to groups and trusted servants around the world by August 2019. Registration will open in September, both online and on paper. Excitement is building as this 85th Anniversary celebratory event draws near!

Julio Espaillat

Regional Forums: The staff member serving the Regional Forums assignment assists with the coordination of content and programming that make up Regional Forums, Local Forums and Special Forums held in the U.S. and Canada. Forum weekends foster wider communication and understanding among A.A. groups, members and trusted servants in a region, the General Service Board, A.A. World Services, Inc., AA Grapevine Corporate Board, and AA Grapevine and General Service Office staff.

Upon the invitation of each region, the General Service Board holds Regional Forums in each region every two years. The locations for Regional Forums are decided upon by each region and host area along with G.S.O.

The Regional Forums staff member coordinates with Forum programming, literature displays, newsletters and final reports. Presentation and workshop topics are suggested by attendees and decided upon jointly by area delegates, G.S.O. staff and the regional trustee. Production of the annual Regional Forum flyers as well as distribution of individual Forum registration forms to trusted servants in each region is handled by the staff member. Additionally, the staff member works closely with the Welcome Contact of each Forum, who is responsible for the coordination of local volunteers to assist during Regional Forum weekends.

While "Additional" Forums were discontinued by the General Service Board as of 2016, Local Forums have continued since 2006, with nine being held to date. The General Service Board continues to encourage regions to support Local Forums, which are structured to meet cultural, accessibility and population considerations within their own A.A. communities. The trustees' Committee on International Conventions/Regional Forums continues annually to approve, at its July meeting, travel of up to two members of the General Service Board and directors of the A.A.W.S. or AA Grapevine Boards or the G.S.O. or Grapevine staff at up to four Local Forums per year.

The General Service Board agreed in 2017 to re-implement Special Forums. Special Forms are designed for remote, sparsely populated or urban areas to serve A.A. members who would not normally be able to attend a Regional Forum as well as when there is an expressed need based on culture, language or geography. Implementation will commence in 2022.

The staff member on the A.A. Regional Forums assignment serves as co-secretary to the trustees' and Conference International Conventions/Regional Forums Committees.

Sandra Wilson

LITERATURE

Trustees' Report: This report offers a summary of the literature projects of the trustees' Committee on Literature since the 2018 General Service Conference.

Projects resulting from 2018 Advisory Actions and Additional Committee Considerations of the General Service Conference:

Completed Projects

The following pamphlets were finalized and made available:

- "Experience, Strength and Hope: Women in A.A. (formerly "A.A. for the Woman")
- "Experience, Strength and Hope: LGBTQ Alcoholics in A.A." (formerly "A.A. and the Gay/Lesbian Alcoholic")
- "Experience, Strength and Hope: A.A. for Alcoholics with Mental Health Issues — and Their Sponsors."
- "Inside A.A.: Understanding the Fellowship and Its Services."
- "G.S.R. General Service Representative: Your Group's Link to A.A. as a Whole." (formerly "G.S.R. General Service Representative: May Be the Most Important Job in A.A.)

The following pamphlet was adopted by A.A.W.S., Inc., finalized and made available:

- "The 'God' Word: Agnostic and Atheist Members in A.A."

The revision to add text (originally included in the 1998 edition of Living Sober*) to the section titled "Note to Medical Professionals" has been implemented in:*

- *Living Sober*

Additionally, the following items were addressed:

- G.S.O.'s Publishing Department is implementing the request to add AA Grapevine literature to the list of A.A. publications noted on the back page of A.A. literature, as additional resources, when appropriate.

- General Service Board Strategic Plan (updated July 2018) — The committee reviewed and discussed the vice chair's progress report on aspects of the General Service Board Strategic Plan relevant to the trustee's Literature Committee. The committee noted that "an inventory of materials and services with an eye for inclusion and acceptance" included in the Strategic Plan may be covered in the Conference Committee on Literature item to review recovery literature. Discussions to "review A.A. literature for targeted audiences" and to "discuss a plan for reviewing literature" will continue at the July 2019 meeting.

- Consider "translating the Big Book, *Alcoholics Anonymous,* into plain language — at a fifth grade or similar reading level" — The committee reviewed and tabled the request for "translating the Big Book, Alcoholics Anonymous into plain language — at a fifth grade or similar reading level." The committee suggested that the General Service Board form a committee to gather information covering a variety of perspectives related to accessibility and other pertinent issues in order to fully evaluate the request. The committee will continue discussions at the July 2019 meeting.

- Consider creating an individualized workbook to accompany *Alcoholics Anonymous* — The committee reviewed and tabled a request to create an individualized workbook to accompany the Big Book, *Alcoholics Anonymous.* The committee suggested that this item also be considered by the proposed General Service Board committee asked to evaluate the request for "translating the Big Book, *Alcoholics Anonymous,* into plain language — at a fifth grade or similar reading level." The committee will continue discussions at the July 2019 meeting.

- Consider the development of a contemporary and comprehensive new workbook to study the Twelve Steps, Traditions and Concepts — The committee considered and tabled a request to develop a contemporary and comprehensive new workbook to study the Twelve Steps, Traditions and Concepts. The committee requested the staff secretary provide the Al-Anon workbook "Reaching for Personal Freedom" as background for the July 2019 trustees' Literature Committee meeting.

Progress reports regarding the following projects were submitted to the 2019 Conference Committee on Literature:

- Update to the pamphlet "Too Young?"
- Update to the pamphlet "Young People and A.A."
- Update to the pamphlet "The Twelve Traditions Illustrated"
- Update regarding language on safety and A.A. to be included in *Living Sober* and "Questions and Answers on Sponsorship"
- Update to the video "Your General Service Office, the Grapevine and the General Service Structure"
- The pamphlet for Spanish-speaking women in A.A.
- The pamphlet based on A.A.'s Three Legacies

Additional Items reviewed, discussed and forwarded to the 2019 Conference Committee on Literature:

- Consider requests to develop a Fifth Edition of the book *Alcoholics Anonymous.*
- Consider the development of a Literature Committee Workbook.
- Review progress report on the update regarding language on anonymity in the pamphlet "Questions and Answers on Sponsorship."
- Consider revising the pamphlet "The A.A. Group."
- Consider revising the foreword to the book *Twelve Steps and Twelve Traditions.*
- Consider suggestion to add "Nonalcoholics may attend open meetings as observers" to the end of the open meeting side of the Primary Purpose (blue) card.
- Review proposed revision to A.A. World Services "Policy on Publication of Literature: Updating Pamphlets and Other A.A. Materials."
- Review matrix of A.A. recovery literature.

No Action Items:

At their quarterly meetings the committee thoroughly discussed and took no action on the following items:

- Request for revision of Chapter 29 in *Living Sober*. The committee discussed a proposal to add a paragraph

to Chapter 29 in *Living Sober* "extolling the positive experience of participation in general service meetings (including business/group conscience meetings)" and took no action. The committee agreed that there is no widely expressed need from the Fellowship to revise *Living Sober* as proposed, and that the "positive experience of participation in general services meetings" may be best addressed in the new pamphlet on the Three Legacies, currently under development.

- Request for service material outlining what "A.A. does not do." The committee discussed a request for a service item that "lists the items from the pamphlet 'The A.A. Group' outlining the things that A.A. does not do in poster form" and took no action. The committee agreed that "what A.A. does not do" is adequately addressed in current literature (e.g., the pamphlet "The A.A. Group" and flyer "Information on A.A.") and that there is no widely expressed need from the Fellowship to provide the information in additional formats.

- Consider creating a pamphlet to help A.A. members and groups apply the Twelve Concepts for World Service at the group level. The committee considered a request to create a pamphlet to help members and groups apply the Twelve Concepts for World Service at the group level and took no action. The committee agreed that there was not a widely expressed need in the Fellowship.

- Consider creating a pamphlet on "service sponsorship." The committee considered a request to create a pamphlet on "service sponsorship" and took no action. The committee noted content on service sponsorship in the pamphlet "Questions and Answers on Sponsorship" and agreed that there was not a widely expressed need in the Fellowship.

- Create a pamphlet on the origins, meaning and application of the Responsibility Statement. The committee considered a request to create a pamphlet on the origins, meaning and application of the Responsibility Statement and took no action. The committee agreed that there was not a widely expressed need in the Fellowship.

- Amend existing literature to reflect the origins, meaning and application of the Responsibility Statement. The committee considered a request to amend existing literature to reflect the origins, meaning and application of the Responsibility Statement and took no action. The committee agreed that there was not a widely expressed need in the Fellowship.

- Consider discontinuing the booklet *Living Sober*. The committee considered a request to discontinue the booklet *Living Sober* and took no action. The committee agreed that there was not a widely expressed need in the Fellowship.

- Consider discontinuing the pamphlet "The 'God' Word." The committee considered a request to discontinue the pamphlet "The 'God' Word" and took no action. The committee noted that it was important to allow time to assess the Fellowship's response to the pamphlet and that in four months over 38,000 copies of the pamphlet have been purchased since its release in October 2018. It was also noted that there was not a widely expressed need in the Fellowship for discontinuation of the pamphlet.

Carole Boerner, Chairperson

Staff Report: As secretary to the trustees' and Conference Committees on Literature and the A.A.W.S. Publishing Committee, the Literature coordinator works closely with the editors, writers and illustrators on reviewing, updating and revising all new and existing recovery pamphlets, books and audiovisuals, in accordance with recommendations from the General Service Conference. Final design and production of all this material is under the auspices of the A.A. World Services Publishing Department.

The Literature desk receives and responds to correspondence from A.A. members and groups about A.A. literature. Many of these inquiries are passed along to our Order Entry Department, our customer service representatives, our publishing staff and our Archives staff. Contact is also maintained with all current area, district and intergroup/central office literature chairpersons. Each newly elected literature chairperson receives a welcoming letter and guidelines to assist them in this vital responsibility. There are currently 67 area, 421 district and 27 intergroup/central office literature chairpersons listed with G.S.O. The Literature assistant is invaluable in supporting and helping facilitate the responsibilities of this aspect of the assignment.

The Literature staff member also gathers sharing for *Box 4-5-9*, working closely with the Publishing Department managing editor and the G.S.O. editorial team. This collection of "news and notes" may include articles containing shared experience from members and A.A. Conference-approved literature that address questions raised in multiple phone calls, emails and letters to G.S.O. G.S.O. always welcomes committee sharing on service from the Fellowship, which also may be included so that *Box 4-5-9* can be an accurate reflection of both Fellowship and G.S.O. activities.

Box 4-5-9 is published in English, French and Spanish, with current quarterly distribution of 65,999 copies in English, 1,624 copies in French and 3,204 copies in Spanish. In addition, there are currently 13,928 English, 542 French and 1,114 Spanish subscribers to the digital delivery service for *Box 4-5-9* available through G.S.O.'s website, aa.org. Also on the website, visitors can find digital copies of every issue going back to the original issue of *Box 4-5-9* from 1956.

Steve Smith

NOMINATING

Trustees' Report: The trustees' Committee on Nominating was first appointed by the chair of the General Service Board on January 18, 1944. At that time, primary responsibilities were to "establish criteria for and to review résumés of trustee candidates and directors and to make recommendations regarding electoral procedures and matters which may affect the composition of the board and election to it." (History and Actions of the trustees' Committee on Nominating)

Since that time, the trustees' Committee on Nominating generally has met three times each year and, with the formation of the General Service Conference in 1951, began to meet annually with the Conference Committee on Trustees. The responsibilities of the committee grew over time to encompass criteria for all vacancies, whether in the ranks of trustees or among key service directors and staff members.

Activities of this committee in the past year:

- *Class A Trustee election:* The committee reviewed the résumés, curriculum vitae and other background material of 34 applicants who had made themselves available to serve as Class A (nonalcoholic) trustees. The committee chose seven applicants to interview in January 2019.

- Following the interviews, the committee recommended to the General Service Board that Sister Judith Ann Karam and Al J. Mooney, M.D., be invited to serve as Class A trustees to succeed Ivan Lemelle and David Morris following the 2019 General Service Conference.

- *Regional Trustee and Trustee-at-Large Canada elections:* The committee recommended to the General Service Board, as eligible for election in May 2019, all candidates submitted for Northeast and Southwest regional trustees and all candidates submitted for trustee-at-large/Canada.

- *Board slates:* The committee reviewed and recommended proposed slates of General Service Board members, officers of the board, and A.A. World Services and AA Grapevine directors to the annual meeting of the members of the General Service Board in May 2019, following presentation at the 2019 General Service Conference for disapproval, if any.

- *A.A.W.S. Directors:* The committee recommended to the General Service Board that Jan Lembke serve as trustee director for a two-year term on A.A. World Services, Inc., following the May 2019 General Service Conference, to succeed Tom Ardolf.

- *AA Grapevine Directors:* The committee recommended that Kathi Fowler serve as trustee director for a two-year term on AA Grapevine, Inc., following the May 2019 General Service Conference, to succeed Cate Wittig.

Committee's Composition, Scope and Procedures: The committee reviewed its Composition, Scope and Procedure and recommended to the General Service Board that the following procedures be updated to include the AA Grapevine magazine as an additional option for placing announcements of Board vacancies:

- No. 1 (Grapevine and A.A.W.S. Boards)
- No. 2 (Appointed Committee Members)
- No. 4 (Class A Trustees)
- No. 11 (Regional Trustees)
- No. 12 (Trustee-at-Large)

Appointed Committee Members: The committee reviewed an update on the status of appointed committee members serving on trustees' committees of the General Service Board for the year 2019–2020 and made the following recommendations to the General Service Board:

- That Allison Callis of Goleta, CA, be appointed for an additional one-year term to serve as an Appointed Committee Member on the trustees' Committee on Public Information beginning with the July 2019 General Service Board weekend.

- That Shari Miller of Ft. Lauderdale, FL, be appointed for an additional one-year term to serve as an Appointed Committee Member on the trustees' Committee on Public Information beginning with the July 2019 General Service Board weekend.

- That Katie Heilmann of Fair Oaks, CA, be appointed for an additional one-year term to serve as an Appointed Committee Member on the trustees' Committee on Literature beginning with the July 2019 General Service Board weekend.

- That Amalia Castillo of Newington, CT, be appointed for a one-year term to serve as an Appointed Committee Member on the trustees' Committee on Literature beginning with the July 2019 General Service Board weekend.

- That George Wright of Louisville, KY, be appointed for an additional one-year term to serve as an Appointed Committee Member on the trustees' Committee on Cooperation with the Professional Community/Treatment and Accessibilities beginning with the July 2019 General Service Board weekend.

Other

Eligibility requirement before standing for chair of the General Service Board: The committee discussed a General Service Board recommendation requiring that no current trustee shall be eligible to stand for the position of chair of the General Service Board until completion of their term as trustee and rotation off the General Service Board and took no action.

General Service Board officer rotation: The committee discussed possible resource material that would be helpful to new General Service Board officers. The committee requested that the general manager and staff coordinator begin the process of collecting a "rotation" memo from current General Service Board officers with the intent that this information can be used to develop job descriptions for General Service Board officer positions.

Class A vacancy announcements: The committee discussed the option of distributing Class A trustee vacancy announcements to professional organizations and took no action. The committee noted the value of reaching professionals who express a deep faith in Alcoholics Anonymous.

Class A trustee recruitment materials: The committee reviewed a draft of the sharing received from current and past Class A trustees regarding their experience serving the General Service Board of Alcoholics Anonymous and requested that the sharing be included with the "Information for Prospective Class A Trustees" document currently distributed to Class A Trustee candidates.

Procedures for partial or total reorganization of the General Service Board, the A.A.W.S. or AA Grapevine Boards: The committee discussed an Additional Committee Consideration from the 2018 Conference Committee on Trustees requesting that the trustees' Committee on Nominating develop procedures for a partial or complete reorganization of the General Service Board, the A.A.W.S. or AA Grapevine boards. The committee requested that the General Service Office staff gather available information relevant to the discussion for review prior to the October 2018 meeting of the committee.

At the October 2018 meeting, the chair appointed a subcommittee comprised of Scott Huyghebaert (chair), Newton Pritchett and Ginger Rhoades Bell to develop steps and procedures for a partial or complete reorganization of the General Service Board and/or Corporate Boards and bring back draft procedures or a progress report to the January 2019 meeting.

At the January 2019 meeting, the committee agreed to forward the draft procedures for a partial or complete reorganization of the General Service Board to the 2019 Conference Committee on Trustees. Additionally, the committee requested that the general manager prepare a memorandum summarizing pertinent information forwarded by legal counsel to accompany the draft procedures.

Survey of Regional Trustees regarding workload of the service commitment: The committee reviewed a memo forwarded to the General Service Board with a suggestion from the trustees' Committee on Nominating to consider a survey of current and past regional trustees regarding the workload of the service commitment and their ability to fulfill all their responsibilities and suggested that the survey include a wider range of questions relevant to service on the General Service Board. The committee agreed to request that the General Service Board postpone implementation of the survey to allow the trustees' Committee on Nominating the opportunity to discuss relevant information that would enhance the usefulness of the survey. Committee members agreed to send their thoughts and questions to the staff secretary for discussion at their October 2018 meeting.

At the October 2018 meeting, the committee had a wide-ranging discussion and determined that it would be best to develop a process to gather shared experience from the Fellowship with respect to serving on the General Service Board, including, but not limited to, workloads, terms of service and rotation. The process could also include the possibility of organizing focused sharing sessions at Regional Forums to obtain feedback.

The committee agreed to define the content and structure of the process, and requested that the staff secretary schedule a committee conference call to take place in the beginning of December 2018.

At the January 2019 meeting, the committee discussed the draft questionnaire designed to explore the current composition and effectiveness of the General Service Board. Pending final revisions, an implementation plan will be designed for review by the trustees' Nominating Committee.

AA Grapevine Board request: The committee discussed a request that the General Service Board make available

issues of AA Grapevine for distribution purposes through the G.S.O. staff assignments, and agreed to continue discussions. At the January 2019 meeting, the committee requested that the staff secretary develop informational packets for Class A candidates that would include AA Grapevine issues and bring back a sample packet to the July 2019 board meeting.

General Service Board Strategic Plan: The committee began discussion of items in the General Service Board Strategic Plan (updated July 2018) relevant to the work of the committee and agreed to first undertake an inventory of its materials, with the goal of reviewing one document per month in teams of two. The committee requested that the staff secretary develop a review schedule, including the list of documents and team assignments.

At the January 2019 meeting, the committee discussed the progress to date of the inventory of its materials. All Nominating Procedures have been reviewed and suggested changes submitted. The committee requested that the staff secretary revise the Procedures to reflect the proposed changes and bring back the draft documents to the July 2019 board meeting for review.

Request that only Class B trustees chair General Service Board committees: The committee discussed a request that — except for the trustees' Finance committee — only Class B trustees chair General Service Board committees, and took no action. The committee agreed that *The Twelve Concepts for World Service* provide the right and responsibility for each trustee committee to determine the best way to carry out their respective business.

Request that the General Service Board develop policy and procedures regarding litigation: The committee discussed a request that the General Service Board develop policy and procedures regarding litigation, and took no action. The committee agreed that a formalized policy might serve to impose constraints that would prevent the trustees from fulfilling their fiduciary responsibilities. The committee also noted the 2018 Conference Committee on Trustees report, specifically the portion regarding the fiduciary responsibility of the General Service Board as it relates to litigation.

Request for a change to the General Service Board composition: The committee discussed a request for a change to the composition of the General Service Board as to the ratio of Class A and Class B trustees, and took no action. The committee noted that they are currently in the beginning phases of an exploration of General Service Board composition and effectiveness.

Request to implement new requirements to the procedures for regional and trustee-at-large elections: The committee discussed a request to implement new requirements to the procedures for regional and trustee-at-large elections, and took no action. The committee agreed that a policy dictating that regional and trustee-at-large candidates neither attend the General Service Conference opening dinner nor visit the General Service Office would not be enforceable.

Tom Ardolf, Chairperson

Staff Report: The staff member on this assignment is responsible to the trustees' Committee on Nominating and to the Conference Committee on Trustees, serving as secretary to these committees as well as to trustees' subcommittees. Since the last Conference, the staff member prepared background, minutes and reports for three quarterly trustees' committee meetings, worked with the trustees' committee on vacancy announcements, and sent time commitment and interest status letters to Class A candidates. Subsequently, the staff member sent follow-up letters to Class A candidates and organized the interview scheduling processes of the search for two new Class A trustees who will succeed Ivan Lemelle and David Morris. The staff member also coordinated the transcription and review of résumés for Class B trustee candidates who made their names available to participate in this year's Conference elections procedure.

Sandra Wilson

PUBLIC INFORMATION

Trustees' Report: The trustees' Committee on Public Information is charged with the responsibility of helping the membership carry the A.A. message of recovery through the general public to the alcoholic who still suffers. The committee does this by recommending and coordinating activities that include: creating a greater public understanding of the Fellowship of Alcoholics Anonymous; producing video and audio public service announcements (PSAs); preparing and distributing press releases on aa.org and other outlets; coordinating health fairs and other community and school exhibits with local P.I. committees; conducting the triennial A.A. Membership Survey; and carrying A.A.'s message through electronic as well as print media.

Activities over the past year have included:

G.S.O.'s website — The committee reviewed and agreed to forward to the 2019 Conference Public Information Committee the annual report of the A.A.W.S. Board regarding G.S.O.'s website aa.org.

AA Grapevine/La Viña website — The committee reviewed and agreed to forward to the 2019 Conference Public Information Committee the annual report of the AA Grapevine Board regarding the AA Grapevine/La Viña website aagrapevine.org.

Public Information Comprehensive Media Plan — The committee reviewed a list of items and activities of the 2018 trustees' committee. The committee also noted that Public Information items from the General Service Board Strategic Plan have been included in the report. The committee reviewed and agreed to forward to the 2019 Conference Public Information Committee a report on the progress of the 2019 Public Information Comprehensive Media Plan. The committee asked that a "Comprehensive Media Plan" subcommittee be formed at the July 2019 meeting to determine a scope of work and action plan.

Video PSAs — In response to a 2018 Advisory Action that in addition to the work of local committees, the video PSA

"Changes" be centrally distributed, tracked and evaluated at a cost not to exceed $42,000 and that the information gathered from the process be forwarded to the 2019 Conference Public Information Committee for their review. The committee reviewed the reports noting that they would be placed on the Conference Public Information Committee agenda for their review.

The committee reviewed the current video PSAs for relevance and usefulness and agreed to forward to the 2019 Conference Public Information Committee a request that the video PSA "My World" be discontinued.

The committee found the remaining video PSAs to be relevant and useful.

Full-Face PSAs — In response to a request, the committee agreed to forward to the 2019 Conference Public Information Committee a request to approve the development of a new PSA in video format that utilizes full-face actors (not members of A.A.).

"Understanding Anonymity" — In response to the 2018 Advisory Action to develop language reflecting that A.A.'s anonymity Traditions are not a cloak protecting criminal or inappropriate behavior and that calling the proper authorities does not go against any A.A. Traditions in the pamphlet "Understanding Anonymity," the committee agreed to forward proposed text to the 2019 Conference Public Information Committee for inclusion in the pamphlet.

"A.A. at a Glance" — The committee reviewed a request to update language in the flyer "A.A. at a Glance." The committee reviewed and agreed to forward possible new text to the 2019 Conference Public Information Committee.

A.A.W.S. YouTube Account — In response to a 2018 Advisory Action, the committee discussed the request that "a progress report including website analytics and the usefulness and effectiveness of the A.A.W.S. YouTube account be brought back to the 2019 Conference Committee on Public Information." The committee reviewed and agreed to forward to the 2019 Conference Public Information Committee a progress report on the A.A.W.S. YouTube account.

The committee also discussed a request for "the immediate removal (cease active use) of the Alcoholics Anonymous World Services YouTube Channel." The committee asked that the item be tabled to the July 2019 meeting. The committee noted that the A.A.W.S. YouTube account is still in its infancy and that more information may be needed before determining its usefulness and effectiveness.

Google AdWords and Google Grants — In response to an Additional Committee Consideration of the 2018 Conference Public Information Committee to "provide a progress report on the use of Google AdWords and Google Grants including information on the cost of implementing a six month trial and the cost of a full year's implementation," the committee reviewed and agreed to forward to the 2019 Conference Public Information Committee a report that includes information requested by the 2018 Conference.

A.A. Membership Survey — At the October meeting the committee met with a potential survey consultant via teleconference to gather information on possible methodologies regarding a new A.A. Membership Survey model. At the January meeting, the committee discussed the report from the "Technical Subcommittee on the A.A. Membership Survey" regarding the survey methodology. The committee reviewed a draft RFP to survey professionals seeking feedback on our current process and additional potential feedback. The committee asked that the staff secretary work with the General Service Office to finalize the RFP language to distribute to survey professionals and bring back a progress report to the July 2019 meeting.

Anonymity Card — The committee discussed the suggestion that the Conference-approved "A.A. Anonymity Card" (F-20) be updated. The committee noted that the "A.A. Anonymity Card" was in need of updated language and tabled their discussion to the July 2019 meeting. The committee also suggested that a review of all anonymity cards be included in this discussion for a broader and consistent review process.

Anonymity Online — The committee discussed updated draft language in the service material "Anonymity Online." The committee suggested that the service piece be updated with the new title "Anonymity Online and Digital Media" with possible additional content to be included.

Posthumous Anonymity Policy — The committee discussed the G.S.O. Public Information Policy on the Co-Founders' Posthumous Anonymity and tabled this item to the July 2019 meeting.

A.A. Videos for Young People Project — The committee noted that the project guidelines are in need of an update and will continue discussion regarding the guidelines at the July 2019 meeting.

P.I. Kit — The Conference-approved flyer "Where Do I Go from Here?" (F-4) will be removed from the P.I. Kit. A link to the "Anonymity in the Digital Age" poster will be added to the kit.

P.I. Banner — In response to local requests, the committee asked that the staff secretary work with Publishing to create a draft public information banner image to be available for local public information committees to create banners locally for exhibits and presentations. The committee will review the draft banner image at the July 2019 meeting.

The committee remains committed to assisting the membership in carrying the message of recovery through the general public to the alcoholic who still suffers and welcomes suggestions from the Fellowship as to what more can be done.

Peter Luongo, Chairperson

Staff Report: The goal of the Public Information assignment at G.S.O. is to assist the Fellowship in seeing that the A.A. message of recovery reaches the still-suffering alcoholic by keeping the general public informed about the A.A. program of hope and recovery from alcoholism.

This assignment is charged with assisting A.A. members

who carry the message to the suffering alcoholic through the general public. These A.A. members share information about A.A. at schools, health fairs, community events and libraries, and through all forms of media.

Below are some of the ways this task is carried out through this assignment:

- Communicates with 840 P.I. committee chairpersons at the area, district, intergroup/central office and group level, providing them with aa.org resources, Workbooks, Guidelines and current shared information on Public Information activity.

- Provides literature to supplement the efforts of local Public Information committees, at local health and community fairs, sharing information about Alcoholics Anonymous.

- Provides P.I. committees with information regarding the production and distribution of video and audio public service announcements (PSAs), including the availability of downloadable HD broadcast-quality versions, in order to enhance their efforts on the local level; also, forwards media requests for PSAs to local committees which serve as A.A. resources.

- Responds to all media inquiries that come to the office providing them with accurate information about Alcoholics Anonymous, and coordinates media coverage of A.A.'s International Conventions, held every five years, and works closely with the Publishing Department regarding timely development and distribution of press releases on matters of public interest.

- Reads and reviews media stories that mention Alcoholics Anonymous and shares relevant information as needed; and receives information from members regarding anonymity breaks at the level of press, radio, films, television and the Internet.

- Passes along instances of anonymity breaks in the media to the delegate in the area in which the break occurred, and provides them with an opportunity to contact the member and share experience regarding our Eleventh Tradition.

- Sends out the Annual Anonymity Letter to the Media. The June 2018 letter was emailed to over 29,000 media outlets in the U.S. and Canada. The email included a link to view a brief video on anonymity on aa.org. The letter was distributed to reporters, editors and publishers at a variety of outlets in print, broadcast and electronic media.

- Coordinates production of new television and radio PSAs, as requested by the Conference, and works with the Publishing Department regarding available formats and delivery options.

- Works closely with the Publishing Department regarding development and updating of Conference-approved literature and assignment-related service material.

- Coordinates the A.A. Membership Survey and works with the Publishing Department to publish the Survey results in pamphlet form and as a table display for information about Alcoholics Anonymous at public events.

- Participates as a member of the G.S.O. Website Committee, which reviews suggested changes to the aa.org website, a key aspect of our Public Information efforts.

Racy Joseph

STAFF COORDINATOR

Staff Report: The General Service Office provides services to A.A. groups and members and shares A.A. experience when available. Thirteen A.A. members comprise the "G.S.O. Staff," with each person responsible for a functional assignment in addition to responding to requests from a specific region in Canada and the United States, or from other countries. The staff coordinator shares responsibility for corresponding with members from the Southwest region, covering the busy six months of the year for the Conference coordinator.

In 2018, the staff received 82,496 pieces of correspondence by mail, email and fax. Additionally, the staff answered over 10,344 phone calls. The staff coordinator helps to assure that letters are answered when staff members are involved in large projects or are away from the office to attend A.A. events, or at times of illness or vacation. Mail, email, faxes, etc., are responded to within ten business days.

G.S.O. staff benefits from the experience of A.A. groups gathered over many years. These resources are passed on to members who seek guidance for their group, central office, district or area assembly. Questions and requests for sharing from the Fellowship are often brought to weekly staff meetings, so that responses reflect either research from A.A. literature or service material or the collective experience of G.S.O. staff and archives. Our weekly staff meetings provide a forum for sharing ideas on how to better serve A.A. groups and members and how to provide the most complete answers to Fellowship inquiries.

G.S.O. staff members serve as secretaries to trustees' and Conference committees and also are voting members of the General Service Conference. The staff coordinator is secretary to the Conference Policy/Admissions Committee.

In 2018, G.S.O. welcomed a total of 3,007 individuals, including many English- and Spanish-speaking groups ranging in size from 10 to 40, to the General Service Office. Each visitor had an opportunity to see and hear "how G.S.O. works" and view a display of Grapevine materials during a tour of G.S.O. Visiting members and guests often attend the open A.A. meeting held at G.S.O. at 11:00 a.m. on Fridays. This is an opportunity for the G.S.O. staff to welcome A.A. members from all over the world or from around the corner.

The staff coordinator has the privilege of serving as a director on A.A. World Services, Inc., in accordance with Concept IV, and also serves as liaison between staff members and other G.S.O. departments. None of these activities would be possible without the dedication and skill of a very capable support staff.

Mary Cumings

◼ G.S.O. Department Reports

Administration and Services — *Albin Zezula, Director*: The director of administration and services reports directly to the general manager and is responsible for planning and management of the General Service Office (G.S.O.) staff functions and for providing oversight and functional guidance to the administrative services, all in fulfillment of the mission of the General Service Conference and the boards to support the Fellowship of Alcoholics Anonymous. He or she also handles special projects and committee responsibilities as needed.

The principal duties and responsibilities of this position are the following:

- Develops, in consultation with the general manager, staff and the appropriate Conference and trustees' committees, the short- and long-term plans for each staff function. Coordinates the development and implementation of departments' strategic planning, policies and initiatives necessary to meet the objectives of the G.S.O.

- Ensures that plans and programs developed by staff functions are consistent with the service goals and objectives established by the Conference and the boards.

- Provides direction, guidance and leadership to G.S.O. staff, ensuring sound performance management and the implementation of effective evaluation procedures. Assists general manager in selection, hiring and training of staff members.

- Coordinates budgeting and monitors the annual budget for the Services group. Recommends staffing, expenditures and efficient operation. Works with controller to ensure that accounting for staff programs and activities is accurate and timely.

- Oversees the Administrative Services Department (staff assistants, Support Services, Records, Files and office management). Collaborates with the administrative services manager to provide administrative support to Staff Services and database management. Ensures staff functions are effectively and efficiently supported.

- Serves on the Senior Management Group. Participates in office operations, policies and procedures decisions. Leads and participates with assigned projects and A.A.W.S. committees, as needed.

- Ensures ongoing support in the coordination of the General Service Board meetings.

- Ensures effective and clear communication of G.S.O. services to the Fellowship, boards and external sources. Communicates the mission of the G.S.O., where appropriate, through participation at General Service and other Fellowship activities, when required.

- Stays abreast of issues and matters of concern to the general manager in order to provide meaningful advice and consultation on board, Conference, corporate and legal matters. Acts effectively in place of the general manager when and as requested.

Administrative Services — *Karen Hale, Assistant Director*: The assistant director of administrative services reports directly to the director of administration and services and is responsible for the overall operation of the Records, Support Services, staff assistants, Office Services and

Meetings, Events and Travel Departments. This responsibility is carried out through oversight of the day-to-day operations of the several departments to ensure that they are operating effectively and efficiently.

The manager of administrative services is also the direct link from G.S.O. to area registrars, coordinating database system changes as well as providing periodic database training and maintenance of any database user manuals.

The Records staff handle the daily operations of the department, assisting G.S.O. staff and other departments and serving the Fellowship. Their duties include but are not limited to the updating of thousands of group and individual records, the processing of new group applications, responding to email/phone inquiries, maintenance of all G.S.O. mailing lists, and providing information and direction on database usage. The work of the department ensures the accuracy and timely availability of the information required for production of the various A.A. Directories. The Records Department staff members serve as "subject matter experts" regarding A.A. databases and provide operational support and continued assistance to new area record keepers working in the database system.

The staff assistants and Support Services Department perform a variety of administrative duties regarding the specific A.A. staff member desk to which each is assigned. In addition to these assignment-specific administrative duties, they provide ongoing assistance to other departments. The fact that many staff assistants and Support Services Department personnel are bilingual provides both the A.A. staff and the Fellowship an additional dimension of service. Support Services personnel also provide necessary support throughout the office, as required. The receptionist/tour guide/lead telephone operator greets visitors and provides information, conducts tours of G.S.O. and answers calls to the switchboard.

The administrative services team assists the manager of administrative services by providing daily oversight of the Records, staff assistants and Support Services departments. Their duties include managing departmental workflow, cross-training and ensuring adequate department coverage.

The Meetings, Events and Travel Services function provides quality, cost-efficient services for G.S.O. meetings and events.

The Office Services function handles day-to-day office operations that include purchasing office materials and furnishings, overseeing the running of the copy center, scheduling of meeting rooms on the floor or within the building and off-premises when necessary, catering needs of the organization, and acquiring vendor quotes for various office services. The Office Services manager acts as liaison between the Interchurch Building management and the G.S.O./Grapevine, ensuring the ongoing and proper maintenance of office space.

Archives — *Michelle Mirza, Archivist*: The mission of the Alcoholics Anonymous General Service Office Archives is to document permanently the work of Alcoholics Anonymous, to make the history of the organization accessible to A.A. members and other researchers, and to provide a context for understanding A.A.'s progression, principles and traditions.

Consistent with A.A.'s primary purpose of maintaining sobriety and helping other alcoholics achieve recovery, the Archives of Alcoholics Anonymous will:

- Receive, classify and index all relevant material, such as administrative files and records, correspondence, and literary works and artifacts considered to have historical importance to Alcoholics Anonymous;

- Hold and preserve such material;

- Provide access to these materials, as determined by the archivist in consultation with the trustees' Archives Committee, to members of Alcoholics Anonymous and to others who may have a valid need to review such material, contingent upon a commitment to preserve the anonymity of all A.A. members;

- Serve as a resource and laboratory to stimulate and nourish learning;

- Provide information services to assist the operations of Alcoholics Anonymous;

- Promote knowledge and understanding of the origins, goals and programs of Alcoholics Anonymous.

Finance and Accounting — *Robert Slotterback, Director*: The Finance and Accounting group consists of several units: contributions, accounts receivable, accounts payable and inventory valuation. The common goal of these finance units is to process information that allows the office to carry on the day-to-day business and recording of transactions that ultimately result in the preparation of monthly, quarterly and annual financial statements. Additional responsibilities of this group traditionally have involved G.S.O. budgeting; assistance with International Convention planning, budgeting, management and reporting; as well as providing information necessary for trusted servants to make appropriate decisions about the General Service Board's Reserve Fund and the A.A.W.S. and AA Grapevine employee retirement plans.

The responsibilities of the accounts receivable unit include balancing daily cash receipts for literature orders, preparation of bank deposits, recording of accounts payments, collection of outstanding balances, and control of credit for accounts receivable. Responsibilities also include account research and sending accounts receivable statements to customers. We continue to encourage purchasers to provide email addresses as we have the ability to email invoices and statements to purchasers. Emailing invoices and statements is an important way to help reduce the cost of operations.

The contributions unit is responsible for processing daily receipts of contributions and making sure contributions are accepted only from A.A. members; posting contributions to group accounts, making sure they are all acknowledged; answering inquiries; and doing any research necessary regarding contributions. Statistical reports generated for contributions by delegate area are included in the Conference material; they are also generated for the quarterly statements that are sent to all groups.

During 2018, approximately 82,000 contributions were received in various forms. These include contributions received in the mail and online, both individually entered transactions and recurring contributions. This compares with 84,000 received in 2017 and approximately 81,000 received in 2016. In 2010, we activated an online system for contributions and in 2014 added a feature for recurring contributions.

During 2018, the department processed approximately 12,000 online contributions, which compares with approximately 11,500 processed in 2017; 7,400 in 2016; 4,600 during 2015; 3,500 during 2014; 3,000 in 2013; and 2,300 in 2012.

The recurring contribution function appears to be growing in usage. Members can set up an account to automatically charge their credit card monthly, quarterly or annually. At the beginning of 2015, there were only 139 members actively using this function. But the word is getting out at Regional Forums and other service events, and as of December 2018, there are approximately 632 active users.

Several years ago, the Contributions Department implemented an email function for contribution acknowledgments and group Quarterly Contribution Statements. Approximately 8,000 to 9,000 email acknowledgments for group and individual contributions have been sent out annually for the past few years.

There are email addresses associated with approximately 30,000 groups for contribution purposes. Approximately 15,500 contributing and 14,600 non-contributing groups have received their quarterly contribution statements via email.

Using the Internet offers the possibility of reducing or mitigating increases in the costs for postage and handling of acknowledgments and statements. Additionally, the Contributions Department has been able to identify repetitive contributions from groups or members, allowing department staff to more quickly process approximately 80% of the contributions, while some 20% — such as bank and postal money orders that some groups and members use to send contributions — still require research and manual data entry to process.

The Finance Department is responsible for maintaining the books of account of A.A. World Services, Inc. and the General Service Board of A.A., Inc., the Reserve Fund and the International Convention financials. This unit ensures proper distributions of expenses among the corporations. Checks are issued through a vouchers payable system that records the expenses in the appropriate accounts. This unit assists in summarizing income and expense transactions, account analysis, bank accounts reconciliations and preparation of financial reports on a monthly, quarterly and annual basis.

The inventory valuation process ensures that appropriate, generally accepted accounting principles are followed in the valuation of A.A.W.S. inventory.

The payroll unit, which is now part of the Human Resources Department, frequently consults with the Finance group on various matters as it processes the biweekly payroll. The payroll process, which includes direct deposit or the issuance of payroll checks, is accomplished via Internet-connected data transfers to an outside service bureau.

In addition to the routine work of the Finance and Accounting group, there traditionally have been additional responsibilities related to assisting with the planning of A.A. International Conventions. Currently there is work ongoing for the next two International Conventions in different stages of planning.

One of the numerous continuing goals for the past few years has been to identify additional ways of reducing postage and mailing costs. Digital delivery of various publications (accessible from aa.org) was implemented partly for this purpose. If every group had an email address, conceivably a wide spectrum of materials — such as letters, memos and various periodicals — could be distributed electronically, thereby saving a significant amount of money in printing and mailing costs.

Human Resources — *Olga Mesonjnik, Director*: The primary goal of the Human Resources Department is to promote a comprehensive and effective program of human resources management embracing recruitment, compensation and benefits, employee relations, executive and professional development, training, payroll, and regulatory and legal compliance. The Human Resources Department supports the ability of G.S.O. to attract, retain, develop, motivate and reward a highly competent and effective workforce.

The Human Resources Department ensures that all

aspects of the overall G.S.O. employment program are in conformity with all applicable federal, state and local laws and regulations. Also, Human Resources ensures effective communication of all policies, programs and procedures to all managerial, professional and non-managerial employees; advises the general manager on industry trends and developments in compensation and employee benefits; and makes revisions to existing plans and policies.

In order to recruit and retain an effective workforce, Human Resources works closely with appropriate senior managerial and supervisory personnel to attract qualified candidates for employment using the most cost-effective means. Orientation programs, training and development are conducted for all employees. In addition to training and development, the Human Resources Department orchestrates recognition, awards and organization-wide events for employees.

The department provides resources to AA Grapevine, as well, on an as-requested basis.

Information Technology Services — *Cynthia S. Garippa, Director*:

The primary goal of the Information Technology Services Department is to provide technical and customer service support to the employees of G.S.O. The Information Technology Services Department also provides technical and customer service support to those in the Fellowship who use our databases, access our dashboards or make Seventh Tradition contributions online.

The Information Technology Services Department is responsible for all technology software and hardware, from installation to maintenance to training. The department designs, updates and maintains our website, aa.org. The department also ensures that all applications are up to date with the latest versions and that all hardware and software are compliant by industry standards, preserving the anonymity of our data with tight security and maintaining a healthy digital environment with anti-virus and anti-intrusion detection programs.

The IT Services group provides leadership and expertise to the entire organization on company-wide projects such as the enterprise resource planning (ERP) conversion that was undertaken in 2018.

Mail/Shipping/Receiving — *Aubrey Pereira, Supervisor*:

The Shipping and Mail Department is responsible for processing annually over 77,110 pieces of incoming and 75,465 pieces of outgoing mail. This department also ships literature orders from New York.

Mail/Shipping assembles, wraps and ships more than 40 different complimentary (no-charge) packages, including Conference and D.C.M. Kits and Public Information packages, which are available in English, Spanish and French. This department completes an average of 112 literature orders per week at our pick-pack operation in New York and is also responsible for gathering and mailing literature for Regional Forums and health fairs.

Additional responsibilities include support of AA Grapevine's Mail/Shipping Department.

Each person in the department is trained to assemble the various items, such as discount packages and workbooks.

Duties also include stocking and replenishing literature supplies and packing material. This requires receiving weekly quantities of literature from our warehouses, enabling us to fill orders shipped from G.S.O.

As we enter into 2019, this department continues to explore methods to better serve the Fellowship and help carry the message through efficient distribution of printed material.

Publishing — *David Rosen, Publishing Director*:

All of the Publishing Department's efforts continue to serve the mission and primary purpose of A.A.W.S., Inc., with this overarching imperative: to maintain the highest-quality editorial and production and distribution standards while implementing economies of best industry-wide practices. Publishing Department divisions are: Editorial, Production, Order Entry, Customer Service, Inventory Control, International Licensing and Translation, Intellectual Property and Permissions, Spanish Translation, French Translation (this year a full-time in-house French editor joined our team), and Mail/Shipping. The Publishing Department coordinates all aspects of publishing literature, translating literature, providing permissions for approved excerpts of literature or linking to the website, creating various formats and providing related services, including supplying content for G.S.O.'s website, aa.org.

The managing editor, associate editor, French and Spanish editors work closely with each G.S.O. staff member to provide editorial direction and expertise regarding Conference-approved literature, service material and newsletters. Copyediting manuscripts; incorporating board, Conference committee and staff suggestions for changes; and rewriting and preparing copy for the printer are the responsibility of these editors. Freelance writers and artists, who are sometimes also A.A. members, are hired to develop material and design covers and layouts.

The production manager works with the production coordinator to ensure optimum manufacturing quality of literature and audiovisual materials at the most competitive prices. Bids are gathered from a variety of vendors, and printers are selected who will produce quality products on time and at a reasonable cost. Paper costs, often quite volatile, are monitored and negotiated. The production manager supplies the publishing director and director of finance with cost information for proposed new A.A.W.S. formats, for Conference projects, and for the A.A.W.S. board's pricing decisions. The production manager works closely with the editors and the Order Entry and Inventory Control divisions in setting up schedules and meeting press dates.

The publishing director works with the Finance Department to determine Publishing Department budget requirements and sales projections. Regular reports are presented by the publishing director to the A.A.W.S. Publishing Committee. In addition, it is the responsibility of the Publishing Department to meet overall publishing goals determined by the General Service Board, A.A. World Services, Inc., and the General Service Conference. Notably in 2018, work continued to refine our detailed P&L/pricing matrix to reflect weighted averages across

English, French and Spanish items.

A note about Spanish and French translation: Under the project management of the associate editor (an in-house editorial position originated in 2017), our enhanced French and Spanish freelancer pools successfully provided 2018 Conference background material under tight deadlines — and well under the anticipated budget.

The intellectual property administrator is responsible for screening requests to reprint A.A.W.S., Inc. copyright-protected materials as well as for handling A.A.W.S., Inc.-owned trademark and domain name registrations and renewals. Additionally, this position administers the investigation of reported abuses of A.A.W.S., Inc. copyrights and trademarks and other intellectual property interests.

In a strategic effort to meet the pressing demands presented by adhering to best-practice publishing business requirements and to accommodate a contemporized body of emerging publishing formats and distribution channels (for audio, e-book, video and other digital modes as well as innovations in print media), during the past year the Publishing Department enlisted the help of a best-in-class industry publishing consulting firm to help apprise the organization of the shifting landscapes. This work is ongoing, with regular reporting to the boards. A particular focus on addressing access and consumption via libraries, subscription services, educators, professionals and institutions (especially in Corrections venues) is underway.

Of particular note were these significant activities: a) addressing accessibility and attraction in the format and design of book and pamphlet cover images and content; b) completing particular new projects and revisions to items of A.A. Conference-approved literature and service material under Advisory Actions, including the pamphlets "Women in A.A.," "LGBTQ Alcoholics in A.A.," "A.A. for Alcoholics with Mental Health Issues — and Their Sponsors," "Access to A.A." and the "Americanization" of the United Kingdom–originated pamphlet "The 'God' Word" for printing and distribution in the U.S./Canada. Also, newly designed large-print versions of these pamphlets were produced: "A.A. for the Older Alcoholic," "Frequently Asked Questions," and "This Is A.A."

A new cover design for the book *Daily Reflections* (in both its regular and large-print editions) saw a steady sales uptick in 2018. The revised and updated American Sign Language video productions of the Big Book and "Twelve and Twelve" were taped in early 2018 and post production will conclude in early 2019. The audiobook re-recordings of the Big Book, "Twelve and Twelve" and *Living Sober* were completed in English and Spanish, and recording continues in 2019 for the French editions. The A.A.W.S., Inc. audiobook strategy, regarding the production of audiobooks and their distribution (via all available venues and outlets to all who may need them), is under ongoing review by the A.A.W.S. board.

Much diligent ongoing teamwork (especially in the areas of production, inventory management, order entry and customer service) has focused on participating in the new unified ERP project build, testing and training.

The new General Service Conference–approved book, *Our Great Responsibility: A Selection of Bill W.'s General Service Conference Talks, 1951–1970,* moved toward production in English, French and Spanish editions, with an off-press date of April 15, 2019 and on sale May 7.

A special "*Twelve Concepts for World Service* Audio project," to be made available on our website (aa.org), completed its professional production in English, French and Spanish in 2018, and entered final post-production review in early 2019.

The video "A New Freedom" dubbing in French and Spanish completed in 2018, with a new DVD to be made available in early 2019.

The 2018–2020 edition of *The A.A. Service Manual combined with the Twelve Concepts for World Service* was published in English, French and Spanish. A working group has been assembled to address the redesign of this material proposed by the 2018 General Service Conference.

The routine monitoring and protecting of A.A.W.S., Inc. copyrights and trademarks continued, as did meeting the steady stream of intellectual property requests for granting of permission to reprint copyrighted material. A new helpful document for non-A.A. twelve-step programs was developed.

The licensing administrator, with the assistance of an in-house temp assistant, addressed the continual surge in queries regarding international translation and licensing of A.A.W.S., Inc. and AA Grapevine, Inc. copyrighted material.

Sales: Total net sales of A.A. literature for 2018 stand at $14,020,147, which is above estimate of $13,780,000 and above the 2017 total, which was $13,693,372.

In 2018, A.A.W.S., Inc. distributed 898,271 copies of *Alcoholics Anonymous* (Fourth Edition, English) in print form, a decrease over 2017's total of 901,484; plus 15,222 as e-books, a downturn from 2017's total of 15,736 (and consistent with industry-wide "e-book fatigue").

Digital book publishing program: More than 55,000 e-book units have been sold through our three distributors (Apple, Amazon and Barnes & Noble). All of our English titles have been converted from print. The Big Book and "Twelve and Twelve" are the two most downloaded titles.

Holiday gift set offer — "A.A. History Shelf": With the approval of A.A.W.S., Inc., the successful Holiday Gift Set special offer of 2016 and 2017 was offered again in 2018 via special flyer and through the online stores October 1, 2018 — January 15, 2019. Sales totaled 1,269 sets (English: 1,157; French: 17; and Spanish: 95), with $38,070 net sales and 5,076 total individual books distributed.

AA.org website: The Publishing Department works closely with the Communication Services desk responsible for web services for the Fellowship and with the web manager to address content changes and corrections called for by the G.S.O. Website Committee.

International translations and licensing: A.A.W.S., Inc. holds and manages nearly 1,500 active registered copyrights in trust for the worldwide Fellowship. In 2018, the trending surge in the volume of international requests continued, and projects moved forward for several different language communities, including: Arabic-speaking, Belgium and French-speaking Europe, Bulgaria, China, Costa Rica, Croatia, Czech Republic, Denmark, Hungary, Iceland, India, Italy, Japan, Lithuania, Poland, Russia, Thailand and Zambia, among many others. Twenty-five reviews of translation submissions from international entities abroad across 17 languages were completed in 2018. Renewals saw a major increase of 263% over 2017.

Notable for 2018 was the completion of the translation and audiobook recording of the much-anticipated Navajo Big Book (a spoken language), with 1,130 copies distributed in 2018, and two manufacturings since its debut in May 2018.

Publishing Operations — *Malini Singh, Manager:*

Inventory and Warehousing: This department monitors inventory on hand at the warehouses and reviews the rates of depletion to project future inventory requirements. The department determines reorder points based on average monthly distribution and advises the production manager when items are up for reordering. The department ensures that inventory is kept at optimal levels at all warehouses and updates and maintains the item maintenance file on Traverse. New items are issued and set up as needed. Inventory sets up safety stock for each item and reviews the safety-stock alert report daily. This department peruses the goods-received reports from the warehouses and resolves inconsistencies, posting all receipts and transfers to and from all distribution points. Inventory also reviews warehouse activity reports monthly and reconciles significant variances.

The Inventory Department is responsible for researching and negotiating with freight companies to guarantee that A.A.W.S. is getting the most competitive pricing and to secure new freight vendors as needed. Another function of this department is to audit the freight invoices to ensure that shipments are charged at the correct rates and that truckers' discounts are properly applied. The department assigns freight carriers for all shipments from the printers/manufacturers to the distribution points; reviews and processes invoices received from the printer or manufacturer; and updates the production log when goods and invoices are received. The Inventory Department reviews the warehousing invoices and investigates discrepancies.

Customer Service: This unit manages and troubleshoots all customer-related issues that arise in the order fulfillment process. They handle and control all warehousing, shipping and literature delivery issues to ensure smooth operations and timeliness. The Customer Service Department also troubleshoots all issues relating to the online stores and the online ordering process.

Order Entry: This unit is responsible for processing and posting all orders and balancing daily, monthly and yearly sales reports. The Order Entry Department processes orders received each day from the United States, Canada and overseas. The orders are received by mail, phone, fax, email and online. Orders processed through our warehousing facilities represent about 95% of the total dollar value of literature sales. Overseas orders are processed from the Canadian warehouse.

Cash deposits are made daily by the Accounting Department, and the orders are then entered on the computer by Order Entry. After the orders are posted, we generate numerous reports, including a daily sales report, invoices for charge and credit card orders, pick-pack slips for the Shipping Department and daily warehouse shipment reports for the Inventory Department. Orders being sent from our warehouses are emailed to them for shipment.

This department is also responsible for taking all phone orders. In 2018, 4,411 calls were taken, including credit card orders. The department gives price quotes and provides callers with general information regarding the ordering of literature. In 2018, 26,789 paid literature orders were processed. Credit card orders totaled 18,008, almost 67% of all paid orders and 80% of all telephone orders.

The department also processes all complimentary literature initiated by staff, which includes new group, new G.S.R. and other complimentary literature. Last year, over 20,000 complimentary orders were processed. In 2018, 3,606 orders were placed online by intergroup/central offices and area and district committees. We currently have over 600 customers signed up to use the bulk-order online bookstore. The consumer online bookstore for the public had 15,348 orders. Web sales made up 64% of total sales.

■ Literature Distributed — 2018

ENGLISH

Books

Alcoholics Anonymous	422,754
Alchololics Anonymous (soft cover)	303,689
Alcoholics Anonymous (large print)	42,895
Alcoholics Anonymous (pocket abridged)	109,256
Alcoholics Anonymous (large print/abridged)	19,677
Daily Reflections	123,000
Daily Reflections (large print)	16,180
Twelve Steps and Twelve Traditions (reg. ed.)	135,563
Twelve Steps and Twelve Traditions (gift ed.)	3,983
Twelve Steps and Twelve Traditions (soft cover)	144,722
Twelve Steps and Twelve Traditions (large print)	25,792
Twelve Steps and Twelve Traditions (pocket ed.)	27,025
A.A. Comes of Age	7,639
As Bill Sees It	20,873
As Bill Sees It (soft cover)	22,849
As Bill Sees It (large print)	7,091
Dr. Bob and the Good Oldtimers	7,594
'Pass It On'	6,123
Experience, Strength & Hope	7,072
Total	**1,453,777**

Booklets

The A.A. Service Manual/ Twelve Concepts for World Service	21,417
Living Sober	108,226
Living Sober (large print)	9,271
Came to Believe	29,864
Came to Believe (large print)	3,544
A.A. in Prisons: Inmate to Inmate	14,223
Total	**186,545**

Pamphlets

A.A. and the Armed Services	10,940
LGBTQ Alcoholics in A.A.	32,304
A.A. as a Resource for the Health Care Professional	29,431
A.A. for the Native North American	13,413
Women in A.A.	62,632
The A.A. Group	73,572
A.A. in Your Community	37,029
A.A. in Correctional Facilities	12,848
A.A. in Treatment Settings	16,691
The A.A. Membership Survey	17,133
The A.A. Member — Medications and Other Drugs	61,471
A.A. Tradition — How It Developed	16,741
A.A.'s Legacy of Service	8,675
A Brief Guide to Alcoholics Anonymous	95,959
Circles of Love and Service	33,929
Bridging the Gap	25,549
Members of the Clergy Ask About A.A.	15,796
The Co-Founders of Alcoholics Anonymous	7,978
Do You Think You're Different?	70,670
Frequently Asked Questions	146,608
Frequently Asked Questions (large print)	8,264
G.S.R.	32,486
Grapevine — Our Meeting in Print	12,870
How A.A. Members Cooperate	13,019
How It Works	46,448
If You Are a Professional…	31,399
Inside A.A.	29,025
A.A. for the Black and African-American Alcoholic	18,612
Is A.A. for You?	286,354
Is A.A. for Me?	84,812
Is There a Problem Drinker in the Workplace?	14,655
Is There an Alcoholic in Your Life?	42,133
It Happened to Alice	19,721
It Sure Beats Sitting in a Cell	30,901
The Jack Alexander Article	11,640
Let's Be Friendly with Our Friends	4,688
A Member's-Eye View of A.A.	27,726
Memo to an Inmate Who May Be an Alcoholic	23,024
A Message to Corrections Professionals	9,632
A Newcomer Asks	260,208
Problems Other Than Alcohol	76,036
Questions and Answers on Sponsorship	225,918
Speaking at Non-A.A. Meetings	10,197
The Twelve Concepts for World Service Illustrated	26,335
The Twelve Steps Illustrated	47,564
Twelve Traditions Flyer	6,576
The Twelve Traditions Illustrated	47,789
This Is A.A.	196,160
This Is A.A. (large print)	5,639
A.A. for the Older Alcoholic (Large Print)	40,200
Too Young?	37,082
Understanding Anonymity	46,096
What Happened to Joe	19,292
Young People and A.A.	65,062
Access to A.A.: Members share on overcoming barriers	17,846
Many Paths to Spirituality	48,997
The "God" Word — Agnostic and Atheist members in A.A.	26,031
A.A. for Alcoholics with Mental Health Issues — and their Sponsors	14,538
Total	**2,754,344**

Miscellaneous

Wallet cards-two-fold	191,856
Wallet cards-I Am Responsible	33,619
Wallet cards-Anonymity	25,549
Anonymity Display Card	1,876
Parchment scrolls	1,417
Placards	554
C.P.C. Workbook	1,163
Archives Workbook	479
Corrections Workbook	855
P.I. Workbook	1,547
Treatment Committee Workbook	1,243
Treatment Committee Kit	438
Accessibilities Workbook	412
Twelve and Twelve on CD	5
A.A. Guidelines	75,959
Group Handbook	2,039
Wire Racks	1,471
Cassettes (tape cassettes)	2
Audio CDs	452
DVDs	3,182
Alcoholics Anonymous (cassette album)	10
Alcoholics Anonymous (4th Ed cassette album)	4
Alcoholics Anonymous (4th Ed CD album)	1,414
A.A. Comes of Age (CD album)	215
Twelve Steps and Twelve Traditions (cassette album)	12
Twelve Steps and Twelve Traditions (CD album)	656
TV Public Service Announcements	118
Radio Public Service Announcements	50
Twelve Steps Shade displays	1,244
Twelve Traditions Shade displays	1,167
A.A. Fact File	1,634
Table Top Display 12 & 12	360
Anonymity in the Digital Age Poster — medium 11x17	489
Anonymity in the Digital Age Poster — small 8.5x11	470
Pioneers of AA (CD album)	34
Living Sober (CD album)	171
Total	**352,166**
Grand Total	**4,746,832**

SPANISH

Libros

Alcohólicos Anónimos (Alcoholics Anonymous soft cover)	11,073
Alcohólicos Anónimos (Alcoholics Anonymous hardcover)	9,432
Alcohólicos Anónimos (Alcoholics Anonymous abridged pocket size)	5,008
Alcohólicos Anónimos (Alcoholics Anonymous large print)	3,811
Alcohólicos Anónimos (Alcoholics Anonymous large print/abridged)	1,089
Como Lo Ve Bill (As Bill Sees It)	4,181
A.A. llega a su mayoría de edad (A.A. Comes of Age)	2,475
El Dr. Bob y los buenos veteranos (Dr. Bob and the Good Oldtimers)	2,184
Transmítelo (Pass it On)	2,426
Reflexiones diarias (Daily Reflections)	7,804
Viviendo sobrio (Living Sober)	10,466
El Manual de Servicio de A.A./ Doce Conceptos para el Servicio Mundial (A.A. Service Manual/Twelve Concepts)	2,785
Doce Pasos y Doce Tradiciones (Twelve Steps and Twelve Traditions)	13,384
Llegamos a creer (Came to Believe)	4,621
A.A. en prisiones de preso a preso (Inmate to Inmate)	4,415
Doce Pasos y Doce Tradiciones (pocket ed.)	2,826
Doce Pasos y Doce Tradiciones (large print)	5,196
De las tinieblas hacia la luz (From Darkness Toward Light)	3,694
Total	**96,870**

Folletos

A.A. en Su Comunidad (A.A. in Your Community)	5,020
Preguntas frecuentes acerca de A.A. (Frequently Asked Questions)	15,100
Esto es A.A. (This is A.A.)	13,154
¿Es A.A. para usted? (Is A.A. for You?)	47,230
¿Hay un alcohólico en su vida? (Is There an Alcoholic in Your Life?)	5,855
Carta a un preso que puede ser alcohólico (Memo to an Inmate)	1,378
El punto de vista de un miembro de A.A. (A Member's-Eye View)	1,129
Alcohólicos Anónimos por Jack Alexander (Jack Alexander Article)	510
Seamos amistosos con nuestros amigos (Let's be Friendly with our Friends)	1,088
Un principiante pregunta (A Newcomer Asks)	7,212
Como funciona el programa (How It Works)	2,767
Lo que le sucedió a José (What Happened to Joe)	4,225
Comprendiendo el Anonimato (Understanding Anonymity)	2,055
El grupo de A.A. (The A.A. Group)	6,546
Preguntas y respuestas sobre el apadrinamiento (Questions and Answers on Sponsorship)	6,618
El miembro de A.A. — los medicamentos y otras drogas (The A.A. Member — Medications and Other Drugs)	2,767
Las Doce Tradiciones Ilustradas (The Twelve Traditions Illustrated)	2,863
A.A. en centros de tratamiento (A.A. in Treatment Centers)	1,144
A.A. para el Nativo Norteamericano (AA for the Native North American)	16
Los jóvenes y A.A. (Young People and A.A.)	8,379
La Tradición de A.A. — cómo se desarrolló (A.A. Tradition — How It Developed)	1,497
Una breve guía a A.A. (A Brief Guide to A.A.)	8,440
A.A. en las Instituciones Correccionales (A.A. in Correctional Facilities)	679
Problemas diferentes del alcohol (Problems Other Than Alcohol)	3,838
Es mejor que estar sentado en una celda (It Sure Beats Sitting In a Cell)	1,788
¿Cómo cooperan los miembros de A.A.? (How A.A. Members Cooperate)	1,188
Dentro de A.A. (Inside A.A.)	1,429
A.A. como recurso para los profesionales de la salud (A.A. as a Resource for the Health Care Professional)	683
Un ministro religioso pregunta acerca de A.A. (The Clergy Asks)	864
R.S.G. (G.S.R.)	1,606
¿Se cree usted diferente? (Do You Think You're Different?)	5,389
Le sucedió a Alicia (It Happened to Alice)	3,421
Hablando en reuniones no-A.A. (Speaking at non-A.A. Meetings)	569
Las mujeres en A.A. (Women in A.A.)	7,220
Encuesta sobre los miembros de A.A. (A.A. Membership Survey)	1,578
¿Hay un bebedor problema en el lugar de trabajo? (Is there a problem drinker in the workplace?)	2,064
¿Es A.A. para mi? (Is A.A. for Me?)	9,701
A.A. para el alcohólico de edad avanzada (A.A. for the older alcoholic)	3,649
Los Doce Pasos Ilustrados (The Twelve Steps Illustrated)	2,373
Círculos de amor y servicio (Circles of Love & Service)	2,628
Uniendo las orillas (Bridging the Gap)	516
A.A. y las fuerzas armadas (A.A. and the Armed Services)	150
Los Doce Conceptos Ilustrados (Twelve Concepts Illustrated)	1,039
Los alcohólicos LGBTQ en A.A. (LGBTQ Alcoholics in A.A.)	1,169
El legado de servicio de A.A. (A.A.'s Legacy of Service)	864
Si usted es un profesional (If you are a Professional...)	698
A.A. para el alcohólico negro y afroamericano (A.A. for the Black & African-American Alcoholic)	3
El Grapevine y La Viña:nuestras reuniones impresas (Grapevine and La Viña: Our Meetings in Print)	1,135
Esto es A.A. (This is AA — large print)	15
Preguntas frecuentes acerca de A.A. (Frequently Asked Questions — large print)	15
¿Demasiado joven? (Too Young?)	2,848
Accessibilidad para todos (Access to AA: Overcoming Barriers)	1,488
Muchas sendas hacia espiritualidad (Many Paths to Spirituality)	2,247
La palabra "Dios" — Los miembros de A.A. agnósticos y ateos (The "God" Word — Agnostic and Atheist members in A.A.)	67
A.A. para los alcohólicos con problemas de salud mental — y sus padrinos (A.A. for Alcoholics with Mental Health Issues — and their Sponsors)	396
Total	**208,310**

Diverso

Guias (Guidelines)	12,910
Carteles	257
Tarjetas tamaño billetera (wallet cards)	8,883
Alcohólicos Anónimos (casetes) (Big Book on cassette)	13
Alcohólicos Anónimos (CD album) (Big Book on CD)	361
Doce Pasos y Doce Tradiciones (CD album)	425
El anonimato en la era digital — Pósters de exhibición (11x17) (Anonymity in the Digital Age Poster — medium 11x17)	11
El anonimato en la era digital — Pósters de exhibición (8.5x11) (Anonymity in the Digital Age Poster — small 8.5x11)	11
Total	**22,888**
Gran Total	**328,068**

FRENCH

Livres

Les Alcooliques Anonymes (Alcoholics Anonymous — format relié)	3,613
Les Alcooliques Anonymes (Alcoholics Anonymous — format souple)	1,150
Les Alcooliques Anonymes (Alcoholics Anonymous — format poche)	481
Les Alcooliques Anonymes (Alcoholics Anonymous — gros caractères)	541
Les Alcooliques Anonymes (Alcoholics Anonymous — gros caractères/abrégé)	190
Les douze étapes et les douze traditions (Twelve & Twelve — format relié)	1,298
Les douze étapes et les douze traditions (Twelve & Twelve — format souple)	609
Les douze étapes et les douze traditions (Twelve & Twelve — gros caractères)	243
Les douze étapes et les douze traditions (Twelve & Twelve — format poche)	248
Le mouvement des AA devient adulte (A.A. Comes of Age)	245
Réflexions de Bill (As Bill Sees It)	1,407
Réflexions quotidiennes (Daily Reflections)	3,171
Dr Bob et les pionniers (Dr. Bob and the Good Oldtimers)	264
Expérience, force & espoir (Experience, Strength and Hope)	61
Transmets-Le (Pass It On)	291
Les AA en Prison (A.A. in Prison)	342
Total	**14,154**

Livrets

Nous en sommes venus a croire (Came to Believe)	664
Vivre... sans alcool! (Living Sober)	2,353
Le manuel du service et les douze concepts	1,109
Total	**4,126**

Brochures

Voici les A.A. (This is A.A.)	9,917
Foire aux questions sur les AA (Frequently Asked Questions)	2,012
Les AA: sont-ils pour vous? (Is A.A. for You?)	10,771
Les femmes des AA (Women in A.A.)	1,993
Collaboration des membres des AA (How A.A. Members Cooperate)	617
Y a-t-il un buveur à problème dans votre milieu de travail? (Is there Problem Drinker in the workplace?)	930
Le membre des AA face aux medicaments et a la drogue (The A.A. Member — Medications & Other Drugs)	697
L'article de Jack Alexander sur les AA (The Jack Alexander Article)	119
Collaborons avec nos amis (Let's Be Friendly With Our Friends)	118
Questions et reponses sur le parrainage (Questions and Answers on Sponsorship)	3,161
Les AA: Une ressource pour les professionels de la santé (A.A. as a Resource for the Health Care Professional)	893
Les AA dans les établissements de traitement (A.A. in Treatment Settings)	439
La Tradition des AA et son developpement (A.A. Tradition/How It Developed)	161
Vous vous occupez professionnelement d'alcoolisme? (If You Are a Professional)	1,161
L'histoire de Nicole (It Happened to Alice)	331
Jean face a son problème d'alcool (What Happened to Joe)	327
Les AA dans votre milieu (A.A. in Your Community)	945
Problémes autres que l'alcoolisme (Problems Other Than Alcohol)	1,287
Point de vue d'un membre sur les AA (A Member's-Eye View of A.A.)	387
Les douze traditions illustrées (The Twelve Traditions Illustrated)	1,595
Les AA dans les établissements correctionnels (A.A. in Correctional Facilities)	385
Ça vaut mieux que de poireauter en prison (It Sure Beats Sitting in a Cell)	752
Petit guide pratique sur les AA (A Brief Guide to A.A.)	1,407
Les membres du clergé se renseignent (Members of the Clergy Ask About A.A.)	268
Les deux fondateurs des AA (The Co-founders of A.A.)	355
Message à l'intention d'un detenu (Memo to an Inmate)	1,023
Message aux professionnels d'établissements correctionnels (Message to Corrections Professionals)	299
Le groupe des AA (The A.A. Group)	2,129
Les Douze Concepts illustrés (Twelve Concepts Illustrated)	1,281
Le sens de l'anonymat (Understanding Anonymity)	1,292
Y-a-t-il un alcoolique dans votre vie? (Is There an Alcoholic in Your Life?)	1,324
Le RSG (The G.S.R.)	2,028
Causeries a l'exterieur des AA (Speaking at Non-A.A. Meetings)	354
Trop jeune? (Too Young?)	896
La Structure des AA (Inside A.A.)	1,239
L'héritage du service chez les AA (A.A.'s Legacy of Service)	418
Cercles d'amour et de service (Circles of Love & Service)	726
Vous croyez-vous différent? (Do You Think You're Different?)	904
Sondage sur les membres des AA (The A.A. Membership Survey)	787
Les jeunes et les AA (Young People & A.A.)	1,306
Votre BSG (Your G.S.O.)	1,250
AA pour l'alcoolique plus âgé (A.A. for the Older Alcoholic)	1,193
Un nouveau veut savoir (A Newcomer Asks)	5,684
Les AA sont-ils pour moi? (Is A.A. for Me?)	1,054
Favoriser le rapprochement (Bridging the Gap)	182
Les AA et les forces armées (A.A. and the Armed Service)	675
Les Douze Etapes Illustrées (Twelve Steps Illustrated)	731
Voici les AA (This Is AA — large print)	15
Les alcooliques LGBTQ des AA (LGBTQ Alcoholics in A.A.)	837
Les AA et les Autochtones d'Amérique du Nord (A.A. and the Native North American)	279
L'accès aux AA (Access to A.A.: Overcoming Barriers)	758
Différentes avenues vers la spiritualité (Many Paths to Spirituality)	6,033
Lignes de conduite des AA (Guidelines)	1,629
Le mot « Dieu » — Membres agnostiques et athées des AA (The "God" Word — Agnostic and Atheist members in A.A.)	100
Les AA pour les alcooliques atteints de maladie mentale — et ceux qui les parrainent (A.A. for Alcoholics with Mental Health Issues — and their Sponsors)	100
Total	**77,554**

Divers

12 & 12 (cassette album)	2
12 & 12 (CD album)	220
Les Alcooliques Anonymes (CD album)	286
Carte 12 Étapes/12 Traditions (Wallet card 12 Steps & 12 Traditions)	807
Carte anonymat (Francais/anglais) (Anonymity wallet card)	450
Carte je suis responsable (I am responsible wallet card)	403
DVDS	18
Notre Méthode (How It Works)	13,574
Manuel de Groupe	22
Pochette de l'Information publique	21
Pochette des centres de détention	9
Pochette de la CMP	18
Prière de la sérénité (12x16) (Parchment Serenity Prayer)	20
Pochette des centres de traitement	9
Dossier d'Information sur les AA (Fact File)	199
L'anonymat à l'ère du numérique — affiches (11x17) (Anonymity in the Digital Age Poster — medium 11x17)	49
L'anonymat à l'ère du numérique — affiches (8.5x11) (Anonymity in the Digital Age Poster — small 8.5x11)	61
Total	**16,168**
Somme final	**112,002**

■ AA Grapevine Literature Distributed — 2018

Books

Best of Bill — Hard Cover (Discontinued)	4
Best of Bill (soft cover)	4,741
Best of Bill (large print)	1,013
Best of the Grapevine I — soft cover	1
The Language of the Heart (hard cover)	2,412
El Lenguaje del Corazón	2,407
A.A. Around the World (soft cover)	0
The Language of the Heart (soft cover)	3,653
Thank You for Sharing (soft cover)	395
Spiritual Awakening (soft cover)	2,464
The Home Group — Revised (soft cover)	1,106
I Am Responsible: The Hand of AA (soft cover)	912
Emotional Sobriety (soft cover)	5,821
Language of the Heart (large print)	751
In Our Own Words	608
Beginners Book	2,962
Voices of Long-Term Sobriety	1,444
A Rabbit Walks Into a Bar	2,247
Spiritual Awakenings Vol II	1,158
Step by Step (soft cover)	1,513
Emotional Sobriety II (soft cover)	2,867
Young & Sober	1,042
Into Action	1,488
Happy, Joyous & Free	1,710
Happy, Joyous & Free — Fr & Sp	1,476
One on One	1,441
No Matter What	1,633
Grapevine Daily Quote Book	2,279
Sober & Out	957
Forming True Partnerships	1,476
Best of Bill — French (soft cover)	927
The Home Group — French (soft cover)	333
Le Langage du Coeur	233
En Tête a Tête	300
Best of Bill — Spanish (soft cover)	2,722
Lo Mejor de la Viña	819
El Grupo Base	1,166
Un Día A La Vez	946
Our Twelve Traditions	1,523
Making Amends	2,269
Voices of Women in AA	6,813
AA in the Military	3,353
One Big Tent	6,275
Frente A Frente	2,740
Total:	**82,400**

E-books

Language of the Heart	923
Best of Bill	254
Lo Mejor de Bill	52
Step by Step	31
Emotional Sobriety I	549
Emotional Sobriety II	192
Spiritual Awakenings I	102
Spiritual Awakenings II	40
Young & Sober	13
Into Action	27
Happy, Joyous & Free	36
Forming True Partnerships	57
Un Día a la Vez (One Day at a Time)	46
Our Twelve Traditions	61
Making Amends	62
Voices of Women in AA	247
AA in the Millitary	28
Frente a Frente	4
One Big Tent	221
Other	366
Total:	**3,311**

CDs – English	975
CDs – Spanish	1,357
Total:	**2,332**
Miscellaneous	15,375
Grand Total	**103,418**

GRAPEVINE SUBSCRIPTIONS* — Geographical Breakdown

	APRIL 2019	APRIL 2018	INCREASE/ DECREASE
UNITED STATES*			
Alabama	420	436	(16)
Alaska	315	305	10
Arizona	1,379	1,439	(60)
Arkansas	334	357	(23)
California	5,991	6,049	(58)
Colorado	1,132	1,111	21
Connecticut	888	901	(13)
Delaware	267	253	14
District of Columbia	96	101	(5)
Florida	3,547	3,855	(308)
Georgia	1,571	1,552	19
Hawaii	395	400	(5)
Idaho	468	482	(14)
Illinois	1,886	1,995	(109)
Indiana	981	969	12
Iowa	684	628	56
Kansas	586	589	(3)
Kentucky	478	527	(49)
Louisiana	443	465	(22)
Maine	354	379	(25)
Maryland	857	875	(18)
Massachusetts	1,310	1,363	(53)
Michigan	1,870	1,994	(124)
Minnesota	1,619	1,673	(54)
Mississippi	180	207	(27)
Missouri	984	1,050	(66)
Montana	435	463	(28)
Nebraska	526	497	29
Nevada	629	704	(75)
New Hampshire	455	472	(17)
New Jersey	1,846	1,834	12
New Mexico	424	431	(7)
New York	3,592	3,732	(140)
North Carolina	1,508	1,567	(59)
North Dakota	274	265	9
Ohio	1,372	1,423	(51)
Oklahoma	442	435	7
Oregon	1,094	1,131	(37)
Pennsylvania	3,489	3,346	143
Rhode Island	226	226	0
South Carolina	607	611	(4)
South Dakota	190	205	(15)
Tennessee	672	677	(5)
Texas	2,224	2,354	(130)
Utah	385	405	(20)
Vermont	220	236	(16)
Virginia	1,493	1,567	(74)
Washington	1,883	1,977	(94)
West Virginia	212	236	(24)
Wisconsin	1,685	1,707	(22)
Wyoming	166	161	5
Puerto Rico	10	7	3
U.S. Possessions/APO	33	40	(7)
Virgin Islands	15	24	(9)
Subtotal US	**55,142**	**56,688**	**(1,546)**
CANADA*			
Alberta/NWT	528	592	(64)
British Columbia/YKN	764	767	(3)
Manitoba	215	241	(26)
New Brunswick/PEI	202	192	10
Nova Scotia/ Newfoundland/Labrador	229	258	(29)
Ontario	2,288	2,328	(40)
Quebec	221	212	9
Saskatchewan	277	265	12
Subtotal CANADA	**4,724**	**4,855**	**(131)**
FOREIGN*	509	527	(18)
Grand Total	**60,375**	**62,070**	**(1,695)**

LA VIÑA SUBSCRIPTIONS*

	Mar./Apr. '19	Mar./Apr. '18	Diff.
Total	7,345	7,452	(107)

(*does not include monthly orders)

Dorothy Goes to the International Convention
(a G.S.O. production loosely based on *The Wizard of Oz*)

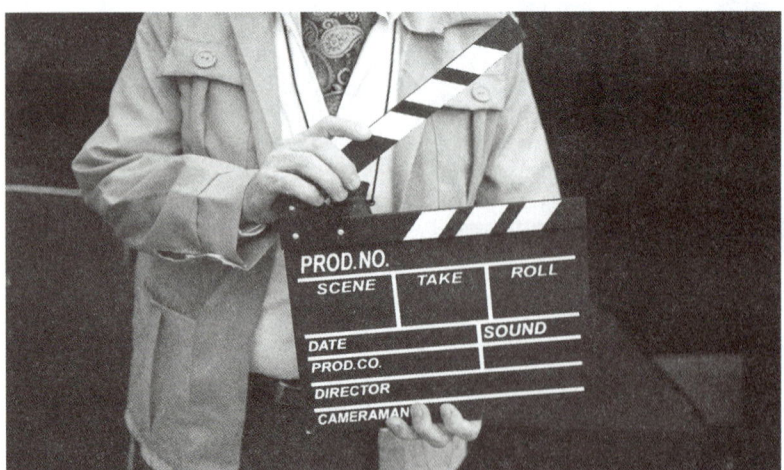

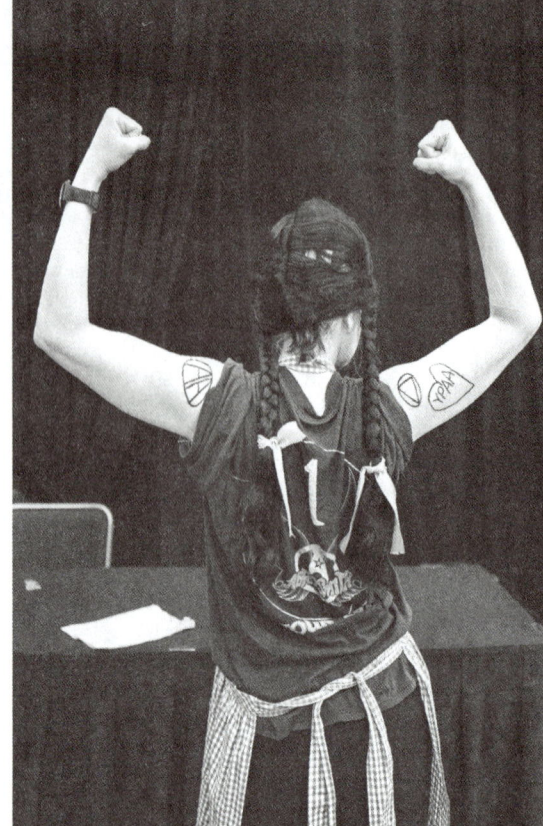

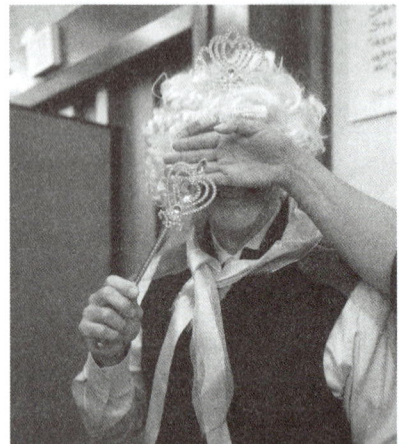

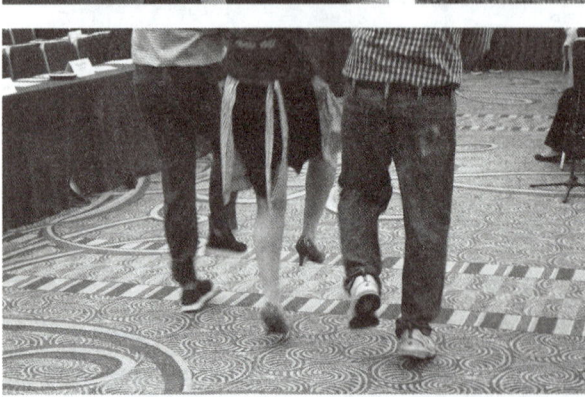

*Performed by the 475 Riverside Players
in honor of the upcoming
2020 International Convention
to be held in Detroit, MI, July 2–5, 2020.*

■ Report of the Independent Auditor

Independent Auditor's Report

May 7, 2019

The Board of Trustees
  The General Service Board of
  Alcoholics Anonymous, Inc.
475 Riverside Drive, New York, New York 10115

Members of the Board:

We have audited the accompanying consolidated financial statements of The General Service Board of Alcoholics Anonymous, Inc. and its Affiliates, Alcoholics Anonymous World Services, Inc. and Alcoholics Anonymous Grapevine, Inc. (collectively, the "Organization"), which comprise the consolidated statement of financial position as of December 31, 2018, and the related consolidated statements of activities, functional expenses and cash flows for the year then ended, and the related notes to the consolidated financial statements.

Management's Responsibility for the Financial Statements

Management is responsible for the preparation and fair presentation of these consolidated financial statements in accordance with accounting principles generally accepted in the United States of America; this includes the design, implementation, and maintenance of internal control relevant to the preparation and fair presentation of consolidated financial statements that are free from material misstatement, whether due to fraud or error.

Auditors' Responsibility

Our responsibility is to express an opinion on these consolidated financial statements based on our audit. We conducted our audit in accordance with auditing standards generally accepted in the United States of America. Those standards require that we plan and perform the audit to obtain reasonable assurance about whether the consolidated financial statements are free from material misstatement.

An audit involves performing procedures to obtain audit evidence about the amounts and disclosures in the consolidated financial statements. The procedures selected depend on the auditors' judgment, including the assessment of the risks of material misstatement of the consolidated financial statements, whether due to fraud or error. In making those risk assessments, the auditors consider internal control relevant to the entity's preparation and fair presentation of the consolidated financial statements in order to design audit procedures that are appropriate in the circumstances, but not for the purpose of expressing an opinion on the effectiveness of the entity's internal control. Accordingly, we express no such opinion. An audit also includes evaluating the appropriateness of accounting policies used and the reasonableness of significant accounting estimates made by management, as well as evaluating the overall presentation of the consolidated financial statements.

We believe that the audit evidence we have obtained is sufficient and appropriate to provide a basis for our audit opinion.

Opinion

In our opinion, the consolidated financial statements referred to above present fairly, in all material respects, the financial position of the Organization as of December 31, 2018, and the changes in its net assets and its cash flows for the year then ended in accordance with accounting principles generally accepted in the United States of America.

Emphasis of Matter

As discussed in Note 2 to the consolidated financial statements, during the year ended December 31, 2018, the Organization adopted Accounting Standards Update 2016-14, "Not-for-Profit Entities." Our opinion is not modified with respect to this matter.

Prior Year Financial Statements

The prior year summarized comparative information has been derived from the Organization's December 31, 2017 consolidated financial statements, which were audited by other auditors whose report dated March 27, 2018, expressed an unmodified opinion on those consolidated financial statements.

Other Matters

Our audit was conducted for the purpose of forming an opinion on the consolidated financial statements as a whole. Supplementary information is presented for purposes of additional analysis of the consolidated financial statements and is not a required part of the consolidated financial statements. Such information is the responsibility of management and was derived from and relates directly to the underlying accounting and other records used to prepare the consolidated financial statements. The information has been subjected to the auditing procedures applied in the audit of the consolidated financial statements and certain additional procedures, including comparing and reconciling such information directly to the underlying accounting and other records used to prepare the consolidated financial statements or to the consolidated financial statements themselves, and other additional procedures in accordance with auditing standards generally accepted in the United States of America. In our opinion, the information is fairly stated in all material respects in relation to the consolidated financial statements as a whole.

Marks Paneth LLP

Marks Paneth
Accountants and Advisors
New York, NY

THE GENERAL SERVICE BOARD OF ALCOHOLICS ANONYMOUS, INC. ALCOHOLICS ANONYMOUS WORLD SERVICES, INC. ALCOHOLICS ANONYMOUS GRAPEVINE, INC. NOTES TO CONSOLIDATED FINANCIAL STATEMENTS DECEMBER 31, 2018

Note 1 — Organization and Nature of Activities: The General Service Board of Alcoholics Anonymous, Inc., ("G.S.B.") and its affiliates A.A. World Services, Inc. ("A.A.W.S.") and A.A. Grapevine, Inc. ("A.A.G.V.") (collectively, the "Organization") are not-for-profit organizations organized in New York for the purpose of assisting in the formation of A.A. groups and coordinating the A.A. program of rehabilitating alcoholics throughout the world, and publishing books, magazines, pamphlets and other material directly related to that purpose. The trustees of G.S.B. are ex officio members of A.A.W.S. and A.A.G.V., and as such, elect their boards of directors. As members, they also have the sole right to amend the A.A.W.S. and A.A.G.V. bylaws and approve their budgets.

G.S.B., A.A.W.S. and A.A.G.V. are exempt from federal income taxes under Section 501(c)(3) of the Internal Revenue Code.

The activities of G.S.B. are conducted in five separate funds, as follows:

GENERAL FUND — This fund is comprised of those assets not included in any of the other funds and may be used for any purpose for which the Organization was formed. These purposes presently include activities related to communication and information services to A.A. groups and members, public information, cooperation with the professional community and regional, national and international meetings, conferences and conventions.

RESERVE FUND — This fund was established in 1954 for the purpose of accumulating a prudent operating reserve, which during 1977, was redefined by a special General Service Board Committee as the prior year's combined operating expenses of A.A.W.S., A.A.G.V. and the general fund of G.S.B. The committee also recommended that all investment activities of the operating entities be consolidated into the Reserve Fund. That advisory action was approved by the Board of Trustees and since that time, all funds of the operating entities in excess of those required for working capital have been transferred to the Reserve Fund. Included in such transfers from A.A.G.V. have been amounts held for unfulfilled subscriptions reflected as a liability of the Reserve Fund on the accompanying consolidated statement of financial position. Any withdrawals from the Reserve Fund must be specifically authorized by the Board of Trustees upon recommendation of the Trustee's Finance and Budgetary Committee.

CAPITAL PROJECTS FUND — This fund accounts for the cost of leasehold improvements and computer hardware and software incurred under major capital projects and records depreciation on such assets.

POSTRETIREMENT MEDICAL FUND — In 2016, a goal of accumulating assets was established to fund 100% of the liability by 2025.

CONVENTION FUND — A separate fund established to record the direct revenue and expenses of international A.A. conventions held every five years. These events are separate from the regular operations of the General Service Office ("GSO"), but the general fund receives any excess of revenue and pays any excess of expense resulting from the activity.

From a historical perspective, the net direct result of all conventions held to date is approximately an excess of income of $1,350,000 and presently resides with all other income not required for working capital in the Reserve Fund.

Note 2 — Summary of Significant Accounting Policies:

A. *Basis of Consolidation* — The consolidated financial statements of the Organization have been prepared by consolidating the financial statements of G.S.B., A.A.W.S. and A.A.G.V. All material intercompany transactions and balances (when applicable) have been eliminated in the consolidation.

B. *Basis of Presentation* — The accompanying consolidated financial statements of the Organization have been prepared on the accrual basis of accounting. The Organization adheres to accounting principles generally accepted in the United States of America ("U.S. GAAP").

C. *Net Assets* — The Organization maintains its net assets under the following classes:

Without donor restrictions — This represents net assets not subject to donor-imposed stipulations and that have no time restrictions. Such resources are available for support of the Organization's operations over which the Board of Directors has discretionary control.

With donor restrictions — This represents net assets subject to donor-imposed stipulations that will be met by actions of the Organization or by the passage of time. When a stipulated time restriction ends or purpose restriction is accomplished, such net assets with donor restrictions are reclassified to net assets without donor restrictions and reported in the consolidated statement of activities as net assets released from restrictions.

All net assets of the Organization are net assets without donor restrictions as of December 31, 2018 and 2017.

D. *Cash and Cash Equivalents* — The Organization considers all highly liquid investments with a maturity of three months or less when acquired to be cash equivalents.

E. *Investments* — Investments are stated at fair value. Interest, dividends and gains and losses on investments are reflected in the accompanying consolidated statements of activities as increases and decreases in net assets without donor restrictions.

F. *Fair Value Measurements* — Fair value measurements are based on the price that would be received to sell an asset or paid to transfer a liability in an orderly transaction between market participants at the measurement date. In order to increase consistency and comparability in fair value measurements, a fair value hierarchy prioritizes observable and unobservable inputs used to measure fair value into three levels, as described in Note 5.

G. *Inventory* — Inventory is valued at the lower of cost or market using the first-in, first-out method of valuation. Literature distributed without charge is included in the cost of printing as a reduction of inventory. Inventory costs include paper, printing, binding and shipping.

H. *Property and Equipment* — Property and equipment are stated at cost less accumulated depreciation and amortization. These amounts do not purport to represent replacement or realizable values. The Organization capitalizes property and equipment with a useful life of one year or more and a cost of at least $1,000. Depreciation is provided on a straight-line basis over the estimated useful lives of the assets. Leasehold improvements are amortized over the lesser of the estimated useful life or the term of the lease.

I. *Revenue Recognition* — The Organization earns revenue from the publication of magazines and distribution of literature. Magazine revenue is recorded as subscriptions are fulfilled. Revenue from the distribution of other publications is recognized when goods are shipped. Payments received in advance related to subscriptions are reflected as deferred revenue on the accompanying consolidated statement of financial position.

J. *Contributions* — The Organization accepts donations from A.A. groups and members. Contributions are recorded as increases in net assets with or without donor restrictions, depending on the existence and/or nature of any donor restrictions. Contributions that are restricted by the donor are considered as increases in net assets without donor restrictions if the restrictions are satisfied in the period in which the contributions are recognized. The Organization does not receive or solicit pledges, so contributions are recorded as revenue when cash is received. For the years ended December 31, 2018 and 2017, all contributions were included in net assets without donor restrictions.

K. *Allowance for Uncollectible Receivables* — The Organization provides a reserve for uncollectible accounts receivable based on management's assessment of the current status of individual accounts outstanding, the creditworthiness of its customers, the aged basis of the receivable and prior historical experience. As of December 31, 2018 and 2017, the Organization determined an allowance of approximately $21,000 was necessary for accounts receivable.

L. *Functional Allocation of Expenses* — The cost of providing the various program and supporting services has been summarized on a functional basis in the accompanying consolidated statement of functional expenses. Accordingly, certain costs have been allocated among the program and supporting services benefited. The Organization only considers costs that are directly spent for the fellowship as program expenses. Other expenses are not indirectly allocated and are considered as supporting services.

M. *Use of Estimates* — The preparation of consolidated financial statements in conformity with U.S. GAAP requires management to make estimates and assumptions that affect the reported amounts of revenues and expenses during the reporting period. Actual results could differ from those estimates.

N. *Operating Measure* — The Organization includes in its definition of operations all revenues and expenses that are an integral part of its programs and supporting activities. Changes in retirement liabilities, support for La Viña, and intercompany and interfund transfers are recognized as non-operating activities.

O. *Recent Accounting Pronouncements* — Financial Accounting Standards Board ("FASB") Accounting Standards Update ("ASU") 2016-14, "Not-for-Profit Entities" was adopted for the year ended December 31, 2018. ASU 2016-14 provides for a number of changes, including the presentation of two classes of net assets and enhanced disclosure on liquid resources and expense allocation. The changes were adopted retrospectively and had no impact on the change in net assets for the year ended December 31, 2017. Net assets as of December 31, 2017 were reclassified to conform to the new presentation.

Note 3 — Liquidity and Availability of Resources for Operating Expenditures:

A.A.W.S. regularly monitors its financial assets available to meet general expenditures during the course of twelve months. It operates within a budget and anticipates collecting sufficient revenue to cover general expenditures. A.A.W.S. and G.S.B. have six non-interest-bearing accounts that enable them to meet these needs.

The Reserve Fund was established in 1954 for the purpose of accumulating a prudent operating reserve, which, during 1977 was re-defined as one year's combined operating expenses of A.A.W.S., A.A.G.V. and the General Fund of G.S.B. Since the inception of this fund, the one-year target has changed to nine to twelve months of combined operating expenses. To assure liquidity, the Reserve Fund shall contain investment instruments having maturities of one year or less in an amount equal to the sum of the unearned A.A.G.V. subscription liability and the operating cash requirements of the service entities. The balance of the Reserve Fund shall be invested in instruments with maturities of between zero and ten years, provided that at no time shall more than 50% of the principal amount of such balance consist of investments having maturity dates of five or more years.

The Organization considers all expenditures related to its ongoing program as well as services undertaken to support these activities to be general expenditures.

As of December 31, 2018, the Organization's financial assets were as follows:

Cash and cash equivalents	$3,396,035
Investments	21,762,993
Accounts receivable, net	378,577
	$25,537,605

As of December 31, 2018, the Organization's financial assets available to meet general expenditures of the next twelve months were as follows:

Cash and cash equivalents	$3,396,035
Accounts receivable, net	378,577
	$3,774,612

The Reserve Fund is not considered available for operations.

Note 4 — Investments: As described in Note 1, all funds of the Organization not required for working capital are invested in the Reserve Fund of G.S.B. In accordance with established policy, the Reserve Fund invests in certificates of deposit.

The postretirement medical fund holds investments designed to assist in reaching the stated goal of accumulating assets equal to 100% of the accrued postretirement health benefits by December 31, 2025. This fund invests in bond and equity mutual funds.

As of December 31, 2018 and 2017, investments were as follows:

	2018	2017
Reserve fund:		
Certificates of deposit	$16,325,250	$15,311,789
Postretirement medical fund:		
Mutual funds — bond funds	1,997,301	1,871,202
Mutual funds — equity funds	3,440,442	3,580,605
	5,437,743	5,451,807
	$21,762,993	$20,763,596

Investments are subject to market volatility that could substantially change their carrying value in the near term. Investment activity consisted of the following for the years ended December 31, 2018 and 2017:

	2018	2017
Interest and dividends	$392,213	$285,811
Unrealized (loss) gain	(361,747)	534,172
Investment expenses	(35,105)	(34,389)
	$ (4,639)	$785,594

Note 5 — Fair Value Measurements: The fair value hierarchy defines three levels as follows:

Level 1: Valuations based on quoted prices (unadjusted) in an active market that are accessible at the measurement date for identical assets or liabilities. The fair value hierarchy gives the highest priority to Level 1 inputs.

Level 2: Valuations based on observable inputs other than Level 1 prices such as quoted prices for similar assets or liabilities; quoted prices in inactive markets; or model-derived valuations in which all significant inputs are observable or can be derived principally from or corroborated with observable market data.

Level 3: Valuations based on unobservable inputs are used when little or no market value data is available. The fair value hierarchy gives the lowest priority to Level 3 inputs.

In determining fair value, the Organization utilizes valuation techniques that maximize the use of observable inputs and minimize the use of unobservable inputs to the extent possible in its assessment of fair value. Investments in mutual funds are valued on quoted market prices and valued at Level 1. Investments in certificates of deposit are valued using observable market data and are valued at Level 2.

The availability of observable market data is monitored to assess the appropriate classification of financial instruments within the fair value hierarchy. Changes in economic conditions or model-based valuation techniques may require the transfer of financial instruments from one fair value level to another. In such instances, the transfer is reported at the end of the reporting period. For the years ended December 31, 2018 and 2017, there were no transfers.

Financial assets carried at fair value as of December 31, 2018 are classified as follows:

	Level 1	Level 2	Total
Reserve fund:			
Certificates of deposit		$16,325,250	$16,325,250
Postretirement medical fund:			
Mutual funds — bond funds	1,997,301		1,997,301
Mutual funds — equity funds	3,440,442		3,440,442
	$5,437,743	$16,325,250	$21,762,993

Financial assets carried at fair value as of December 31, 2017 are classified as follows:

	Level 1	Level 2	Total
Reserve fund:			
Certificates of deposit		$15,311,789	$15,311,789
Postretirement medical fund:			
Mutual funds — bond funds	1,871,202		1,871,202
Mutual funds — equity funds	3,580,605		3,580,605
	$5,451,807	$15,311,789	$20,763,596

Note 6 — Property and Equipment:

Property and equipment consisted of the following as of December 31:

	2018	2017	Estimated Useful Lives
Furniture and equipment	$948,764	$979,614	8 years
Computers and software	1,812,958	2,132,704	3-5 years
Leasehold improvements	4,131,917	4,099,532	Life of lease
Total cost	6,893,639	7,211,850	
Less: accumulated depreciation and amortization	(5,366,156)	(5,402,625)	
Net book value	$1,527,483	$1,809,225	

Depreciation and amortization expense amounted to $502,128 and $418,592 for the years ended December 31, 2018 and 2017, respectively. Fully depreciated property and equipment amounting to $538,598 was disposed of during the year ended December 31, 2018.

Note 7 — Concentration:
Cash and cash equivalents that potentially subject the Organization to a concentration of credit risk include cash accounts with a bank that may exceed the Federal Deposit Insurance Corporation ("FDIC") insurance limits. Accounts are insured up to $250,000 per depositor. As of December 31, 2018 and 2017, cash and cash equivalents held in banks exceeded FDIC limits by approximately $900,000 and $2,200,000, respectively.

Note 8 — Postretirement Health Benefits:
The Organization provides health care benefits for retired employees, substantially all of whom become eligible if they attain retirement age while working at the General Service Office. Benefits are provided through health insurance contracts maintained by the Organization.

For employees hired before 2004, 25% of the cost is borne by the retirees.

For employees hired after January 1, 2004 through June 30, 2016, there is a three-tier structure in the level of group medical insurance premiums paid for on behalf of employees who retire directly from the GSO. For employees with 5-9 years of service, the Organization pays 25%, 10-15 years, 50% and more than 15 years, 75%.

In March 2016, the Organization decided to no longer provide health care benefits upon retirement for employees hired after June 30, 2016.

The assumed health care cost trend rate used to measure the expected cost of benefits covered by the plan was 5.1% and 6.0% as December 31, 2018 and 2017, respectively. A discount rate of 4.26% and 3.55% has been used to measure the accrued postretirement health benefit obligation reflected on the accompanying consolidated statement of financial position as of December 31, 2018 and 2017, respectively.

As described in Note 1, a postretirement medical fund has been created by the Board with the purpose of accumulating assets to fund 100% of the postretirement health benefits liability. As of December 31, 2018 and 2017, this fund had assets with a fair value of $5,487,251 and $5,498,363, respectively. As required under U.S. GAAP, such assets are not reported net of the related postretirement benefit obligation on the accompanying consolidated statement of financial position.

The benefit obligation amounted to $6,836,634 and $7,373,680 as of December 31, 2018 and 2017, respectively. The net change in the retirement liability is reported as non-operating activity in the accompanying consolidated statement of activities and amounted to $1,032,682 and $638,213 for the years ended December 31, 2018 and 2017, respectively.

The net periodic benefit cost for the years ended December 31, 2018 and 2017, amounted to $495,636 and $92,133, respectively.

The expected postretirement benefits to be paid for the next ten years are as follows:

2019	$ 270,587
2020	278,274
2021	294,063
2022	314,306
2023	327,003
2024-2028	1,846,476

Note 9 — Retirement Plan:
The Organization adopted a defined benefit pension plan (the "Plan") effective January 1, 1965 to provide retirement benefits to eligible employees who have completed one year of service.

The Plan provides an annual benefit equal to two percent of final average compensation multiplied by years of service (not to exceed 35 years), less 0.65% of average social security earnings multiplied by years of service (not to exceed 30 years). The social security offset cannot reduce the gross benefit by more than 50%.

During 2017, the Plan was amended to provide a limited window from October 10 through November 22, 2017 to allow deferred vested participants the opportunity to elect to receive a lump sum distribution if the present value of their benefit was less than $100,000 as of December 1, 2017.

The components of the net periodic benefit cost for the years ended December 31 are as follows:

	2018	2017
Change in benefit obligation:		
Benefit obligation at beginning of the year	$36,894,234	$35,158,955
Service cost	562,966	554,396
Interest cost	1,284,233	1,387,019
Actuarial (gain) loss	(1,851,266)	2,105,667
Benefits paid	(1,652,075)	(2,311,803)
Benefit obligation at end of year	35,238,092	36,894,234
Fair value of plan assets	33,059,042	34,770,101
Funded status	$(2,179,050)	$(2,124,133)
Accrued pension benefit obligation recognized in the consolidated statement of financial position	$(2,179,050)	$(2,124,133)

The funding status of the Plan as of December 31 is as follows:

	2018	2017
Service cost	$562,966	$554,396
Interest cost	1,284,233	1,387,019
Expected return on plan assets	(2,422,441)	(2,084,466)
Amortization of prior service cost	22,214	22,214
Amortization of actuarial loss	877,086	949,517
Net Periodic cost	$324,058	$828,680

Other changes in plan assets and benefit obligations recognized in the change in net assets without donor restrictions for the years ended December 31 are as follows:

	2018	2017
Actuarial gain/(loss)	$(2,130,159)	$229,385
Amortization of prior service cost	22,214	22,214
Amortization of actuarial loss	877,086	949,517
Net Periodic cost	$(1,230,859)	$1,201,116

Weighted-average assumptions used to determine benefit obligations as of December 31, 2018 and 2017 were as follows:

	2018	2017
Discount rate	4.21%	3.55%
Salary increases	4.0%	3.0%
Expected long-term return on assets	7.0%	7.0%

Weighted-average assumptions used to determine net periodic pension cost for the years ended December 31, 2018 and 2017, were as follows:

	2018	2017
Discount rate	3.55%	4.05%
Salary increases	3.0%	3.0%
Expected long-term return on assets	7.0%	7.0%

The expected rate of return on plan assets is determined by those assets' historical long-term investment performance, current asset allocation, and estimates of future long-term returns by asset class.

The fair value of plan assets as of December 31, 2018 were classified as follows:

	Level 1	Total
Cash and cash equivalents	$930,500	$930,500
Mutual funds — domestic equity	17,825,496	17,825,496
Mutual funds — international equity	3,582,646	3,582,646
Mutual funds — bond funds	10,720,400	10,720,400
	$ 33,059,042	$33,059,042

The fair value of plan assets as of December 31, 2017 were classified as follows:

	Level 1	Total
Cash and cash equivalents	$939,184	$939,184
Mutual funds — domestic equity	19,770,248	19,770,248
Mutual funds — international equity	4,186,944	4,186,944
Mutual funds — bond funds	9,873,725	9,873,725
	$34,770,101	$34,770,101

The expected benefits to be paid for the next ten years are as follows:

2019	$1,813,253
2020	1,829,640
2021	1,858,920
2022	1,912,602
2023	1,962,456
2024-2028	10,714,400

For the years ended December 31, 2018 and 2017, the Organization contributed $1,500,000 and $2,750,000, respectively to the Plan. The Organization expects to contribute $1,500,000 to the plan next year.

Effective January 1, 2013, the Organization implemented a soft freeze of the Plan. Employees in the Plan as of December 31, 2012 continue to accrue benefits; however, employees hired after that date are eligible to participate in a new defined contribution plan. The Organization contributes 5% of eligible salary plus a 50% match on employee contributions up to a maximum of 5% of eligible salary. For the years ended December 31, 2018 and 2017, contributions to the defined contribution plan amounted to approximately $194,000, and $186,000, respectively.

Note 10 — Commitments and Contingencies:

A. The Organization has a lease agreement for the office space at 475 Riverside Drive in New York City expiring on December 31, 2025. Future minimum annual rent payments related to the lease for each of the five years ended after December 31, 2018 are as follows:

2019	$900,000
2020	912,000
2021	917,789
2022	909,741
2023	922,346
Thereafter	1,815,000
	$6,376,876

Rent expense for real property amounted to $846,761 and $994,207 for the years ended December 31, 2018 and 2017, respectively.

B. The Organization believes it had no uncertain tax positions as of December 31, 2018 and 2017, in accordance with Accounting Standards Codification ("ASC") Topic 740, "Income Taxes," which provides standards for establishing and classifying any tax provisions for uncertain tax positions.

Note 11 — Intercompany and Interfund Transactions: As of December 31, 2018 and 2017, G.S.B. owed A.A.W.S. $4,666,903 and $2,155,593, respectively, for various organizational expenses.

The Reserve Fund of G.S.B. includes transfers from A.A.G.V. that represent amounts held for unfulfilled subscriptions. This balance amounted to $1,943,500 as of December 31, 2018 and 2017, and is reflected as an asset of A.A.G.V. and a liability of the Reserve Fund of G.S.B. on the accompanying consolidated statement of financial position. In addition, as of December 31, 2018 and 2017, the Reserve Fund owes A.A.G.V. an additional $19,560 and $5,800, respectively.

As described in Note 1, funds of the operating entities in excess of those required for working capital are transferred to the Reserve Fund. For the years ended December 31, 2018 and 2017, such transfers made to the Reserve Fund were as follows:

	2018	2017
Transferred from A.A.W.S.	$1,400,000	$3,362,828
Transferred (to) from A.A.G.V.	(44,000)	40,000
	$1,356,000	$3,402,828

Additionally, $251,000 and $1,001,000 were transferred from the General Fund and A.A.W.S. to the Postretirement Medical Fund for the years ended December 31, 2018 and 2017, respectively. Funds of $32,386 and $223,210 were transferred from the General Fund and A.A.W.S. to the Capital Projects Fund for the years ended December 31, 2018 and 2017, respectively.

Note 12 — Subsequent Events: Management has evaluated, for potential recognition and disclosure, events subsequent to the date of the consolidated statement of financial position through May 7, 2019, the date the consolidated financial statements were available to be issued.

The General Service Board of Alcoholics Anonymous, Inc.
Alcoholics Anonymous World Services, Inc. • Alcoholics Anonymous Grapevine, Inc.
CONSOLIDATED STATEMENT OF FINANCIAL POSITION
Year Ended December 31, 2018 (with comparative totals for 2017)

| | General Service Board of A.A. | | | | | | | | | |
	General Fund	Reserve Fund	Capital Projects Fund	Postretirement Medical Fund	Pension Benefits	A.A. World Services, Inc.	A.A. Grapevine, Inc.	Eliminations	Consolidated Total 2018	Consolidated Total 2017
ASSETS										
Cash and cash equivalents (Notes 2D & 7)	$1,145,536	$1,332,942		$49,508		$522,219	$345,830		$3,396,035	$4,638,578
Investments (Notes 2E, 2F, 4, 5 & 8)		16,325,250		5,437,743					21,762,993	20,763,596
Accounts receivable, net (Note 2K)						245,124	133,453		378,577	313,458
Inventory (Note 2G)						1,630,990	239,591		1,870,581	1,872,108
Prepaid expenses and other assets	466,881	240,199				298,360	44,765		1,050,205	693,866
Due from affiliates/intercompany funds (Note 11)						4,671,183	1,943,500	(6,614,683)		
Property and equipment, net (Notes 2H & 6)			1,143,030			224,264	160,189		1,527,483	1,809,225
Total Assets	1,612,417	17,898,391	1,143,030	5,487,251		7,592,140	2,867,328	(6,614,683)	29,985,874	30,090,831
LIABILITIES										
Accounts payable and accrued expenses (Note 11)	4,673,687	1,963,060				929,489	246,756	(6,614,683)	1,198,309	1,289,433
Deferred revenue (Note 2)						80,815	1,725,701		1,806,516	1,864,952
Postretirement benefit (Note 8)				6,836,634					6,836,634	7,373,680
Accrued pension benefit (Note 9)					2,179,050				2,179,050	2,124,133
Total Liabilities	4,673,687	1,963,060		6,836,634	2,179,050	1,010,304	1,972,457	(6,614,683)	12,020,509	12,652,198
COMMITMENTS AND CONTINGENCIES (Note 10)										
NET ASSETS – WITHOUT DONOR RESTRICTIONS (Note 2)	(3,061,270)	15,935,331	1,143,030	(1,349,383)	(2,179,050)	6,581,836	894,871		17,965,365	17,438,633
Total Liabilities and Net Assets	1,612,417	17,898,391	1,143,030	5,487,251		7,592,140	2,867,328	(6,614,683)	29,985,874	30,090,831

The accompanying notes are an integral part of these financial statements.

The General Service Board of Alcoholics Anonymous, Inc.
Alcoholics Anonymous World Services, Inc. • Alcoholics Anonymous Grapevine, Inc.
CONSOLIDATED STATEMENT OF ACTIVITY
Year Ended December 31, 2018 (with comparative totals for 2017)

	General Service Board of A.A.						A.A. Grapevine, Inc.				
	General Fund	Reserve Fund	Capital Projects Fund	Postretirement Medical Fund	Pension Benefits	A.A. World Services, Inc.	Grapevine	La Viña	Total	Consolidated 2018	Consolidated 2017
OPERATING REVENUE AND SUPPORT:											
Gross sales revenue (Note 2I)						$14,235,594	$2,812,933	$140,824	$2,953,757	$17,189,351	$16,861,005
Less: Discounts						(215,445)				(215,445)	(205,178)
Net Sales						14,020,149	2,812,933	140,824	2,953,757	16,973,906	16,655,827
Cost of Literature Distributed											
Printing						(2,799,471)	(203,681)	(55,176)	(258,857)	(3,058,328)	(2,983,371)
Direct shipping and warehousing						(1,768,063)	(725,118)	(4,913)	(730,031)	(2,498,094)	(2,284,658)
Gross Profit from Literature						9,452,615	1,884,134	80,735	1,964,869	11,417,484	11,387,798
Contributions (Note 2J)	8,385,009									8,385,009	8,409,452
Investment income (Notes 2E & 3)		226,713		(262,112)			30,760		30,760	(4,639)	785,594
TOTAL OPERATING REVENUE AND SUPPORT	8,385,009	226,713		(262,112)		9,452,615	1,914,894	80,735	1,995,629	19,797,854	20,582,844
OPERATING EXPENSES (Note 2L):											
Program services	6,582,772		268,045	495,636	324,058	2,671,905	1,537,529	229,202	1,766,731	11,021,408	10,446,333
Supporting services	3,848,030					2,765,236	350,532		350,532	8,051,537	6,280,473
TOTAL OPERATING EXPENSES	10,430,802		268,045	495,636	324,058	5,437,141	1,888,061	229,202	2,117,263	19,072,945	16,726,806
OPERATING SURPLUS (LOSS)	(2,045,793)	226,713	(268,045)	(757,748)	(324,058)	4,015,474	26,833	(148,467)	(121,634)	724,909	3,856,038
NON-OPERATING ACTIVITIES AND OTHER (Note 2N):											
G.S.B. support for La Viña	(148,467)							148,467	148,467		
Intercompany and interfund transfers (Note 11)	(924,023)	1,356,000	32,386	251,000	1,500,000	(2,083,363)	(132,000)		(132,000)		
CHANGE IN NET ASSETS BEFORE PENSION-RELATED CHANGES	(3,118,283)	1,582,713	(235,659)	(506,748)	1,175,942	1,932,111	(105,167)		(105,167)	724,909	3,856,038
Pension and post-retirement changes other than net period costs				1,032,682	(1,230,859)					(198,177)	838,329
CHANGE IN NET ASSETS WITHOUT DONOR RESTRICTIONS	(3,118,283)	1,582,713	(235,659)	525,934	(54,917)	1,932,111	(105,167)		(105,167)	526,732	4,694,367
Net Assets — Without donor restrictions — Beginning of Year	57,013	14,352,618	1,378,689	(1,875,317)	(2,124,133)	4,649,725	1,000,038		1,000,038	17,438,633	12,744,266
NET ASSETS — WITHOUT DONOR RESTRICTIONS — END OF YEAR	$(3,061,270)	$15,935,331	$1,143,030	$(1,349,383)	$(2,179,050)	$6,581,836	$894,871		$894,871	$17,965,365	$17,438,633

The accompanying notes are an integral part of these financial statements.

The General Service Board of Alcoholics Anonymous, Inc.
Alcoholics Anonymous World Services, Inc.
Alcoholics Anonymous Grapevine, Inc.

	Literature Distribution	Literature Development	Group Services	Public Information	Cooperation with Profes. Community	Treatment/ Accessibility	Correctional Facilities	Loners and Overseas Service	General Service Conference	Regional Forums
									Program Services	
Salaries	$1,307,970	$153,359	$933,494	$148,495	$103,596	$60,079	$150,849	$275,140	$217,091	$135,599
Payroll taxes and benefits (Notes 8 and 9)	633,932	81,286	480,363	88,577	85,578	56,298	84,291	118,509	107,694	99,409
Total Personnel Costs	1,941,902	234,645	1,413,857	237,072	189,174	116,377	235,140	393,649	324,785	235,008
Printing		208,716	9,891	6,388	600	20,294	7,515	59,317	21,306	3,455
Mailing, labor, etc.			95,279		1,425		2,080	1,800	3,286	3,200
Postage and express shipping	5,836	1,144	202,737	1,534	9,318	3,104	14,597	3,845	26,863	21,160
Editorial services	99,391		18,997	15,835		225	30,970		7,760	5,343
Foreign literature assistance								10,344		
Selling expenses	190,775									
Professional fees										
Contracted services	200,892	7,750	56,291	36,966	70,076	3,391	5,665	29,733	103,667	25,770
Occupancy	191,744	11,038	112,035	11,038	11,038	5,204	11,038	16,242	11,038	3,164
Telephone and communications	11,677	1,706	26,455	11,579	1,641	890	1,804	6,863	3,534	1,895
Equipment maintenance	7,154		1,058							
Depreciation (Note 6)	57,589	1,624	15,547	4,861	1,336	662	1,784	1,998	4,795	1,336
Stationery and office supplies	5,843	357	62,699	325	843	127	2,047	547	13,517	5,215
Office services and expenses	13,628	1,173	17,977	1,877	1,031	775	1,144	1,361	116,758	26,063
Travel, meals and accommodations	15,426	866	3,617	5,402	4,593	(289)	2,331	26,593	760,005	103,277
Bad debts										
Delegate fees									(343,162)	
Total expenses before pension and capital projects	2,741,857	260,303	2,235,265	336,380	296,863	131,066	328,894	500,490	1,092,163	452,737
Less: contribution to retirement plans	(244,215)	(31,455)	(194,670)	(35,505)	(50,490)	(7,695)	(33,885)	(47,250)	(43,875)	(39,150)
Less: contributions to post-retirement plans	(48,510)	(6,075)	(27,135)	(5,355)	(4,770)	(2,453)	(4,995)	(7,425)	(5,783)	(6,728)
Plus: net periodic pension and post-retirement cost										
Plus: capital projects depreciation										
TOTAL EXPENSES	$2,449,132	$222,773	$2,013,460	$295,520	$241,603	$120,918	$290,014	$445,815	$1,042,505	$406,859

The accompanying notes are an integral part of these financial statements.

Exhibit C

CONSOLIDATED STATEMENT OF FUNCTIONAL EXPENSES

Year Ended December 31, 2018 (with comparative totals for 2017)

Archives	Nominating	Trustee and Director Activities	World Service Meeting	Grapevine	La Viña	Total Program Services	General Service Board	A.A.W.S.	Grapevine	Total Supporting Services	Total 2018	Total 2017
$381,830	$154,677		$10,544	$782,386	$151,927	$4,967,036	$1,931,418	$1,420,997	$126,303	$3,478,718	$8,445,754	$7,507,954
198,112	100,562			369,973	55,309	2,559,893	901,773	652,306		1,554,079	4,113,972	3,931,595
579,942	255,239		10,544	1,152,359	207,236	7,526,929	2,833,191	2,073,303	126,303	5,032,797	12,559,726	11,439,549
	455				337,937					337,937	410,262	
						107,070					107,070	119,286
2,277	394	2,332	9,724	5,141		310,006	17,756	12,364		30,120	340,126	430,003
						178,521	2,851	1,943		4,794	183,315	86,304
						10,344					10,344	37,983
				190,815	14,844	396,434	17,732	12,079		29,811	426,245	703,070
							314,762	193,508	88,082	596,352	596,352	660,042
64,332	5,817		30,806	144,950		786,106	530,973	365,666		896,639	1,682,745	1,330,873
85,622	4,415			84,447		558,063	216,904	150,765	68,479	436,148	994,211	897,007
11,507	366	2,120	1,533			83,570	21,806	15,103		36,909	120,479	136,725
14,009						22,221	22,605	15,399	17,314	55,318	77,539	98,732
9,662						101,194	49,329	33,605	49,955	132,889	234,083	170,640
5,105	158	1,428	7,432			105,643	53,114	36,290		89,404	195,047	229,046
13,746	1,808	60,465	22,897	106,678	1,580	388,961	73,939	81,741	28,767	184,447	573,408	373,754
1,463	947	534,048	234,549		5,542	1,698,370	34,191	22,182		56,373	1,754,743	1,235,722
									771	771	771	5,676
			(114,773)			(457,935)					(457,935)	(305,633)
791,120	269,144	600,848	202,712	1,684,390	229,202	12,153,434	4,189,153	3,013,948	379,671	7,582,772	19,736,206	18,059,041
(79,920)	(40,905)			(125,166)		(974,181)	(285,660)	(215,325)	(24,834)	(525,819)	(1,500,000)	(1,500,000)
(11,453)	(5,468)			(21,695)		(157,845)	(55,463)	(33,387)	(4,305)	(93,155)	(251,000)	(1,001,000)
							819,694			819,694	819,694	921,173
							268,045			268,045	268,045	247,592
$699,747	$222,771	$600,848	$202,712	$1,537,529	$229,202	$11,021,408	$4,935,769	$2,765,236	$350,532	$8,051,537	$19,072,945	$16,726,806

2018 Contributions From Groups, Individuals, Specials, Special Meetings — by Delegate Area (in U.S. Dollars)

AREA #	GENERAL SERVICE CONFERENCE AREA	#GPS. REPORTED	#GPS. CONTRIB.	% OF GPS. CONTRIB.	TOTAL GROUP CONTRIB.	MEMBERSHIP	CONTRIBUTION PER CAPITA	INDIVIDUAL MEMBERS	MEMORIAL	SPECIALS[1]	SPECIAL MEETINGS[2]	TOTAL AREA CONTRIBUTIONS	PER CAPITA
1.	Alabama/N.W. Florida	468	203	43.38%	$47,343.32	10,459	4.53	$5,018.77	–	$200.00	$200.00	$52,762.09	$5.04
2.	Alaska	190	101	53.16%	26,064.97	2,954	8.82	2,189.71	50.00	243.33	–	28,548.01	9.66
3.	Arizona	1,093	542	49.59%	146,630.10	25,375	5.78	16,429.75	10.00	12,851.10	569.41	176,490.36	6.96
4.	Arkansas	263	123	46.77%	30,320.72	4,867	6.23	1,966.00	–	3,949.85	–	36,236.57	7.45
	California												
5.	Southern	1,471	543	36.91%	144,809.98	48,704	2.97	27,917.74	2,000.00	3,509.86	173.80	178,411.38	3.66
6.	Northern Coastal	2,180	1,227	56.28%	340,806.38	61,826	5.51	42,254.53	–	11,464.53	222.68	394,748.12	6.38
7.	Northern Interior	1,081	469	43.39%	115,783.13	31,846	3.64	19,215.53	33.00	6,827.53	–	141,859.19	4.45
8.	San Diego/Imperial	1,096	506	46.17%	106,116.70	28,500	3.72	13,753.12	3,200.00	1,912.48	1,219.14	126,201.44	4.43
9.	Mid-Southern	2,239	1,060	47.34%	229,563.29	65,606	3.50	23,131.79	2,070.00	5,241.39	397.00	260,403.47	3.97
10.	Colorado	970	466	48.04%	123,235.63	21,265	5.80	29,641.00	178.00	27,554.49	–	180,609.12	8.49
11.	Connecticut	1,467	600	40.90%	140,224.75	32,993	4.25	23,697.29	1,440.00	19,648.92	1,083.89	186,094.85	5.64
12.	Delaware	283	141	49.82%	46,323.35	4,286	10.81	4,166.38	–	–	–	50,489.73	11.78
13.	District of Columbia	545	205	37.61%	53,423.49	14,589	3.66	3,431.59	200.00	–	–	57,055.08	3.91
	Florida												
14.	North	1,074	489	45.53%	146,355.22	21,719	6.74	14,524.08	5,425.00	18,695.00	450.00	185,449.30	8.54
15.	So. Florida/Bahamas/ US V.I./Antigua	2,296	1,003	43.68%	249,410.08	44,703	5.58	35,566.36	261.00	114,312.85	–	399,550.29	8.94
16.	Georgia	805	480	59.63%	127,711.48	19,984	6.39	9,791.74	100.00	3,441.11	33.20	141,077.53	7.06
17.	Hawaii	298	179	60.07%	46,485.68	5,142	9.04	617.39	–	673.02	18.00	47,794.09	9.29
18.	Idaho	295	119	40.34%	26,452.64	5,425	4.88	5,158.30	500.00	1,859.86	787.23	34,758.03	6.41
	Illinois												
19.	Chicago	1,329	356	26.79%	76,867.04	25,990	2.96	15,303.57	500.00	2,288.20	25.00	94,983.81	3.65
20.	Northern	1,349	495	36.69%	80,580.13	23,626	3.41	13,868.81	5,025.00	31,546.59	62.00	131,082.53	5.55
21.	Southern	470	184	39.15%	31,312.75	7,821	4.00	3,579.40	2,000.00	1,217.00	256.84	38,365.99	4.91
	Indiana												
22.	Northern	719	253	35.19%	46,582.57	10,185	4.57	4,338.17	162.00	914.80	–	51,997.54	5.11
23.	Southern	741	308	41.57%	45,972.97	12,389	3.71	9,958.92	41.00	1,420.41	400.00	57,393.30	4.63
24.	Iowa	689	312	45.28%	62,329.92	14,529	4.29	3,476.09	–	401.00	–	66,607.01	4.58
25.	Kansas	366	158	43.17%	36,799.69	8,502	4.33	7,400.66	–	3,195.00	–	47,395.35	5.57
26.	Kentucky	826	319	38.62%	76,950.46	13,565	5.67	7,282.80	–	7,605.76	–	91,839.02	6.77
27.	Louisiana	717	173	24.13%	46,952.51	13,124	3.58	1,976.70	100.00	460.46	–	49,489.67	3.77
28.	Maine	582	214	36.77%	29,136.79	9,014	3.23	4,091.00	50.00	9,961.35	100.00	44,353.14	4.92
29.	Maryland	1,050	463	44.10%	99,462.77	15,889	6.26	12,986.91	1,650.00	3,290.11	1,114.00	117,449.79	7.39
	Massachusetts												
30.	Eastern	1,608	592	36.82%	133,246.58	47,000	2.84	19,447.40	5,410.00	990.00	60.00	159,093.98	3.38
31.	Western	314	150	47.77%	19,401.11	5,452	3.56	2,556.27	–	–	–	21,957.38	4.03
	Michigan												
32.	Central	668	267	39.97%	43,315.99	14,842	2.92	4,267.83	352.00	1,842.00	–	49,777.82	3.35
33.	Southeastern	1,016	297	29.23%	58,619.62	20,658	2.84	1,883.50	5,280.00	–	–	65,783.12	3.18
34.	Western	674	229	33.98%	50,006.43	13,366	3.74	1,969.71	–	4,770.00	–	56,746.14	4.25
	Minnesota												
35.	Northern	566	268	47.35%	39,687.51	8,528	4.65	4,505.76	–	500.00	–	44,693.27	5.24
36.	Southern	1,200	499	41.58%	107,420.64	28,600	3.76	10,435.36	50.00	12,092.17	–	129,998.17	4.55
37.	Mississippi	248	80	32.26%	21,885.25	4,874	4.49	2,250.00	–	240.56	250.00	24,625.81	5.05
	Missouri												
38.	Eastern	637	313	49.14%	69,865.15	10,006	6.98	6,694.37	105.00	1,367.00	–	78,031.52	7.80
39.	Western	234	114	48.72%	26,344.97	6,752	3.90	5,563.25	–	280.00	–	32,188.22	4.77
40.	Montana	276	131	47.46%	36,076.78	5,440	6.63	2,735.81	5,000.00	1,064.00	124.65	45,001.24	8.27
41.	Nebraska	711	269	37.83%	47,251.83	15,046	3.14	7,551.14	–	1,538.06	–	56,341.03	3.74
42.	Nevada	686	220	32.07%	50,920.00	14,867	3.43	9,949.00	5,000.00	1,967.00	–	67,836.00	4.56
43.	New Hampshire	613	273	44.54%	49,001.30	9,137	5.36	4,976.34	–	6,560.00	–	60,537.64	6.63
	New Jersey												
44.	Northern	1,382	607	43.92%	181,200.89	41,396	4.38	22,338.70	5,945.00	1,220.00	–	210,704.59	5.09
45.	Southern	600	286	47.67%	78,778.11	9,584	8.22	8,877.31	120.00	549.54	–	88,324.96	9.22
46.	New Mexico	388	170	43.81%	38,875.73	7,121	5.46	6,359.43	328.33	3,404.23	–	48,967.72	6.88
	New York												
47.	Central	794	291	36.65%	54,820.31	10,606	5.17	3,345.59	11,150.00	812.62	–	70,128.52	6.61
48.	H./M./B.	839	331	39.45%	47,918.97	12,044	3.98	3,903.00	100.00	6,796.09	–	58,718.06	4.88
49.	Southeast	1,867	820	43.92%	307,703.25	55,834	5.51	45,552.52	7,596.00	1,551.58	1,266.63	363,669.98	6.51
50.	Western	329	119	36.17%	26,393.35	5,164	5.11	1,128.00	100.00	2,130.38	60.00	29,811.73	5.77
51.	North Carolina	1,177	599	50.89%	184,116.61	21,324	8.63	28,717.60	2,000.00	12,349.88	50.00	227,234.09	10.66
52.	North Dakota	168	79	47.02%	23,936.11	3,485	6.87	1,413.40	200.00	5,994.73	–	31,544.24	9.05
	Ohio												
53.	Central & Southeast	931	251	26.96%	33,480.25	11,010	3.04	1,297.02	80.00	553.42	–	35,410.69	3.22
54.	Northeast	1,674	375	22.40%	51,303.50	19,801	2.59	5,468.35	150.00	2,790.00	150.00	59,861.85	3.02
55.	Northwest	316	109	34.49%	13,498.63	4,285	3.15	542.00	50.00	122.06	–	14,212.69	3.32
56.	Southwest	575	286	49.74%	51,229.97	10,264	4.99	7,196.62	5,200.00	678.95	–	64,305.54	6.27

57.	Oklahoma	426	166	38.97%	47,394.68	8,898	5.33	3,307.30	35.00	419.89	–	51,156.87	5.75
58.	Oregon	1,252	527	42.09%	120,369.55	22,962	5.24	20,045.85	5,050.00	3,762.36	50.00	149,277.76	6.50
	Pennsylvania												
59.	Eastern	1,675	860	51.34%	221,239.34	32,473	6.81	20,674.49	904.33	8,053.25	–	250,871.41	7.73
60.	Western	828	371	44.81%	69,131.56	10,427	6.63	6,729.42	36.00	1,835.59	–	77,732.57	7.45
61.	Rhode Island	287	115	40.07%	25,020.51	5,665	4.42	4,802.51	80.00	1,611.67	–	31,514.69	5.56
62.	South Carolina	440	213	48.41%	70,550.61	10,308	6.84	8,051.41	50.00	1,690.00	–	80,342.02	7.79
63.	South Dakota	159	61	38.36%	9,830.13	4,401	2.23	895.65	–	1,372.94	–	12,098.72	2.75
64.	Tennessee	610	262	42.95%	64,182.30	12,735	5.04	7,100.18	2,200.00	739.87	40.00	74,262.35	5.83
	Texas												
65.	Northeast	531	197	37.10%	104,324.37	18,647	5.59	11,464.56	–	6,903.47	–	122,692.40	6.58
66.	Northwest	300	65	21.67%	14,664.87	6,805	2.16	5,126.40	75.00	2,955.72	–	22,821.99	3.35
67.	Southeast	733	296	40.38%	85,682.75	17,990	4.76	11,294.87	202.48	400.00	–	97,580.10	5.42
68.	Southwest	668	277	41.47%	100,394.05	16,303	6.16	17,613.16	169.00	5,782.60	–	123,958.81	7.60
69.	Utah	440	178	40.45%	50,030.46	7,868	6.36	4,035.30	30.00	–	300.00	54,395.76	6.91
70.	Vermont	298	131	43.96%	29,443.19	4,724	6.23	3,934.70	–	4,906.40	–	38,284.29	8.10
71.	Virginia	1,602	746	46.57%	188,628.51	27,606	6.83	32,317.29	560.00	4,059.22	678.25	226,243.27	8.20
72.	Western Washington	1,606	655	40.78%	174,661.37	32,012	5.46	29,276.79	5,025.00	17,051.81	100.00	226,114.97	7.06
73.	West Virginia	283	103	36.40%	16,988.32	3,024	5.62	5,930.70	–	314.95	–	23,233.97	7.68
	Wisconsin												
74.	N. Wisc./Upper Penn. Mich.	761	260	34.17%	30,807.70	11,181	2.76	530.00	–	576.00	–	31,913.70	2.85
75.	Southern	1,161	508	43.76%	70,080.01	19,457	3.60	4,838.42	100.00	1,327.47	–	76,345.90	3.92
76.	Wyoming	106	52	49.06%	10,193.38	1,848	5.52	1,135.50	28.00	3,248.15	–	14,605.03	7.90
77.	Puerto Rico	130	48	36.92%	5,866.40	1,242	4.72	146.00	–	435.00	–	6,447.40	5.19
78.	Alberta/N.W.T.	566	229	40.46%	59,587.63	9,417	6.33	2,948.04	–	6,567.50	–	69,103.17	7.34
79.	B.C./Yukon Canada	828	423	51.09%	114,585.86	14,643	7.83	3,368.55	2,000.00	6,723.47	159.25	126,837.13	8.66
80.	Manitoba Canada	124	40	32.26%	12,063.00	3,161	3.82	46.08	–	189.45	–	12,298.53	3.89
81.	N.B./P.E.I.	184	78	42.39%	12,861.44	2,835	4.54	1,253.08	–	2,026.05	0.39	16,140.96	5.69
82.	N.S./Nfld/Lab.	206	89	43.20%	18,070.87	3,045	5.93	–	–	3,325.58	–	21,396.45	7.03
	Ontario												
83.	Eastern	563	243	43.16%	59,599.57	13,472	4.42	3,411.23	–	11,652.73	222.32	74,885.85	5.56
84.	Northeast	155	56	36.13%	10,490.35	1,687	6.22	125.00	321.98	4,377.38	–	15,314.71	9.08
85.	Northwest	60	16	26.67%	3,529.57	895	3.94	58.40	–	11,526.58	–	15,114.55	16.89
86.	Western	613	280	45.68%	78,657.92	10,300	7.64	1,907.48	–	11,888.09	424.75	92,878.24	9.02
	Quebec												
87.	Southwest	512	127	24.80%	15,904.25	8,558	1.86	1,965.06	–	42,573.16	–	60,442.47	7.06
88.	Southeast	183	11	6.01%	1,317.40	2,658	0.50	4,686.01	–	13,237.05	–	19,240.46	7.24
89.	Northeast	346	7	2.02%	1,922.07	4,056	0.47	143.00	–	37,989.13	–	40,054.20	9.88
90.	Northwest	373	37	9.92%	2,820.79	6,187	0.46	1,426.82	–	34,624.31	–	38,871.92	6.28
91.	Saskatchewan Canada	308	115	37.34%	22,422.83	3,255	6.89	530.00	78.17	5,327.81	–	28,358.81	8.71
92.	Washington State East	530	222	41.89%	43,322.65	6,608	6.56	2,771.70	–	2,694.92	–	48,789.27	7.38
93.	Central California	1,188	534	44.95%	118,884.61	29,461	4.04	11,730.06	654.96	7,071.89	94.00	138,435.52	4.70
	Total U.S. & Canada	68,478	28,314	41.35%	6,711,832.22	1,418,177	4.73	819,280.39	96,811.25	636,091.73	11,042.43	8,275,058.02	5.83

Online and telephone groups	8,454.96
Total groups	6,720,287.18
Individual, in-memoriam & special meetings	927,134.07
Specials	636,091.73
Total groups, individual, memorial, special and special meeting	$8,283,512.98
OTHER	
Loners	189.32
International Lawyers in A.A.	1,000.00
Foreign individuals, WSM, other	99,998.86
Hospital	201.68
Prison	106.00
Grand Total	$8,385,008.84

CONTRIBUTION COMPARISON – 2017-2018 *(in U.S. dollars)*

	#GPS. REPORTED	#GPS. CONTRIB.	% OF GPS. CONTRIB.	TOTAL GROUP CONTRIB.	MEMBERSHIP	TOTAL PER CAPITA INCLUDING SPECIALS, ETC.
U.S. & Canada 2018	68,478	28,314	41.35%	$6,711,832.22	1,418,177	$5.83
U.S. & Canada 2017	66,860	29,219	43.70%	$6,738,945.82	1,381,954	$6.00
Increase (Decrease)	1,618	(905)	-2.35%	(27,113.60)	36,223	$(0.17)

	2018	2017
EST. COST OF SERVICES PER CAPITA	$8.06	$7.40

(1) A Special contribution is one that comes from any number of A.A. entities that is not an A.A. group. For example, a conference, a committee, an area, a district, an intergroup, etc.

(2) A Special Meeting is a meeting that does not want to be a group but does want to contribute to the General Service Board.

The General Service Board of Alcoholics Anonymous, Inc.

Alcoholics Anonymous World Services, Inc.
Alcoholics Anonymous Grapevine, Inc.

Consolidated Statement of Cash Flows

Year Ended December 31, 2018
(with comparative totals for 2017)

CASH FLOWS FROM OPERATING ACTIVITIES:	2018	2017
Change in net assets	$526,732	$4,694,367
Adjustments to reconcile change in net assets to net cash provided by operating activities:		
Pension related changes other than net periodic pension cost	1,230,859	(1,201,116)
Postretirement related changes other than net periodic cost	(1,032,682)	(638,213)
Unrealized loss (gain) on investments	361,747	(534,172)
Bad debt	771	5,676
Depreciation and amortization	502,128	418,592
Sub-total	1,589,555	2,745,134
Changes in assets and liabilities:		
Decrease (increase) in assets:		
Accounts receivable, net	(24,196)	27,922
Inventory	(49,596)	(142,244)
Prepaid expenses and other assets	(305,217)	(257,128)
Increase (decrease) in liabilities:		
Accounts payable and accrued expenses	(132,817)	392,167
Deferred revenue	(58,436)	(59,413)
Postretirement benefit	495,636	343,133
Accrued pension benefit	(1,175,942)	(1,921,320)
Net Cash Provided by Operating Activities	338,987	1,128,251
CASH FLOWS FROM INVESTING ACTIVITIES:		
Purchases of investments	(1,361,144)	(4,839,343)
Proceeds from sales of investments		3,774,043
Acquisition of property and equipment	(220,386)	(454,232)
Net Cash Used in Investing Activities	(1,581,530)	(1,519,532)
NET DECREASE IN CASH AND CASH EQUIVALENTS	(1,242,543)	(391,281)
Cash and cash equivalents — beginning of period	4,638,578	5,029,859
CASH AND CASH EQUIVALENTS — END OF PERIOD	$ 3,396,035	$ 4,638,578

The accompanying notes are an integral part of these consolidated financial statements.

The General Service Office
2019 OPERATING BUDGET

INCOME	2018 Budget	2018 Actual	2019 Budget
GROSS SALES	$14,000,000	$14,235,594	$15,000,000
Discounts Allowed	220,000	215,445	225,000
Net Sales	13,780,000	14,020,149	14,775,000
Cost of Literature Distributed			
Manufacturing	2,725,000	2,799,471	3,100,000
Royalties	0	0	0
Gross Margin	11,055,000	11,220,678	11,675,000
DIRECT SHIPPING AND WAREHOUSING	1,794,755	1,768,063	1,900,000
Gross Profit from Literature	9,260,245	9,452,615	9,775,000
	67.20%	67.40%	66.16%
Contributions Received	8,200,000	8,385,009	8,384,721
Interest Income	0	0	0
Total Revenue	$17,460,245	$17,837,624	$18,159,721
OPERATING EXPENSES			
Salaries	7,182,468	7,385,138	7,850,000
Payroll taxes	550,000	566,285	580,000
Insurance	1,285,000	1,281,952	1,400,000
Retirement expense	1,861,000	1,840,453	1,875,000
Other program printing	417,400	337,938	350,000
Mailing, labor, etc.	119,500	107,070	120,000
Postage & express	402,800	334,986	420,000
Editorial Services	235,000	183,314	90,000
Other literature assistance	40,000	10,344	40,000
Selling expenses	224,450	220,586	300,000
Professional fees	457,500	508,270	360,000
Contracted services	1,204,549	1,537,794	1,200,000
Occupancy	843,758	841,285	860,000
Telephone	116,480	120,479	130,000
Equipment maintenance	66,750	60,225	56,000
Furniture & equipment	168,200	184,128	150,000
Stationery & office expense	179,600	195,045	205,000
Office service & expense	361,706	436,385	450,000
Travel, meals, & accommodations	1,239,891	1,291,266	1,220,000
Bad debts	2,500	0	2,500
TOTAL OPERATING EXPENSES	16,958,552	17,442,943	17,658,500
INCOME (LOSS) FOR PERIOD	$ 501,693	$ 394,681	$ 501,221

AA Grapevine, Inc.
2019 BUDGET

	GRAPEVINE			LA VIÑA		
	2018 Budget	2018 Actual	2019 Budget	2018 Budget	2018 Actual	2019 Budget
PAID CIRCULATION—						
AVERAGE # OF Print COPIES	62,322	66,857	69,139	9,188	9,635	9,709
On-Line Circulation	3,280	3,390	3,894			
GV Subscription App	2,500	2,053	3,053			
INCOME FROM CONTENT PRODUCTION						
Subscription income	$1,672,134	$1,799,074	$1,879,674	$102,675	$109,752	$115,292
Single copies and back issues	30,171	36,569	41,568	9,244	10,768	10,768
GV Online	95,447	100,366	114,944			
GV Subscription APP	43,131	41,825	59,755			
Books	644,024	739,538	861,037	20,435	15,624	13,280
Content Related Items	87,317	95,558	95,559	4,315	4,682	3,979
Total income	2,572,223	2,812,930	3,052,537	136,669	140,825	143,319
DIRECT COSTS FROM CONTENT PRODUCTION						
Magazine Costs	575,376	624,469	648,203	46,670	55,176	57,266
GV Online	19,512	24,244	26,000			
GV Subscription APP	5,500	7,425	8,500			
Books/Content Related Items	220,559	272,661	304,061	6,212	4,913	4,176
Total direct costs	820,947	928,799	986,764	52,882	60,090	61,443
GROSS PROFIT ON CONTENT PRODUCTION	1,751,277	1,884,132	2,065,773	83,787	80,735	81,877
COSTS AND EXPENSES						
EDITORIAL COSTS						
Salaries, including temporary help	456,716	416,663	539,294	101,955	106,195	118,251
Payroll taxes and benefits	136,033	131,369	138,983	33,912	35,024	34,587
Occupancy costs	40,684	40,755	41,814			
Office supplies and expenses	16,227	20,055	20,576	1,765	1,034	1,065
Product development & Web	105,000	49,415	60,000			
Total Editorial	754,660	658,256	800,667	137,632	142,252	153,903
CIRCULATION AND BUSINESS						
Salaries, including temporary help	334,322	365,723	466,739	47,133	45,732	47,936
Payroll taxes and benefits	262,431	238,604	289,116	24,428	20,391	24,878
Fulfillment	147,359	158,475	160,535	7,307	7,389	7,610
Occupancy costs	43,763	43,692	44,260			
Office supplies and expenses	98,162	86,626	87,753			
Selling expense-regular	89,359	79,540	80,574	8,124	7,456	7,679
— Outreach/Rep Program	51,640	48,335	48,963			
Postage	6,051	5,141	5,208			
Total Circulation and Business	1,033,088	1,026,136	1,183,147	86,991	80,968	88,104
GENERAL AND ADMINISTRATIVE						
Computer Consulting	30,000	17,314	15,000			
Insurance	8,784	8,377	8,712			
Severance Pay		126,303				
Professional fees	60,000	88,082	60,000		440	
Meetings and conferences	70,008	60,102	60,883	4,972	5,542	5,708
Furniture and equipment	53,000	49,955	62,000			
Canadian exchange and other	4,633	20,020	20,281			
Bank service charges	18,418	8,747	8,861			
Bad debts	10,000	771	781			
Total General and Administrative	254,842	379,670	236,518	4,972	5,982	5,708
TOTAL COSTS AND EXPENSES	2,042,590	2,064,063	2,220,332	229,595	229,202	247,715
Add: Interest earned	20,000	30,760	20,000			
Support from General Service Board General Fund				145,809	148,467	165,838
NET INCOME (LOSS) FOR PERIOD	($271,313)	($149,171)	($134,559)	$0	$0	$0

■ 2019 Conference Committees

Agenda
PANEL 68
Jenny Cmar** — Area 56, Southwest Ohio
Roxane Rollins* — Area 8, San Diego/Imp. CA
Mike Silva — Area 31, W. Massachusetts
PANEL 69
Coleen Ashworth — Area 17, Hawaii
Bobby Davis — Area 21, Southern Illinois
Lorraine Payette — Area 85, Northwest Ontario
Steve Shuffield — Area 57, Oklahoma
Susan Vlajk — Area 73, West Virginia
Secretary: Patrick Claymore

Cooperation with the Professional Community
PANEL 68
Chuck Beinhauer** — Area 50, Western New York
Kathi Cullen* — Area 76, Wyoming
Colleen Halverson — Area 84, Northeast Ontario
PANEL 69
Cynthia Bars — Area 33, Southeast Michigan
Barb Dove — Area 71, Virginia
Alan Foster — Area 72, Western Washington
Brad Moore — Area 4, Arkansas
Gail Patterson — Area 79, BC/Yukon
Secretary: Diana Lewis

Corrections
PANEL 68
Anthony Flores — Area 63, South Dakota
Teresa Jacks — Area 46, New Mexico
Becky Parker — Area 78, Alberta/NWT
Don Strachan* — Area 48, H/M/B New York
Lisa Whittington** — Area 37, Mississippi
PANEL 69
Brad Albright — Area 22, Northern Indiana
Ken Dennison — Area 59, E. Pennsylvania
Jeff Gulack — Area 93, Central California
Secretary: Julio Espaillat

Finance
PANEL 68
Jay Baez — Area 77, Puerto Rico
Henry Coombs** — Area 55, Northwest Ohio
Vera Farrell — Area 58, Oregon
Eric Parent — Area 90, Northwest Québec
Rose Sellnow* — Area 45, Southern New Jersey
PANEL 69
Troy Bush-DiDonato — Area 67, Southeast Texas
Missy Patterson — Area 36, Southern Minnesota
Margie Stanislaw — Area 60, W. Pennsylvania
Secretary: Bob Slotterback

Grapevine
PANEL 68
Don Bridges** — Area 29, Maryland
Earl Cronin — Area 81, New Brunswick/PEI
Allen DenAdel — Area 92, Washington East
Sara Plansky-Pecor — Area 74, N. WI/Upper Pen. MI
Roger Wheatley* — Area 26, Kentucky

PANEL 69
Jeff Bernknopf — Area 44, Northern New Jersey
Jenny Donovan — Area 39, Western Missouri
Rhonda Fairchild — Area 42, Nevada
Stephen Shelton — Area 53, Central SE Ohio
Secretary: Jon Witherspoon

Literature
PANEL 68
Erika Hanson* — Area 41, Nebraska
Jim Magee — Area 43, New Hampshire
Rick McNamara** — Area 16, Georgia
Marge Miller — Area 23, Southern Indiana
Jonathan Smith — Area 68, Southwest Texas
PANEL 69
Shyrl Blair — Area 54, Northeast Ohio
Matt Dyer — Area 69, Utah
Katy Patterson — Area 51, North Carolina
Serge Vigneux — Area 88, Southeast Québec
Secretary: Steve Smith

Policy/Admissions
PANEL 68
Christine Gerth* — Area 35, Northern Minnesota
Mary Kenney — Area 61, Rhode Island
Mike Kim — Area 7, Northern Interior CA
Dave Ruhlen** — Area 25, Kansas
PANEL 69
Barb Chambers — Area 47, Central New York
Lori Conant — Area 32, Central Michigan
Alain Gelinas — Area 89, Northeast Québec
Kevin Hawkins — Area 1, Alabama/NW Florida
Ray McCallum — Area 91, Saskatchewan
Secretary: Mary Cumings

Public Information
PANEL 68
Amy Bailey* — Area 62, South Carolina
David Craig** — Area 12, Delaware
Jesus Olivas — Area 9, Mid-Southern CA
Robert Snipes — Area 20, Northern Illinois
PANEL 69
Michelle García — Area 13, Washington, D.C.
Tina Palmer — Area 65, Northeast Texas
Shirley Parrado — Area 15, S. FL/Bhms/VI/Antigua
Kirk Stone — Area 82, Nova Scotia/NL
Curt Winmill — Area 52, North Dakota
Secretary: Racy Joseph

Report and Charter
PANEL 68
Noni McLean* — Area 80, Manitoba
Dee Payton** — Area 3, Arizona
Dale Sharp — Area 86, Western Ontario
PANEL 69
Annette Dahl — Area 14, North Florida
Dan Geels — Area 24, Iowa
Jean Kerivan — Area 30, E. Massachusetts
Gene Marshall — Area 38, Eastern Missouri
Brian Tenenbaum — Area 19, Chicago, Illinois
Secretary: Jeff Wine

Treatment and Accessibilities
PANEL 68
Alicia Hughes — Area 66, Northwest Texas
Rick Padgett** — Area 34, Western Michigan
Jan Rowe* — Area 70, Vermont
Alizon White — Area 2, Alaska
PANEL 69
Teddy Basham-Witherington
   — Area 6, Northern Coastal CA
Jane Ehrich — Area 49, Southeast New York
Rob McArthur — Area 83, Eastern Ontario
Sue Tart — Area 27, Louisiana
Secretary: Rick Walker

Trustees
PANEL 68
Shannon Coburn — Area 18, Idaho
Robin Gasparino — Area 28, Maine
Lucien Jean* — Area 87, Southwest Québec
Jon Phillips** — Area 64, Tennessee
PANEL 69
John Dussault — Area 11, Connecticut
Kris Krueger — Area 75, Southern Wisconsin
Paul Lamb — Area 40, Montana
Scott Meiklejohn — Area 10, Colorado
Thomas Sells — Area 5, Southern California
Secretary: Sandra Wilson

Archives[1]
PANEL 68
Allen DenAdel — Area 92, Washington East
Teresa Jacks* — Area 46, New Mexico
Dale Sharp** — Area 86, Western Ontario
Roger Wheatley — Area 26, Kentucky
PANEL 69
John Dussault — Area 11, Connecticut
Kris Krueger — Area 75, Southern Wisconsin
Gail Patterson — Area 79, BC/Yukon
Missy Patterson — Area 36, Southern Minnesota
Secretary: Michelle Mirza

International Conventions/ Regional Forums[1]
PANEL 68
Earl Cronin — Area 81, New Brunswick/PEI
Anthony Flores — Area 63, South Dakota
Alicia Hughes** — Area 66, Northwest Texas
Rick McNamara* — Area 16, Georgia
Becky Parker — Area 78, Alberta/NWT
PANEL 69
Teddy Basham-Witherington
   — Area 6, Northern Coastal CA
Lori Conant — Area 32, Central Michigan
Jane Ehrich — Area 49, Southeast New York
Secretary: Julio Espaillat, Sandra Wilson

*Chair
**Alternate Chair

[1]Members of this committee serve on this as a secondary committee assignment.

■ 2019 Conference Members

CLASS A (NONALCOHOLIC) TRUSTEES

Leslie Sanders Backus (Savannah, GA) was elected Class A trustee in April 2015. Leslie's professional background is in volunteer leadership and fund development. She is currently chief executive officer in an outpatient substance abuse treatment facility. Leslie is currently chair of the International Conventions/Regional Forums Committee and serves on the Corrections, Compensation, Finance & Budgetary Committees.

Christine Carpenter (Columbia, MO) was elected Class A trustee in April 2016. Judge Carpenter retired from the bench in 2017 and is now a Senior Judge for the 13th Judicial Circuit Court of Missouri. She is continuing to accept trial assignments and also works as a consultant and lecturer for the National Drug Court Institute. She is chair of the Corrections Committee and serves on the Public Information and C.P.C./Treatment-Accessibilities Committees.

Michele Grinberg (Charleston, WV) was selected as chair of the General Service Board following the 67th General Service Conference. Michele, an attorney who focuses on health care compliance as well as nonprofit governance, joined the General Service Board following the 60th General Service Conference in April 2010. Michele is an ex-officio member of all trustees' committees.

*The Hon. Ivan L. R. Lemelle (New Orleans, LA) was elected Class A trustee in April 2013. An honors graduate of Xavier University and Loyola University School of Law, New Orleans, former public and private practitioner, Ivan currently serves as a Senior U.S. District Judge in New Orleans, with occasional assignments to other federal courts in the nation. He is active in reentry court and drug court programs, and lectures often at national and international forums. Ivan serves on the C.P.C/Treatment-Accessibilities, Nominating and International Committees.

Peter F. Luongo, Ph.D. (Germantown, MD) was elected Class A trustee in April 2015. Pete's professional background is in public health services at state and local levels. He is currently executive director, Institute for Research, Education and Training in Addictions (IRETA). Pete chairs the Public Information Committee and serves on the Archives and Conference Committees.

Nancy McCarthy (St. Louis, MO) was approved by Conference for the position of Class A Trustee in 2016. Nancy retired from the Missouri Department of Corrections, Board of Probation and Parole in 2017 after 33 years of service. She started as a probation and parole officer and was promoted into a number of supervisory roles working primarily with individuals with substance use disorders. In 2004, Nancy was promoted to the position of regional administrator for the St. Louis area. As a Class A trustee, Nancy has served as a member of the trustees' committees for International and Public Information. She chaired the trustees' committee on Corrections in 2018 and currently serves as the chair for CPC/Treatment and Accessibilities. In 2018, Nancy was approved by Conference to serve as a director for Grapevine.

*David M. Morris, CPA (New York, NY) was elected Class A trustee in April 2013. Currently, David is the owner of Morris Consulting, a practice that focuses on providing financial and accounting guidance. He is retired from the position of senior vice president, JPMorgan Chase Bank. David chairs the Finance & Budgetary and Audit Committees and serves on the Archives, Compensation and International Conventions/Regional Forums Committees.

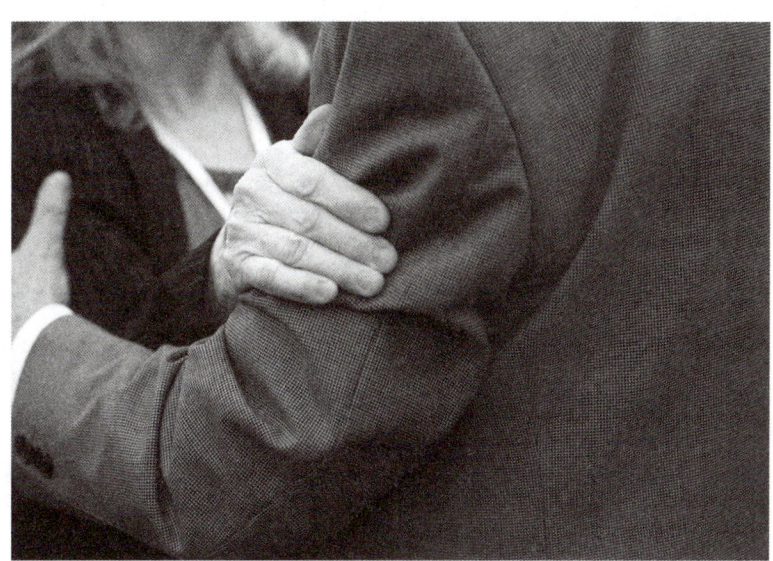

ALCOHOLIC (CLASS B) TRUSTEES

Thomas L. Ardolf (Waite Park, MN) was elected West Central regional trustee in April 2016. Tom was a Panel 50 delegate. Prior to his election, he served on a number of nonprofit boards. Together with his wife, Susie, Tom launched and sold three technology businesses over the past 30 years. He is still involved in real estate, and does product testing and evaluation for an international marine technology firm. He chairs the Nominating Committee and serves on the Finance and International Conventions/Regional Forums Committees. He is also a member of the A.A.W.S. board.

Cathy Beckham (Morgantown, WV) was elected Southeast regional trustee in April 2017. A Panel 63 delegate, Cathy is actively involved in sponsorship and her home group, as well as the area's website committee. Cathy retired last year in September after a career in IT and the transit industry. She is a member of the A.A.W.S. board and also serves on the Conference, International Conventions/Regional Forums, Literature, Finance and Compensation Committees.

extensive employment experience as an editor and writer, and has owned and operated a communications company as well as an event management company. She serves on the International Conventions/Regional Forums, Literature, International and Retirement Committees.

Deborah Koltai (Durham, NC) was elected A.A.W.S. director in April 2017. A Panel 59 delegate, Deborah remains active in her area. She is a clinical neuropsychologist and associate professor at a major university medical center. She serves on the trustees' Conference, Public Information and C.P.C./Treatment-Accessibilities Committees.

Homer Moeller (Winston-Salem, NC) was elected A.A.W.S. Board director in April 2016. A Panel 63 delegate, Homer is active in his home group and in his area. Homer is now retired from a long career in manufacturing and operations management. Homer also serves on the Public Information, International, Finance and Retirement Committees.

Carolyn Walsh (Surrey, BC) was elected A.A.W.S. director in April 2018. A Panel 63 delegate, Carolyn remains active in her area. As regional administrator for a large health care organization, she is responsible for operations and financial performance and is the privacy officer for the organization's 50-plus locations in British Columbia. From 1988 to 1996, Carolyn was in the Canadian Armed Forces. She serves on the International Conventions/Regional Forums, Archives and Corrections Committees.

Class A Trustees elected by the General Service Board following 2019 Conference

Sr. Judith Ann Karam, CSA, FACHE (Richfield, Ohio) was elected Class A trustee in May 2019. Sister Judith Ann is the congregational leader of the Sisters of Charity of St. Augustine and the immediate past president and CEO of the Sisters of Charity Health System. Begun in 1962, her healthcare career has included working as a clinical pharmacist as well as numerous executive positions and leadership roles in healthcare administration, among them serving as board chair of the Catholic Health Association of the United States. She has won many awards and distinctions along the way and is a Fellow of the American College of Healthcare Executives.

Al J. Mooney, III, MD, FAAFP, FASAM (Cary, North Carolina) was elected Class A trustee in May 2019. He has provided medical care in the specialties of family, behavioral, community and addiction medicine for over 40 years. A noted author and a respected pioneer in the field, Al helped establish the certification standards for addiction medicine in the United States in the 1980s. For most of his career, Al has held an adjunct faculty position with the Department of Family Medicine at the University of North Carolina. Currently, he is involved in projects promoting addiction awareness worldwide.

Class B Trustees elected by the General Service Board following 2019 Conference

James (Jimmy) Dean (Dallas, Texas) was elected Southwest regional trustee in May 2019. A Panel 59 delegate, Jimmy is actively involved in sponsorship as well as many group commitments. Currently senior vice president of support services of a corporation that markets proprietary software, Jimmy has extensive experience in business operations and financial planning. He has also served a range of local nonprofits in various capacities.

Francis H. Gilroy (Chelmsford, Massachusetts) was elected Northeast regional trustee in May 2019. A Panel 57 delegate, Francis remains active in his area's young people's activities and serves as hotel liaison to the 2021 Northeast Regional Forum. Now retired, Francis has extensive experience as a CPA, having performed field audits for major defense corporations in New York and Massachusetts. He volunteers for several organizations in his community, among them the Chelmsford Commission on Disabilities.

Patricia (Trish) LaNauze (Vancouver, BC, Canada) was elected trustee-at-large/Canada in May 2019. A Panel 57 delegate, Trish is active in her district and area, facilitating workshops and inventories. Now retired, she was executive director of a nonprofit charitable organization and has extensive experience in communication and other leadership positions. Trish currently serves on several advisory boards in her community.

AREA DELEGATES

What do panel numbers mean? Delegates to each Conference are made up of two "panels." One is even-numbered and includes those elected to start serving in an even year. The other is odd-numbered and includes those elected to start serving in an odd year. The 69th Conference includes Panel 68 (delegates now serving for their second year) and Panel 69 (new delegates).

UNITED STATES

State	Area no.	Panel		
Alabama/N.W. Florida	1	69	Kevin Hawkins	Anniston, AL
Alaska	2	68	Alizon White	Ketchikan, AK
Arizona	3	68	Dee Payton	Mesa, AZ
Arkansas	4	69	Brad Moore	Tontitown, AR
California				
Southern	5	69	Thomas Sells	Inglewood, CA
Central	93	69	Jeffrey (Jeff) Gulack	Santa Clarita, CA
Northern Coastal	6	69	Teddy Basham-Witherington	Oakland, CA
Northern Interior	7	68	Michael (Mike) Kim	Sacramento, CA
San Diego/Imperial	8	68	Roxane Rollins	Valley Center, CA
Mid-Southern	9	68	Jesus Olivas	Bellflower, CA
Colorado	10	69	Scott Meiklejohn	Golden, CO
Connecticut	11	69	John Dussault	Farmington, CT
Delaware	12	68	David Craig	Dagsboro, DE
District of Columbia	13	69	Michelle García	Beltsville, MD
Florida				
North	14	69	Annette Dahl	Melbourne, FL
South Florida/ Bahamas/ VI/Antigua	15	69	Shirley Parrado	Bradenton, FL
Georgia	16	68	Rick McNamara	Johns Creek, GA
Hawaii	17	69	Coleen Ashworth	Makawao, HI
Idaho	18	68	Shannon Coburn	Boise, ID
Illinois				
Chicago	19	69	Brian Tenenbaum	Evanston, IL
Northern	20	68	Robert Snipes	Glendale Heights, IL
Southern	21	69	Robert (Bobby) Davis	West Frankfort, IL
Indiana				
Northern	22	69	Bradley (Brad) Albright	Muncie, IN
Southern	23	68	Margaret (Marge) Miller	Indianapolis, IN
Iowa	24	69	Dan Geels	Gladbrook, IA

State	Area no.	Panel		
Kansas	25	68	David (Dave) Ruhlen	Lawrence, KS
Kentucky	26	68	Roger Wheatley	Vine Grove, KY
Louisiana	27	69	Sue Tart	New Orleans, LA
Maine	28	68	Robin Gasparino	Mt. Vernon, ME
Maryland	29	68	Donald (Don) Bridges	Baltimore, MD
Massachusetts				
Eastern	30	69	Jean Kerivan	Weymouth, MA
Western	31	68	Michael (Mike) Silva	Agawam, MA
Michigan				
Central	32	69	Lori Conant	Michigan Center, MI
Southeast Michigan	33	69	Cynthia Bars	Milford, MI
Western	34	68	Rick Padgett	SE Lowell, MI
Minnesota				
Northern	35	68	Christine Gerth	St Cloud, MN
Southern	36	69	Melissa (Missy) Patterson	West Concord, MN
Mississippi	37	68	Lisa Whittington	Jackson, MS
Missouri				
Eastern	38	69	Eugene (Gene) Marshall	Chesterfield, MO
Western	39	69	Jennifer (Jenny) Donovan	Lebanon, MO
Montana	40	69	Paul Lamb	Whitefish, MT
Nebraska	41	68	Erika Hanson	Lincoln, NE
Nevada	42	69	Rhonda Fairchild	Las Vegas, NV
New Hampshire	43	68	James (Jim) Magee	Derry, NH
New Jersey				
Northern	44	69	Jeff Bernknopf	South Bound Brook, NJ
Southern	45	68	Rose Sellnow	Southampton, NJ
New Mexico	46	68	Teresa Jacks	NE Albuquerque, NM
New York				
Central	47	69	Barb Chambers	Ithaca, NY
Hudson/Mohawk/ Berkshire	48	68	Don Strachan	Burke, NY
Southeast	49	69	Jane Ehrich	Kings Park, NY
Western	50	68	Charles (Chuck) Beinhauer	Buffalo, NY
North Carolina	51	69	Katy Patterson	Statesville, NC
North Dakota	52	69	Curtis (Curt) Winmill	Fargo, ND

State	Area no.	Panel	
Ohio			
Central/Southeast	53	69	Stephen Shelton Columbus, OH
Northeast	54	69	Shyrl Blair Euclid, OH
Northwest	55	68	Henry Coombs Toledo, OH
Southwest	56	68	Jennifer (Jenny) Cmar Middletown, OH
Oklahoma	57	69	Steve Shuffield Guthrie, OK
Oregon	58	68	Vera Farrell Bend, OR
Pennsylvania			
Eastern	59	69	Kenneth (Ken) Dennison Kennett Square, PA
Western	60	69	Marjorie (Margie) Stanislaw Jeannette, PA
Rhode Island	61	68	Mary Kenney Wakefield, RI
South Carolina	62	68	Amy Bailey Greenville, SC
South Dakota	63	68	Anthony Flores Rapid City, SD
Tennessee	64	68	Jon Phillips Nashville, TN
Texas			
Northeast	65	69	Tina Palmer Allen, TX
Northwest	66	68	Alicia Hughes El Paso, TX
Southeast	67	69	William (Troy) Bush-DiDonato Rosharon, TX
Southwest	68	68	Jonathan Smith San Antonio, TX
Utah	69	69	Matt Dyer Clearfield, UT
Vermont	70	68	Jan Rowe Shelburne, VT
Virginia	71	69	Barbara (Barb) Dove Front Royal, VA
Washington State			
East	92	68	Allen DenAdel Spokane, WA
Western	72	69	Alan Foster Seattle, WA
West Virginia	73	69	Susan Vlajk Lewisburg, WV
Wisconsin			
N. WI/Up. Penn. MI	74	68	Sara Plansky-Pecor Porterfield, WI
Southern	75	69	Kristi (Kris) Krueger Montello, WI
Wyoming	76	68	Kathleen (Kathi) Cullen Sheridan, WY
Puerto Rico	77	68	Julio (Jay) Baez Aguadilla, PR

CANADA

Province	Area no.	Panel	
Alberta/NWT	78	68	Rebecca (Becky) Parker Olds, AB
British Columbia/Yukon	79	69	Gail Patterson Victoria, BC
Manitoba	80	68	Noni McLean Winnipeg, MB6
New Brunswick/P.E.I.	81	68	Earl Cronin Charlottetown, PEI
Nova Scotia/ Newfoundland/Labrador		69	Kirk Stone St. Peters, NS
Ontario			
Eastern	83	69	Robert (Rob) McArthur Whitby, ON
Northeast	84	68	Colleen Halverson Sault Ste Marie, ON
Northwest	85	69	Lorraine Payette Schreiber, ON
Western	86	68	Dale Sharp N Milton, ON
Québec			
Southwest	87	68	Lucien Jean St. Hyacinthe, QC
Southeast	88	69	Serge Vigneux Pohenegamook, QC
Northeast	89	69	Alain Gelinas Shawinigan, QC
Northwest	90	68	Eric Parent Mont-Laurier, QC
Saskatchewan	91	69	Raymond (Ray) McCallum Prince Albert, SK

A slide from the International presentation, with advice from
the rotating trustee-at-large/Canada.